Delhi

a Lonely Planet
city guide

Hugh Finlay

Delhi
1st edition

Published by
Lonely Planet Publications
Head Office: PO Box 617, Hawthorn, Vic 3122, Australia
Branches: 155 Filbert St, Suite 251, Oakland,
            CA 94607, USA
            10 Barley Mow Passage, Chiswick,
            London W4 4PH, UK
            71 bis rue du Cardinal Lemoine,
            75005 Paris, France

Printed by
Colorcraft Ltd, Hong Kong

Photographs by
Glenn Beanland (GB), Lindsay Brown (LB), Greg Elms (GE),
Richard Everist (RE), Hugh Finlay (HF), Greg
Herriman (GH), Sally Hone (SH), Richard I'Anson (RI),
Avinash Pasricha (AP), Bryn Thomas (BT),
Bahá'í-Verlag (BV), Tony Wheeler (TW)

Front cover: Tika powder (GE)
Front gatefold: Cleaner at the observatory (TW)
                    Bottom: Jama Masjid (HF)
Back gatefold: Street sweeper (BT)

First Published
January 1996

National Library of Australia Cataloguing in Publication Data

Finlay, Hugh
    Delhi city guide

    1st ed.
    Includes index.
    ISBN 0 86442 349 7.

    1. Delhi (India) – Guidebooks.
    I. Title. (Series: Lonely Planet city guide).

    915.4560452

Hugh Finlay

After an unsuccessful foray into academia in Melbourne, Hugh first hit the road in 1976, on a trail which eventually led him to Africa via Asia, Europe and the Middle East in the early '80s.

Since joining Lonely Planet in 1985, Hugh has co-authored with Geoff Crowther the LP travel survival kits to *Kenya*, *East Africa* and *Morocco, Algeria & Tunisia*. Other LP books he has been involved with include *Africa*, *Australia* and *Malaysia, Singapore & Brunei*.

Hugh currently lives in central Victoria with Linda and their two daughters, Ella and Vera, trying to juggle the demands – and pleasures! – of family life, restoring an old farmhouse, writing, raising sheep, gardening and lengthy phone calls from Lonely Planet editors!

From the Author

A book like this requires input from a wide array of sources, and for this I must thank the many people in Delhi who went out of their way to help. In particular, my thanks to Persian scholar Dr Yunus Jaffrey of the Anglo Arabic College. His knowledge of the Mughal period is second to none, and he showed me some interesting corners of the old city which I would otherwise have missed.

William Dalrymple, author of *City of Djinns*, generously opened up his address book for me and put me in touch with a number of people in Delhi. Vinod Kumar and the staff at the Government of India Tourist Office on Janpath helped where they could, and special thanks to Ms Purnima Ray, librarian at the Archaeological Survey of India library, whose no-nonsense approach to her work was a breath of fresh air. She also unearthed some worthwhile maps despite bureaucratic obstacles.

Sanjay Puri, Avnish Puri and Rajendra Kumar each made useful contributions in their own way and so thanks to them also.

From the Publisher

This first edition of *Delhi* was edited by David Meagher and Jenny Missen and taken through production by Linda Suttie. Louise Keppie did the design and layout, and the maps were produced by Louise Keppie with assistance from Chris Love and Sally Woodward. Many thanks to Greg Alford and Jo Horsburgh for helping out with the proofreading, to Simon Bracken and Adam McCrow for designing the cover and to Sharon Wertheim for compiling the index.

Warning & Request

Things change – prices go up, schedules change, good places go bad and bad places go bankrupt – nothing stays the same. So if you find things better or worse, recently opened or long since closed, please write and tell us. Your letters will be used to help update future editions.

We greatly appreciate all information that is sent to us by travellers. Back at Lonely Planet we employ a hard-working readers' letters team to sort through the many letters we receive. The best ones will be rewarded with a free copy of the next edition or another Lonely Planet guide if you prefer. We give away lots of books, but, unfortunately, not every letter/postcard receives one.

Contents

Maps

Introduction

Delhi is the capital of India and its third-largest city – after Bombay and Calcutta. Since the 11th century its fortunes have fluctuated in concert with those who have ruled over the north Indian plains. Its peak came with the Mughals in the mid-17th century, a time when there was wealth and relative peace, circumstances which led to the construction of some of the finest buildings in Asia. It was later the heart of the British Raj, an empire which endowed it with yet more architectural master-pieces. Today it's the administrative heart of the world's second most populous nation.

Delhi actually consists of two distinctly contrasting parts: Delhi, or 'Old' Delhi, was the capital of Muslim India between the mid-17th and late 19th centuries. It is here you will find the mosques, monuments and forts relating to the city's rich Mughal history, as well as lively, teeming and colourful bazaars, narrow streets and barely controlled chaos. The other Delhi is New Delhi, the imperial city created as the capital of India by the British. It is spacious and open with wide, tree-lined avenues, sweeping views to imposing government buildings and a sense of order absent in other parts of the city.

Many visitors to Delhi are not encouraged by their first impression, especially if this is their first foray into Asia. But for those armed with a sense of curiosity and an interest in history, the city has plenty to offer. Any small effort to scratch below the surface reveals a place with a fascinating history, a place where centuries-old traditions still live virtually unchanged, a place which characterises the stark contrasts that are India, where the 20th century clashes head-on with the 17th or even earlier.

In addition to its historic interest and role as the government centre, Delhi is a major travel gateway. It is one of India's busiest entrance points for overseas air-lines, the hub of the north Indian travel network and on the overland route across Asia. It is also an excellent base from which to visit two of the most popular cities in India – Agra, with the incomparable Taj Mahal, is only two hours away by air-conditioned train, while Jaipur, which is chock-full of Rajasthani colour, is less than five hours away.

Facts about Delhi

HISTORY

Delhi has not always been the capital of India but it has played an important role in Indian history. The area has been continuously settled for at least the last 2500 years, and since the 12th century Delhi itself has seen the rise – and fall – of seven major powers who have built themselves a capital here.

Early Hindu Kingdoms

Archaeological evidence discovered in recent years – such as a rock edict carved in the era of the Mauryan emperor Ashoka – show that this area was settled at least 2500 years ago. Ashoka's capital was Pataliputra (near modern-day Patna in Bihar state) and his rule spread right across northern India.

Popular Hindu tradition has it that Delhi was the site of the fabled city of Indraprastha, which featured in the epic poem the *Mahabharata* over 3000 years ago. Here, on the nearby battlefield of Kurukshetra, the Kauravas and the Pandavas, descendants of the lunar race, fought a raging battle for 18 days and nights. The city is said to have been located on the west bank of the Yamuna River, on the site today occupied by the ruins of the Mughal emperor Humayun's fort, Purana Qila. While potsherds found in digs on the site do date back to that period, it is hard to see how a firm site can be attributed to a city that existed in a text based largely on myth.

Getting on to firmer historical ground requires a jump to the 10th century AD, when the area was held by the Tomara Rajputs, a warrior clan based in Rajasthan. In the barren, rocky area now known as Mehrauli on Delhi's southern outskirts, this Hindu clan constructed numerous temples and a substantial settlement started to take shape. The Tomara leader, Anang Pal, is credited with being the builder of Lal Kot, a small citadel which forms the heart of what is now popularly described as the first city of Delhi. Anang Pal is also given the credit for bringing to Delhi and installing the pure Iron Pillar.

The Tomaras were just one of a number of Rajput clans who fought for control of northern and western India, another clan being the Chauhans, who overran the Tomaras in about 1155 AD. They then set about enlarging and fortifying the city, and renamed it Qila Rai

Pithora after their leader Prithviraj (Rai Pithora). At its height the city became the most important Hindu centre in northern India.

Muslim Incursions

The Muslim rulers of central Asia had long held ambitions to extend their influence to the east. By early in the 11th century Mahmud of Ghazni had annexed present-day Pakistan and the Punjab directly north of Delhi. But it wasn't until the rule of Muhammad bin Sam of the obscure Ghor province in Afghanistan that Delhi itself was threatened.

Muhammad of Ghor mounted a powerful expedition in 1191. The invaders swept through present-day Pakistan, were repelled from Gujarat, moved into the Punjab and then attempted to take Qila Rai Pithora.

The various Rajput clans of northern India were very much aware of the dangers posed by the Muslims and for once managed to set aside their differences. Under the leadership of Rai Pithora, they formed a united front against the invading force and repelled them in a battle at Tarain, about 130 km north of Delhi; a region that in the centuries to follow was to become the battleground for at least another three major attacks on Delhi by invaders from the north-west.

The following year Muhammad of Ghor returned better prepared and, at the same spot, routed the Rajput armies. Rai Pithora fled the battle but was captured and killed. Muhammad returned to Ghazni, leaving his new conquests in the hands of Qutb-ud-din Aibak, one of his Turkish slaves.

From a local viewpoint the hero of this era was undoubtedly Rai Pithora, whose great leadership of the Rajputs made him a popular figure, a tradition that exists in stories even today. His romantic exploits added to his appeal – the story goes that he eloped with the daughter of Raja Jaichand, leader of a neighbouring clan.

Qutb-ud-din Aibak occupied Delhi in 1193, and following the death of Muhammad bin Sam in 1203 and his successor in 1206, became the first sultan of Delhi. This ushered in six and half centuries of Muslim rule, which entirely changed the cultural face of north India.

Delhi Sultanate (1206-1526)

In the period known as the Delhi Sultanate, which lasted from the time of Qutb-ud-din's reign in 1206 until the onset of Mughal rule in 1526, five different dynasties ruled Delhi, four of them building their own capital.

Chronological History of Delhi

Dynasty & Date	Rulers	Principal Monuments
Tomara & Chauhan Rajputs		
10th-11th C AD	Anang Pal	Lal Kot
	Rai Pithora	
Slave Dynasty		
1206-90 AD		
1206-10	Qutb-ud-din	Quwwat-ul-Islam Masjid
1211-36	Iltutmish	Qutb Minar
1236-37	Rukn-ud-din	
1237-40	Sultan Raziya	Sultan Raziya's Tomb
1240-42	Bahram Shah	
1242-46	Musaud Shah	
1246-66	Sultan Nasir-ud-din	
1266-86	Sultan Balban	
1286-90	Kai Kubad	
Khalji Dynasty		
1290-1321		
1290-96	Jalan-ud-din	
1296-1316	Ala-ud-din	Hauz Khas
Tughlaq Dynasty		
1321-1414		
1321-25	Ghiyas-ud-din	Tughlaqabad
		Ghiyas-ud-din's Tomb
		Bijai Mandal
1325-51	Muhammad Shah	
1351-88	Feroz Shah Tughlaq	Feroz Shah's Tomb
		Feroz Shah Kotla
		Begumpur Masjid
		Kalan Masjid
		Khirki Masjid
1388-93	Abu Bakr Shah	
1394-1412	Mahmud	
1412-14	Daulat Khan Lodi	
Sayyid Dynasty		
1414-51		
1414-21	Khizr Khan	
1421-33	Mubarak Shah	Mubarak Shah's Tomb
1434-45	Muhammad Shah	Muhammed Shah's Tomb
1445-50	Alam Shah	

Lodi Dynasty
1451-1526

1451-89	Bahlol Lodi	
1489-1517	Sikander Lodi	Moth-ki-Masjid
		Sikander Lodi's Tomb
1517-26	Ibrahim Lodi	Ibrahim Lodi's Tomb

Mughals
1526-40

1526-30	Babur	
1530-40	Humayun	

Afghan
Sur Dynasty
1540-55

1540-55	Sher Shah	Sher Mandal
		Purana Qila
		Qila-i-Kuhna Masjid

Mughals
(2nd time)
1555-1857

1555-56	Humayun (2nd time)	Humayun's Tomb
1556-1605	Akbar	Arab Serai
		Adham Khan's Tomb
1605-27	Jahangir	
1628-58	Shah Jahan	Old Delhi
		Red Fort
		Jama Masjid
1658-1707	Aurangzeb	Moti Masjid
1707-12	(Bahadur) Shah Alam I	Madrasa of Ghazi-ud-din
		Jantar Mantar
1712-13	Jahandar Shah	
1713-19	Faruksiyar	
1719-48	Muhammad Shah	Qudsia Bagh
1748-54	Ahmed Shah	Safdarjang's Tomb
1754-59	Alamgir	
1759-1806	Shah Alam II	
1806-37	Akbar II	St James' Church
1837-57	Bahadur Shah	Hindu Rao's House
		Metcalfe House

British Rule
1857-1947

		Mutiny Memorial
		Coronation Durbar site
		New Delhi

Independent India
1947-

		Raj Ghat
		Lakshmi Narayan Temple
		Bahai House of Worship

Slave Dynasty (1206-1290) Qutb-ud-din's reign
was shortlived, as he died in 1210 after an accident
playing polo. His son and successor, Aram, proved so
ineffectual that his position was quickly taken by his
brother-in-law, Iltutmish (1211-1236), who assumed the
title Shams-ud-din (sun of the religion).

Iltutmish took on the job of completing the great
tower, the Qutb Minar, begun by Qutb-ud-din, and also
made additions to the Quwwat-ul-Islam Masjid, or
Might of Islam Mosque. These two monuments, along
with the tomb of Iltutmish, are the finest reminders of
this period. It was also at this time that Genghis Khan,
the great Mongol leader, started making raids into the
country directly to the north-west of Delhi.

The succession to Iltutmish was a messy affair. His
nominated successor was his daughter, Raziya-ud-din,
but the thought of a female sultan so outraged the nobles
that they had her incompetent brother, Rukn-ud-din,
crowned in her place. His ineffective reign lasted six
months before the citizens rebelled and had Sultan
Raziya crowned, as had been her father's intention. She
only ruled for four years, and is the only woman ever to
have ruled the city.

The next ruler of any note was a former slave of
Iltutmish, Sultan Balban (1266-1286). He not only ruled
in his own right for 20 years, but was the power behind
his predecessor Sultan Nasir-ud-din (1246-1266), who it
seems was quite prepared to leave the running of the
empire to Balban, the most powerful slave in the household.

Balban was powerful and ruthless; indeed he had
reached his position of power largely through shedding
the blood of his fellow slaves, thereby eliminating any
competition. As a ruler he made both his enemies and
his own people suffer. He was threatened by unruly
Hindu clans to the south, a rebelling Turk noble to the
east, and the ever-menacing Mongols in the north. It was
the death of his sons in a battle against the Mongols in
1285 which really defeated him, though, and he died a
year later.

With no obvious successor to Balban in sight, the
Slave dynasty slid into a mire of internal intrigue, which
opened the way for the Khalji Afghan-Turks to assume
control of the empire, which by the time of Balban's
death included the areas that today constitute Uttar
Pradesh, Rajasthan, Sind (in Pakistan) and parts of
Punjab and Madhya Pradesh.

Khalji Dynasty (1290-1321) The first Khalji sultan
was Jalal-ud-din (1290-1296), an officer in the army of

the Slave dynasty. He was already an old man when he took the throne, and was so incapable and unpopular that he dared not even live in Delhi, instead building himself a palace some distance away.

Jalal-ud-din's successor was his nephew and brother-in-law, Ala-ud-din (1296-1316), a ruthless and cruel man who deposed the old ruler by having him executed and his head paraded around the army camp. His reign was equally tyrannical – rebellions were brutally put down, Hindus were heavily taxed so they couldn't become wealthy (and therefore powerful), spies were set up everywhere and possible rivals (real or imagined) and their families were killed.

While Ala-ud-din was conquering new territory to the south, the Mongols in the Punjab were making their presence felt. An attempted conquest by them in 1299 was repulsed by the sultan's forces. At the time there was a large community of Mongols who had taken refuge in Delhi, and they immediately came under suspicion and were massacred.

Although he was exceptionally cruel, Ala-ud-din also had a love of building – he made additions to the Quwwat-ul-Islam Masjid and built Siri, the second city of Delhi. This was the first totally new city built by the Muslims, although the only reminder of it today is Hauz Khas, the city's reservoir.

The death of Ala-ud-din was followed by another messy scramble for the throne, which ultimately led to the nobles backing Ghazi Malik, a Turk Tughlaq who had spent much of his life fighting the Mongols in the Punjab. He marched into Delhi and overthrew the last of the Khalji sultans.

Detail of carving on arches of prayer hall at the Quwwat-ul-Islam Masjid, Qutb Minar Complex (HF)

The Seven Cities of Delhi

Contemporary accounts of Delhi's history often speak of the 'Seven Cities of Delhi'. This refers to the various citadels and forts which have been built over the last 1000 or so years by those who chose to rule and fight from this strategic area on the banks of the Yamuna River.

In chronological order the seven cities are:

Lal Kot - Qila Rai Pithora - a fortified city built in the 12th century by Hindu Rajputs. Sometimes referred to as Old Delhi in early accounts.

Siri - built in the 14th century by Muslims who had invaded from Afghanistan.

Tughlaqabad - a heavily fortified city, also dating from the 14th century.

Jahanpanah - another 14th-century city which was formed basically by joining together Lal Kot and Siri.

Ferozabad - a 14th-century fort on the banks of the Yamuna River.

Purana Qila - Shergarh - 16th-century city started by the Mughal ruler, Humayun, and completed by his Afghan successor, Sher Shah.

Shahjahanabad - the 17th-century city of Mughal emperor Shah Jahan, known today as Old Delhi.

Taking things a step further it could be said that the shady wide avenues and imposing British buildings of 1930s New Delhi are the eighth incarnation of the city, and that today the ninth city is a thriving, bustling sprawl which encompasses all previous eight. ■

Tughlaq Dynasty (1321-1414) Ghazi Malik was proclaimed king and assumed the title Ghiyas-ud-din Tughlaq (1321-1325). He quickly restored order and built the massively fortified Tughlaqabad, the third city of Delhi, in an easily defendable position on the barren hills a few km to the east of Siri. He was also prescient enough to build himself a fortress-like tomb close by, and it wasn't long before he was safely ensconced within: his son, Muhammad-bin-Tughlaq, orchestrated an elaborate 'accident' which killed his father, leaving the way open for him to take charge.

The Tughlaq dynasty would probably not be well remembered were it not for the barbaric behaviour of the extraordinary Muhammad-bin-Tughlaq. Known as Muhammad Shah Tughlaq (1325-1351), he was an erudite scholar, gifted writer and original thinker; he

was also arguably insane. Early in his reign he built
Jahanapanah, the fourth city of Delhi, largely by enclosing the area between Siri and Qila Rai Pithora, even
though Tughlaqabad remained the capital. After consol-
idating and extending the empire to include much of
south India, he then came up with the lunatic scheme of
moving the capital – and its entire population – to
Daulatabad in the Deccan, something over 1000 km
away to the south. Worse still, he force-marched them all
the way back again only four years later!

Muhammad Shah's character was also marred by a
streak of extreme cruelty that earned him almost univer-
sal hatred and caused rebellion throughout the empire,
which by this stage was bigger than at any time during
the Delhi sultanate. Added to this were the economic
pressures placed on the sultanate by fanciful and
extremely costly (and unsuccessful) expeditions to
conquer Persia and China. So Muhammad Shah was
unable to prevent the break up of the empire, and it went
into a decline that wasn't reversed until the arrival of the
Mughals 150 years later.

Feroz Shah Tughlaq (1351-1388), the late sultan's
cousin and successor, was a far less extreme character.
He spent a good deal of time restoring order in the
much-reduced sultanate, but he continued his
predecessor's intolerance of Hindus – temples were
destroyed and Hindus were heavily taxed, which in turn
led to widespread conversion to Islam, as may have been
the intention.

Feroz Shah's greatest loves were history and building
– Ferozabad, the fifth city of Delhi, the ruins of which are
close to the centre of today's New Delhi, was built by
him on the banks of the Yamuna. His curiosity was
sufficiently aroused by inscribed Ashokan stone
columns found elsewhere in northern India to order
them transported to Delhi with great care. One was set
up in Ferozabad, the other on the Ridge to the north
where the ruler had established a hunting lodge (both
survive today). Feroz Shah was also unusual in that he
chose to restore rather than demolish buildings constructed by previous rulers – he repaired and added to
the Qutb Minar, for instance.

The old sultan died in 1388 and the struggle for his
succession seemed to follow what was by now a familiar
pattern – political instability involving in-fighting and
intrigue among the nobles, accompanied by Hindu
rebellion, although this time the problems were far
worse. With each provincial governor virtually declar-
ing himself independent, the empire as such ceased to
exist.

This state of anarchy continued for a decade, and into this political void came the powerful Turk Timur (Tamerlane), the famous sultan of Samarkand who embarked upon years of raids throughout Asia. He had no intention of staying in India, but sensed the chance to make a quick killing – the country was rich and there was no government to speak of. After a series of victories in the country to the north, Timur was proclaimed king of Delhi. The city's residents rebelled and were promptly massacred in an orgy of killing and looting that lasted five days. Mission accomplished, Timur headed back to Samarkand, loaded to the hilt with booty and captives.

Sayyid Dynasty (1414-1451) For 15 years following Timur's raid the sultanate remained virtually without a government until Khizr Khan, a former governor of the Punjab, declared himself a *sayyid*, or descendant of the prophet Muhammad's grandson Husain, and founded the Sayyid dynasty. He was followed by three more Sayyids, but the country they ruled over was far from rich, and by the time the dynasty folded the sultanate was greatly reduced in size.

Although the Sayyids were not patrons of the arts and built no major cities or palaces, their distinctive tombs, such as that of Muhammad Shah (1434-1444), the grandson of Khizr Khan, in the Lodi Garden in New Delhi today, are of great architectural merit.

Lodi Dynasty (1451-1526) The next rulers of Delhi were of the Afghani Lodi clan, and the first sultan, Bahlol Lodi (1451-1489), did much to regain control over territories lost since the invasion by Timur, as did his two successors. The first of these was Sikander Lodi (1489-1517), who had to fight to ascend the throne as the nobles disapproved of the fact that his mother was a Hindu and he was therefore not of good noble blood. He spent most of his time living in Agra.

Following Sikander came the last of the Lodi sultans, Ibrahim Lodi (1517-1526). He found it impossible to get on with his Afghan nobles, and they consequently invited Babur, the Mughal king of Kabul and descendant of both Timur and Genghis Khan, to invade Delhi. The two armies met at Panipat, 90 km north of Delhi, where Babur's well-trained and equipped force of 12,000 men had no difficulty in overpowering Ibrahim (who was killed in the battle) and his 100,000 men.

The demise of the Lodi sultanate brought to an end more than a century of cultural stagnation, a great contrast to the next phase in the history of Delhi which saw the rise of refined rulers – the Mughals.

The Mughals (1526-1857)

Only Ashoka is as giant a figure in Indian history as the Mughal emperors. These larger-than-life individuals ushered in another golden age of building, arts and literature and spread their control over India to an extent rivalled only by Ashoka and the British. Their rise to power was rapid but their decline was equally quick. There were only six great Mughals; after Aurangzeb the rest were emperors in name only.

The Mughals did more than simply rule, however; they had a passion for building that led them to erect some of the greatest monuments in India. Shah Jahan's magnificent Taj Mahal ranks as one of the wonders of the world, and Delhi's Red Fort, Jama Masjid (Friday Mosque) and various Mughal tombs are also exceptional. Art and literature also flourished under the Mughals and the magnificence of their court stunned early European visitors.

Babur (1526-1530) Babur ruled over a fractured empire from Agra, and had to contend with warring Rajputs to the south and Afghan chiefs who held power in Bihar and Bengal to the east. He overcame them, and by the time he died in 1530 the fractured Delhi sultanate had regained some of its former size, but was held together more by personal loyalty to the likeable and energetic Babur than by sheer Mughal might.

Humayun (1530-1540, 1555-1556) Babur's son Humayun ascended the throne but was not made of the same stuff as his father. Provinces beyond the Indus were abandoned to his brothers, and thus weakened he suffered defeats at the hands of the Afghan chief, Sher Shah Sur, who controlled southern Bihar.

Humayun was forced into exile in Sind, Persia and Afghanistan for 15 years, before he was able to re-establish himself at Kabul and move on to take Delhi, which had flourished under the leadership of Sher Shah and his descendants. When Humayun did finally retake Delhi in 1555 he was only there for seven months before he died after slipping on the stone stairs of his library.

Before his exile Humayun had decided to build a new fort in Delhi called Din-Panah (Shelter of the Faith). It was started in 1534 but was still incomplete when Sher Shah took over.

Afghan Sur Dynasty (1540-1555) Sher Shah's reign was brief, but in the five years of his rule he proved himself to be an extremely capable leader and administrator. Humayun's fort of Din-Panah was also completed, and became the centre of Shergarh, the sixth city of Delhi. (When Shah Jahan's Qila-e-Mu'alla (Auspicious Fort, later called Lal Qila, or Red Fort) was built, around a century later, Din-Panah became known as Purana Qila (Old Fort), the name it still holds today.)

Sher Shah died fighting the Rajputs in 1545 and was succeeded by his son, Islam Shah, who ruled without any great distinction for nine years. On his death in 1553, however, there was yet another unseemly scramble among relatives for the throne, and it was this chaos that left the way open for Humayun to retake the city.

Akbar (1556-1605) On his ascension to the throne Akbar first had to overcome the remnants of the Sur dynasty, which included Hemu, a Hindu minister and general at the Sur court who had actually occupied Delhi and Agra. Once again the scene of battle was the plains north of Delhi at Panipat, where only 30 years previously control over north-western India had been contested between Babur and Ibrahim Lodi.

For the next 50 years Akbar ruled with great wisdom and flair. He was probably the greatest of the Mughals, for he not only had the military ability required of a ruler in that time, he was also a man of culture and wisdom with a sense of fairness. He saw, as previous Muslim rulers had not, that the number of Hindus in India was too great to simply subjugate them. Instead he integrated them into his empire and made use of many Hindu advisers, generals and administrators. Akbar also had a deep interest in religious matters and spent many hours in discussion with religious experts of all persuasions, including Parsis and Jesuits. Somewhat surprisingly, he was also illiterate.

Although Akbar ruled from Agra, he went to Delhi regularly to visit his foster-mother, Maham Anga.

Jahangir (1605-1627) Jahangir followed Akbar and maintained his father's toleration of other religions but took advantage of the stability of the empire to spend most of his time in his beloved Kashmir, while leaving the running of the empire to his wife, Nur Jahan. He eventually died while returning to Agra from a trip to Kashmir.

Shah Jahan (1628-1658) Jahangir's son Shah Jahan was an entirely different character. He had already fought one war with his father (and lost), then set about knocking off his brothers and anyone else who might claim the throne. Having secured his position, he devoted much effort and expense to gaining control of the Deccan plateau in the south of India and Kandahar in central Asia (the latter three times without success).

During his reign a new capital was built in Delhi, and in 1648 the official move from Agra was made. That year the walls of Shahjahanabad, the seventh city of Delhi, were also started, and it's this city which forms the basis of Old Delhi today. Shah Jahan was a passionate builder; best known, of course, is the Taj Mahal in Agra, but that was only one of many magnificent buildings. In Delhi he built a palace (the Lal Qila, or Red Fort) and the Jama Masjid (Friday Mosque), both of which still stand today.

Shah Jahan's reign marks the peak of the Mughal Empire. The power of the emperor was unchallenged, architecture and the arts flourished and there was staggering wealth – the amazing Peacock Throne, made of gold, studded with precious stones and seven years in the making, was installed in Delhi's Red Fort.

Despite Shah Jahan's appreciation of the finer things in life, he was a far from brilliant ruler with a cruel streak – justice was harsh and the population were heavily taxed to support the lavish life of the imperial court. He also ditched Akbar's policy of religious tolerance in favour of a return to Islam; yet it was during his reign that the British were granted their trading post at Madras in 1639.

In 1657 the emperor suffered a stroke, and although he recovered, news of his death spread rapidly to the provinces, where three of his four sons were governors. The fourth son and Shah Jahan's favoured successor, Dara Shikoh, stayed with his father in Shahjahanabad. On hearing the news of their father's 'death', the sons all starting manoeuvring for the throne – Shuja enthroned himself in Bengal and minted coins in his name, Murad Baksh did the same in Ahmedabad. The fourth son, Aurangzeb, gathered his army in the Deccan and headed for Delhi, on the way striking a deal with Murad Baksh to join forces and share the spoils.

On behalf of his father, Dara Shikoh led a powerful force which engaged Aurangzeb and Murad Baksh near Agra and was defeated. Aurangzeb, the shrewdest and most able prince, moved quickly: he imprisoned his father in Agra fort for life, turned on Murad Baksh and had him imprisoned and later executed. His next step was to have himself enthroned, a ceremony which took place in 1658 at the beautiful Shish Mahal pavilion in the Shalimar Bagh gardens on the outskirts of northern

Detail of the Taj Mahal, Agra (RE)

Delhi, a building which survives today. Shuja was killed in battle with Aurangzeb in 1660, which just left Dara Shikoh as a possible rival. He was pursued relentlessly, captured and brought to Delhi. Once there, however, he was sentenced to death for being a heretic, having spent much time in earlier years studying the relationship between Hinduism and Islam, and even having the *Upanishads* and the *Bhagavad Gita* translated into Persian. Dara Shikoh was executed and his headless body was paraded through the streets before being buried in Humayun's mausoleum.

Shah Jahan spent his last eight years imprisoned in the Red Fort of Agra, from where he could gaze out over the Taj Mahal, the exquisite mausoleum that he built for his wife, Mumtaz Mahal, and where he himself was buried when he died in 1666.

Aurangzeb (1658-1707) Aurangzeb was the last of the great Mughals. He devoted his resources to extending the empire's boundaries, but it was the punitive taxes he levied on his subjects to pay for his military exploits and his religious zealotry that eventually secured his downfall. It was also during his reign that the empire began to rot rapidly from the inside as luxury and easy living corroded the mettle and moral fibre of the nobles and military commanders. His austere and puritanical beliefs led him to destroy many Hindu temples and erect mosques on their sites, alienating the very people who were such an important part of his bureaucracy.

Aurangzeb spent most of his time in Delhi, and had a great ally in his sister Roshanara, who had sided with Aurangzeb in the struggle for power with the favoured son Dara Shikoh, who in turn had as his ally Shah Jahan's favoured daughter Jahanara. It was Jahanara who became head of her father's vast harem in the Red Fort in Delhi, and later stayed with her father during his internment at the Red Fort in Agra. The jealous Roshanara was one of those who called for the execution of Dara Shikoh.

Later Mughals (1707-1857) Aurangzeb's oppressive style soon caused revolts to break out on all sides, and with his death in 1707 the fortunes of the Mughal Empire – and therefore of Delhi – rapidly declined.

The Ram Yantra at the Jantar Mantar in New Delhi (TW)

When Aurangzeb died there was the usual scramble for power, with the elderly Bahadur Shah (1707-1712) emerging victorious over two brothers, who were killed. He was followed by two puppet-emperors who were in the power of two Sayyid brothers, whose family had served the imperial court since the days of Akbar.

Muhammad Shah's reign (1719-1748) saw the disintegration of the empire, the increasing rise to power of the Hindu Marathas and finally the invasion of Delhi by the Persian king Nadir Shah in 1739. Once again Panipat was the scene of battle, and Muhammad Shah lost 20,000 men in a battle lasting little more than two hours.

The two kings returned together to Delhi and things were temporarily peaceful. However, following a scuffle in Paharganj, a false report that Nadir Shah had been killed led to an uprising of the city's inhabitants during which several hundred of Nadir Shah's soldiers were killed. Nadir Shah's response was vicious: he commanded the city be sacked and its residents slaughtered – a massacre which lasted for nine hours and which Nadir Shah is said to have observed from the Sunehri Masjid in Chandni Chowk. By the end over 100,000 citizens had been indiscriminately murdered and Nadir Shah then set about collecting his ransom – the city's accumulated wealth, valued at the time at £4 million and including the famous Peacock Throne.

The next 60 years saw the final decline of the Mughal Empire. Two governors set themselves up virtually as independent rulers – Asaf Jah became the Nizam-ul-Mulk at Hyderabad in the Deccan and Saadat Khan founded the kingdom of Awadh (Oudh) at present-day Lucknow – and the emperor in Delhi was helplessly caught in the rivalries between the two.

The position of *wazir* (prime minister) of the Delhi court became a hereditary post within the Awadh family. Safdar Jung, the nephew of the first king of Awadh, held the post but was ousted in 1752 by Ghazi-ud-din, the grandson of the *nizam* of Hyderabad. Muhammad Shah had been succeeded by Ahmed Shah (1748-1754), but the real power lay with Ghazi-ud-din – he deposed and blinded the emperor, and installed a relative on the throne, who was styled Alamgir II (the Second Conqueror of the World).

By this stage all there was left to rule was just a few districts around Delhi; the Deccan and Awadh were already gone, and much of the rest of India was in the hands of the Marathas and even the English, in the form of the East India Company.

In 1757 the weak Alamgir (1754-1759) tried to outsmart Ghazi-ud-din and invited the Afghan chief and successor to Nadir Shah, Ahmed Shah Durrani, who already controlled the Punjab, to invade Delhi. Thus Delhi was sacked yet again, and the crafty Ghazi-ud-din, who had ingratiated himself with the Durrani chief, remained in control. Not wishing to be double-crossed again, Ghazi-ud-din had Alamgir murdered at Ferozabad. His fortunes suffered a serious reversal two years later when Ahmed Shah Durrani invaded once again in response to Maratha gains in the Punjab. Ghazi-ud-din fled to Surat and Ahmed Shah Durrani recognised Alamgir's son, Shah Alam (1759-1806), as the new emperor of Delhi.

The increasingly powerful Hindu Marathas and Jats now decided the time was right to drive the Muslims out, and once again Panipat was the scene where, for a second time, the Hindus tried to take control of north India. As was the case in the second battle of Panipat two centuries earlier, the Hindus were outsmarted and out-manoeuvred, and after a siege lasting two months, Ahmed Shah Durrani inflicted a bloody defeat on the Marathas. He was unable to gain any effective control, however, as his troops mutinied and he was forced to return to Kabul.

Shah Alam ruled from Allahabad, and managed to survive largely thanks to an annual pension from the British, who by now had gained considerable influence in eastern India. He returned to Delhi in 1770 with the co-operation of the Marathas, who were occupying the city at that time. In 1788 the final blow to the Mughal Empire was struck when the emperor was blinded by Ghulam Qadir, a rival of the Marathas from the Rohilla clan. The emperor was restored to the throne by the Marathas, but it says something about the sorry state of the Mughal Empire that a blind emperor could rule – in previous times the very act of blinding was an effective way of rendering a rival incapable. In fact, a rhyme was made at the time which made a mockery of the emperor:

From Delhi to Palam
Is the realm of Shah Alam.

Palam is a village only 15 km from Delhi, the site of today's Indira Gandhi International Airport.

The real power now lay with the Marathas, and the next stage in the history of Delhi revolves around their struggle for supremacy with the British. Even so, there were Mughal 'emperors' right up to the time of the Indian Mutiny in 1857, although they had no empire to speak of and were virtually puppets.

The British (1803-1947)

Early Years In 1803 war broke out between the British, in the form of the East India Company which now controlled large parts of eastern and southern India, and the Marathas. After a short siege on the eastern banks of the Yamuna, General Lake marched into the Red Fort and the blind old emperor, Shah Alam, was placed under British protection. With the installation of a full-time British administrator (known as the Resident), Sir David Ochterlony, in the north of Shahjahanabad in today's Civil Lines, the focus of power in Delhi shifted away from the Red Fort for the first time in 150 years.

The British came under siege from the Marathas in 1804, and the crumbling walls of Shahjahanabad offered little protection. The Marathas were repulsed, but having had a nasty shock the British then set about strengthening the walls of the old city and adding a number of bastions.

In the early years of the British administration in Delhi the Mughal emperor ruled undisturbed – although there was in fact very little left to rule – but as time went on and the British grew more powerful the Resident assumed much greater control. As early as 1805 the emperor and his family were on monthly pensions from the British. It soon got to the stage where the large Mughal royal family was something of an embarrassment, and certainly a hindrance to the development of the city's administration.

Shah Alam had been succeeded by his son Akbar Shah in 1806, and he by Bahadur Shah in 1837. In 1856 the Mughals suffered a final indignity: when the heir-apparent died, the British decided that the current emperor, Bahadur Shah was to be the last Mughal ruler – his successor would simply be a Prince of the House of Timur – and they were evicted from the Red Fort.

The early British administrators in Delhi were far from the stuffed shirts that one might expect – Ochterlony had 13 Indian wives and each evening he used to promenade through the city on elephant back, followed by the 13 wives each on her own elephant. The Residency he built used at its core a former Mughal building. Another interesting character was William Fraser, a Persian scholar who arrived in Delhi in 1805 as the Resident's Assistant, and after nearly 30 years in and around the city finally took up the post of Resident in 1833. One of his favourite occupations was hunting Asiatic lions – on foot with a spear. He too had a virtual harem of Indian wives, composed Persian couplets, commissioned a superb collection of Indian miniature paintings, and built himself a mansion on the Ridge. Fraser's closest friend, James Skinner, fought with the Marathas and subsequently raised his own cavalry unit – the famous Skinner's Horse (see Things to See & Do).

Indian Mutiny & Siege of Delhi In 1857, less than half a century after Britain had taken firm control of India, they had their first serious setback. To this day the causes of the 'Indian Mutiny' are hard to unravel – it's even hard to define if it really was the 'War of Independence' by which it is officially referred to in India today, or merely a mutiny. The administration had been run down and there were other more specific causes. The result was a loosely co-ordinated mutiny of the Indian battalions of the Bengal Army.

The Mutiny first broke out in May at Meerut, close to Delhi, and soon spread across north India. Within days Indian soldiers had occupied the old city. The British were caught unprepared and there followed a siege lasting throughout the horrendous heat and humidity of the summer and monsoon. The Mughal emperor, Bahadur Shah, sided somewhat reluctantly with the rebels, perhaps thinking that if the rebels succeeded in overcoming the British he would once again be in charge.

British reinforcements arrived from Punjab in early September and after six days of heavy fighting they had retaken the city. In the process they wreaked a savage revenge on the mutineers and the city – large areas were razed to the ground and the Red Fort was extensively damaged.

The immediate aftermath saw an ugly British response to the Mutiny. The emperor and his sons, who had taken refuge in Humayun's Tomb, were captured; the sons were executed and the emperor himself tried (with dubious legality), found guilty of abetment and exiled to Rangoon, Burma. More than 3000 of the city's inhabitants were tried and executed, often on very little evidence; the rest were turfed out, and the Muslims were not allowed to return for two years. There was even talk of demolishing the Red Fort and the Jama Masjid, but fortunately sanity prevailed.

Post-Mutiny Following the Mutiny, the East India Company was wound up and administration belatedly handed over to the British government. The remainder of the century was the peak period for the empire on which 'the sun never set' and in which India was one of its brightest stars. Although Calcutta was the official capital of India, Delhi retained a prominent commercial role as it was almost equidistant from the three other major cities of India – Calcutta, Bombay and Karachi. After the Mutiny the city's population stood at around 100,000, but by the end of the century it had increased by 50%.

The lavishness of the British Raj of the late 19th century was extreme. In 1877 a huge ceremony, the Imperial Assemblage, was held in Delhi, to proclaim Queen Victoria as Empress of India. This was followed by two equally extravagant ceremonies – the Coronation Durbars of 1903 and 1911; the first to proclaim Edward VII and the second to proclaim George V as Emperor of India. It was here that the announcement was made that the capital would be shifted from Calcutta and a new capital built in Delhi. Foundation stones were laid by King George and Queen Mary at the site of the durbars on the northern outskirts of the city (see Things to See & Do).

20th Century Having made the decision to move the capital, the British set to and built New Delhi, an imposing city of wide, tree-lined avenues and soaring public buildings. It was to be the ultimate stamp of authority, a representation of might born of an era when the empire was everything and the British felt they were destined to rule. The Council Chamber (now Sansad Bhavan – the parliament building) was opened in 1927, but the city officially became the capital in 1931.

During the 1930s the demand for independence became a central issue, and Delhi was obviously a focal point. The July 1945 Labour Party victory in the British elections brought to power leaders who realised that a search for a solution to the Indian problem was imperative. The biggest obstacle was that the country was divided along communal lines; there was just no way the Hindus and Muslims could reconcile their differences.

Independence, Partition & Beyond

The British decided Independence would come by 1948, but the viceroy, Lord Louis Mountbatten, decided to follow a breakneck pace and announced that it would come on 14 August 1947.

The dividing line was drawn and the country was thrown into chaos as millions of Muslims fled west into the newly created Pakistan, while Hindus there fled east to the safety of Hindu-dominated India. Much of Delhi was torched – yet again – and over 300,000 of the city's Muslim inhabitants, most of whom lived in Old Delhi, abandoned their homes and fled, their places being taken by nearly half a million Hindu refugees, most of them from Lahore and other cities.

Prior to Partition the city basically consisted of old Delhi inside the old city wall (and where the bulk of the population lived), Civil Lines north of the old city and New Delhi to the south. With the great influx the refugees spread themselves out and camped wherever they could – gardens, schools, military barracks and railway platforms – and even the Purana Qila became a refugee camp.

A Ministry of Rehabilitation was established simply to deal with this new problem. Most of the outer suburbs and housing estates in Delhi date from this time, when a large building program was undertaken. By 1951 nearly 200,000 refugees had been placed in dwellings abandoned by Muslims fleeing to Pakistan, and another 100,000 in new constructions.

The final stages of Independence held one last tragedy. On 30 January 1948, Mahatma Gandhi, deeply disheartened by Partition and the subsequent bloodshed, was assassinated by a Hindu fanatic in the grounds of the industrialist Birla's house in New Delhi.

Since Independence the city has prospered as the capital of India, and many of the important events in the country's recent history have taken place here. Foremost among these was the assassination of the prime minister, Indira Gandhi, in 1984 by a Sikh member of her bodyguard. The three days of horrendous Hindu-Sikh riots that followed left more than 3000 people dead.

In the past decade Delhi's population has increased by 50%. The increase is largely due to rapid economic expansion and increased job opportunities, but unfortunately many of those attracted are poor and poorly educated rural dwellers who have few prospects left in the village and head for the capital in the hope of finding work. For many the hope remains largely unfulfilled and they live an impoverished existence in the *jhuggis* (shanty settlements) on the east side of the Yamuna River.

The rapid expansion of the city has led to increasing problems of overcrowding, traffic congestion and pollution, although nowhere near the scale of Calcutta. One of the main challenges in the years ahead is to get on top of these problems, thus ensuring that this historical city flourishes yet retains its appeal as a place with much to offer the resident or visitor.

GEOGRAPHY

The 1483-sq-km Union Territory of Delhi lies on the
Indo-Gangetic Plain below the Himalaya and is flat, flat,
flat. The city of Delhi occupies most of the union territory, and the only hills to speak of (and even these don't
amount to much) are those of the Ridge, which is
divided into North and South sections west of the city
centre. These small hills are the northern extent of the
Aravalli Range.

The territory is bordered on the eastern side by the
state of Uttar Pradesh, and on the other three sides by
the state of Haryana.

Rulers wanting to stamp their authority on a city often
like to make use of high points for the construction of
major buildings: Shah Jahan had the Jama Masjid built
on the old city's only hill (albeit an almost imperceptible
one!), while the British built the Secretariat Buildings
and Viceroy's Residence (now Rashtrapati Bhavan) on
the only high point in New Delhi, Raisina Hill, which is
an equally insignificant mound!

The Yamuna (Jumna) River flows north to south along
the eastern edge of city, and eventually joins the Ganges
at Allahabad in Uttar Pradesh, 600-odd km to the south-
east.

CLIMATE

One of Delhi's drawbacks is that for more than half the
year the climate is lousy. For about five months –
November through to the end of March – it is very good,
with daytime temperatures between 21 and 30°C and
night-time minimums of around 7°C. April is the build
up to the blast-furnace heat of summer, and by the end
of the month things are starting to warm up, with temperatures around 38°C. May and June are intolerable,
with daily temperatures well in excess of 45°C – roads
start to melt, birds drop out of the sky and quite a few
people also fail to last the distance.

July brings some relief from the heat but this is
replaced with the enervating humidity of the monsoons
and, as the temperatures are still in the mid-30s, it's
debatable whether this is any more comfortable than the
dry heat of early summer. The monsoon is characterised
more by heavy showers each afternoon than steady
all-day rain. This weather continues throughout August
and September, although by the end of this period the
rain is tailing off and the temperatures coming down to
something approaching tolerable. In these three months
Delhi receives 75% of its annual rainfall of 715 mm.

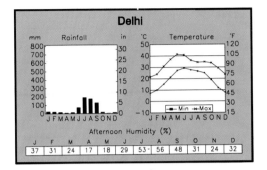

October is quite pleasant, with minimal rainfall and temperatures averaging 33°C.

GOVERNMENT

In 1991 under an act of parliament the Union Territory was provided with a legislative assembly, consisting of 70 elected members and a seven-member council of ministers, headed by a chief minister. Federally the people of Delhi are represented by seven members in the parliamentary lower house (Lok Sabha) and three in the upper house (Rajya Sabha).

The territory is administered by three local authorities: the Delhi Municipal Corporation, New Delhi Municipal Committee and the Cantonment Board.

ECONOMY

Delhi is the economic centre of north India and so is an important light-industrial centre. There are over 80,000 industrial units in the territory, producing everything from TV sets to medicines.

Agriculture still accounts for almost 5% of the territory's land use, but this is decreasing rapidly as the urban sprawl continues apace.

POPULATION & PEOPLE

The population of Delhi currently stands at around 10.1 million, and is growing at the rate of 5% per year. Very few of the city's residents can lay claim to being 'real' Delhi-wallahs, as the population mix was completely changed almost overnight during the trauma of Partition in 1947, when the country was split into Muslim

Pakistan and Hindu India. Delhi went from being a Muslim-dominated city of less than a million to a largely Hindu city of almost two million.

Prior to 1947 the people of the old city were predominantly Muslim, and most of them headed for Pakistan when trouble broke out. Their place was taken by Hindus and to a certain extent by Muslims from elsewhere in India, so while Old Delhi is still basically a Muslim city, it is inhabited largely by people who have been there for less than 50 years. This goes some way to explaining why so many of the fine *havelis* (mansions) of Old Delhi are so poorly maintained – the original owners have long gone, and the new owners have no pride in or sentimental attachment to the buildings. Long-time Muslim residents will tell you with more than a hint of sadness that the city has changed irrevocably – the Urdu spoken in the bazaars these days is a far cry from the classical Urdu which was in use prior to Partition, and many of the old skills, crafts and traditions are rapidly dying out.

The people of New Delhi are basically Hindu Punjabis, many of them originally refugees who fled in the opposite direction during Partition – from Pakistan to India.

ARTS

Dance

Indian dancing relates back to Siva's role as Nataraj, Lord of the Dance. Lord Siva's first wife was Sati and when her father, who disliked Siva, insulted him Sati committed suicide in a sacrifice by fire that later took her name. Outraged, Siva killed his father-in-law and danced the Tandava – the Dance of Destruction. Later Sati reincarnated as Parvati, married Siva again and danced the Lasya. Thus the Tandava became the male form of dance, the Lasya the female form. Dancing was a part of the religious temple rituals and the dancers were known as *devadasis*. Their dances retold stories from the *Ramayana* or the *Mahabharata*.

Temple dancing is no longer practised but classical Indian dancing still has a religious background. Indian dance is divided into *nritta* – the rhythmic elements, *nritya* – the combination of rhythm with expression, and *natya* – the dramatic element. Nritya is usually expressed through eye, hand and facial movements and with nritya makes up the usual dance programmes. To appreciate natya, dance drama, you have to understand and appreciate Indian legends and mythology.

Dance is divided into three major forms known as Bharat Natyam, Kathakali and Kathak. Bharat Natyam is further subdivided into three other classical forms. One of the most popular, it originated in the great temples of the south and usually tells of events in Krishna's life. Bharat Natyam dancers are usually women and, like the sculptures they take their positions from, always dance bent-kneed, never standing upright, and use a huge repertoire of hand movements. Orissi, Mohini Attam and Kuchipudi are variations of Bharat Natyam which take their names from the places where they originated. Kathakali, the second major dance form, originated in Kerala and is exclusively danced by men. It tells of epic battles of gods and demons and is as dynamic and dramatic as Bharat Natyam is austere and expressive. Kathakali dancing is noted for the elaborate make-up and painted masks the dancers wear. They even use special eye drops to turn their eyes a bloodshot red!

The final classical dance type is Kathak, which originated in the north and at first was very similar to the Bharat Natyam school. Persian and Muslim influences later altered the dance from a temple ritual to a courtly entertainment. The dances are performed straight-legged and there are intricately choreographed foot movements to be followed. The ankle bells the dancers wear must be adeptly controlled and the costumes and themes are often similar to those in Mughal miniature paintings.

There are many opportunities to see classical Indian dancing while you are in Delhi. The major hotels often put on performances to which outsiders as well as hotel guests are welcome.

Music

Indian music is most unlike the concept of music in the West. It is very difficult for a Westerner to appreciate it without a lengthy introduction and much time spent in listening.

The two main forms of Indian music are the southern Carnatic and the northern Hindustani traditions. The basic difficulty is that there is no harmony in the Western sense. The music has two basic elements, the *tala* and the *raga*. Tala is the rhythm and is characterised by the number of beats. *Teental* is a tala of 16 beats. The audience follows the tala by clapping at the appropriate beat, which in teental is at one, five and 13. There is no clap at the beat of nine since that is the *khali* or 'empty section' indicated by a wave of the hand. Just as tala is the rhythm, so is raga the melody; just as there are a number

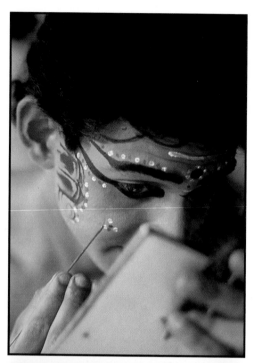

Top : A Kathakali dancer applies makeup.(GE)
Bottom : The tabla provides the tala (rhythm). (GB)

of basic talas so there are many set ragas. The classical Indian music group consists of three musicians who provide the drone, the melody and the rhythm – in other words a background drone, a tala and a raga. The musicians are basically soloists – the concept of an orchestra of Indian musicians is impossible since there is not the harmony that a Western orchestra provides – each musician selects their own tala and raga. The players then zoom off in their chosen directions, as dictated by the tala and the raga selected, and, to the audience's delight, meet every once in a while before again diverging.

Yehudi Menuhin, who has devoted much time and energy to understanding Indian music, suggests that it is much like Indian society: a group of individuals not working together but every once in a while meeting at some common point. Western music is analogous to Western democratic societies, a group of individuals (the orchestra) who each surrender part of their freedom to the harmony of the whole.

Although Indian classical music has one of the longest continuous histories of any musical form, the music had never, until quite recently, been recorded in any written notation. Furthermore, within the basic framework set by the tala and the raga, the musicians improvise – providing variations on the basic melody and rhythm.

Best known of the Indian instruments are the *sitar* and the *tabla*. The sitar is the large stringed instrument popularised by Ravi Shankar in the West – and which more than a few Westerners have discovered is more than just slightly difficult to tune. This is the instrument with which the soloist plays the raga. Other stringed instruments are the *sarod* (which is plucked) or the *sarangi* (which is played with a bow). The tabla, a twin drum rather like a Western bongo, provides the tala. The drone, which runs on two basic notes, is provided by the oboe-like *shehnai* or the *tampura*.

Architecture

The evolution of north Indian architecture can be traced in the many distinctive buildings around the city (see Things to See & Do for more about the buildings described here and how to find them).

Hindu Architecture Early Hindu temples were characterised by rectangular doorways (as against arches which came later), stepped ceilings rather than domes, and a high degree of ornamentation with floral and other natural motifs. White marble was the predominant material used. Examples of this style can still be seen in the courtyard of the 11th-century Quwwat-ul-Islam mosque at the Qutb Minar complex, as the mosque itself was built with material taken from Hindu temples.

Slave & Khalji Dynasties During the Slave and Khalji dynasties the first examples of architectural styles brought in by Muslims from central Asia began to appear. Foremost among these is the use of pointed arches and domes. The problem here was that the local Hindu stonemasons were unfamiliar with these techniques, and so the arches built during this time were not true arches with keystones, but simply arch-shaped openings in a wall. The soaring arches of the Quwwat-ul-Islam mosque were built in this way.

The other feature of Muslim architecture is the carved ornamentation of geometric patterns and Koranic inscriptions. One of the first structures to be decorated in this way after stonemasons were brought in from Afghanistan was the tomb of Iltutmish at the Qutb Minar complex.

Early examples of buildings which combine all three elements of Muslim design – the pointed arch, dome and geometric design – are the Alai Darwaza gateway at the Qutb Minar and the Jama'at Khana mosque by the shrine of Nizam-ud-din.

Tughlaq Style The most striking thing about the Tughlaqabad buildings is the sense of strength and impregnability which they convey. The walls generally slope inwards, reinforcing the impression of strength. This overall appearance was perhaps no accident as, with the Mongols threatening from the north, the plain of Delhi during the time of the Tughlaqs was not the safest of places.

The buildings were generally of local stone faced with plaster, perhaps an indication of the relative modesty of the Tughlaq's wealth and how much their resources were stretched keeping the Mongols at bay; these days the plaster has long since disintegrated, leaving just the bare stone walls.

The Tughlaqs also reintroduced some elements of Hindu design, such as the square doorway pillar and the lotus motif. This was the first sign of the emergence of a purely Indian architectural style.

Good examples of buildings from this period include: the remains of Feroz Shah Kotla, the *madrasa* and Tomb of Feroz Shah at Hauz Khas and the tomb of Ghiyas-ud-din at Tughlaqabad (see under South Delhi in Things to See & Do).

Sayyid & Lodi Style The important buildings of the Sayyid and Lodi periods were limited to tombs and mosques, and showed growing integration of Hindu and Islamic styles.

The earlier tombs were square, squat structures, one of the main features being the two-storey appearance created by the use of two rows of arches on the facades. The low domes were usually covered with coloured tiles and had the lotus design on top. Examples are the Bara Gumbad and Shish Gumbad tombs in the Lodi Garden.

Later Lodi tombs were octagonal, surrounded by a square-pillared veranda with small overhanging *chajjas* (eaves). An innovation with these tombs was the addition of small domes *(chhatris)* surrounding the large dome, which served to blend the curves of the main dome with the harsher angles of the rest of the structure. The tombs of Mubarak Shah and Sikander Lodi in the Lodi Garden and that of Isa Khan by Humayun's Tomb are all good examples.

The mosques of this period feature low, tapering minarets, such as on the Bara Gumbad mosque in the Lodi Garden. The mosques were also finely proportioned, with a large central arch flanked on either side by two smaller ones, and a three-domed roof. The interiors were highly decorated with carved inscriptions, and different coloured stones were used to enhance the external appearance. The two best examples of this are the Moth-ki-Masjid in south Delhi and the Qila-i-Kuhna mosque in the Purana Qila.

The Mughals Easily the most impressive structures in Delhi today are those built by the Mughals. One reason for this is that the Mughals were simply so much wealthier than any previous rulers that they were able to lavish vast sums of money on the finest materials and could afford to employ the most experienced and talented artisans.

During the early Mughal period buildings were of red sandstone with marble details. Square tombs were built on high platforms, and these were surrounded by a formal Persian-style garden. The style was known as *charbagh*, or four-garden, as the huge courtyard surrounding the tomb was quartered by watercourses, and these quarters were then divided by smaller channels. The tombs themselves had marble domes surrounded by small chhatris. Humayun's Tomb, one of the finest buildings in Delhi, is a superb example, and the garden here is one of the very few to still have its original watercourses intact, although they remain empty most of the time.

During the middle period, much more use was made of marble, and buildings had more bulbous domes and towering minarets. The Jama Masjid and the Fatehpuri Masjid are both good examples, but the supreme building from this period is, of course, the Taj Mahal in Agra.

In the later Mughal period the style became over-elaborate and the materials used were inferior as money became scarcer; good examples of this decadent period are the Sunehri Masjid on Chandni Chowk in Old Delhi and the Safdarjang's Tomb, probably the last notable Mughal building.

Film

The Indian film industry is the largest in the world in purely volume terms – in 1992, a massive 836 films were registered for classification with the censorship board! There are more than 12,000 cinemas across the country, and at least five times as many 'video halls'. The vast proportion of what is produced are your average Bollywood 'masala movies' – cheap melodramas based on three vital ingredients: romance, violence and music. Most are dreadful, but it's cheap escapism for the masses, a chance to dream.

However, for all the dross churned out, India has produced some wonderful films from brilliant directors, foremost among them being Satyajit Ray. Other notable Indian directors include Meera Nair, who directed *Salaam Bombay*, Mrinal Sen, Ritwik Ghatak, Shaji N Karuns, Adoor and Aravindan.

Hand-painted billboards advertising films (HF)

Painting & Sculpture

Indian art and sculpture is basically religious in its themes and developments, and appreciation requires at least some knowledge of its religious background. The earliest Indian artefacts are found in the Indus Valley cities in modern-day Pakistan. Pieces are mainly small items of sculpture and it was not until the Mauryan era that India's first major artistic period flowered. This classical school of Buddhist art reached its peak during the reign of Ashoka. The Sungas, who followed the Mauryas, continued their artistic traditions. When this empire ended, the Gandharan period came into its own in the north-west. Close to Peshawar, in today's Pakistan, the Gandharan period combined Buddhism with a strong Greek influence from the descendants of Alexander the Great's invading army. During this period the Buddha began to be represented directly in human form rather than by symbols such as the footprint or the stupa.

Meanwhile in India proper another school began to develop at Mathura, near Delhi. Here the religious influence was also Buddhist but was beginning to be altered by the revival of Brahmanism, the forerunner of Hinduism. It was in this school that the tradition of sculpting *yakshis*, those well-endowed heavenly damsels, began.

During the Gupta period from 320-600 AD, Indian art went through a golden age, and the Buddha images developed their present-day form – even today in Buddhist countries the attitudes, clothing and hand positions have scarcely altered. This was, however, also the end of Buddhist art in India, for Hinduism began to reassert itself.

The following 1000 years saw a slow but steady development through to the exuberant medieval period of Indian Hindu art. Sculpture can be traced from the older, stiff and unmoving Buddhist sculptures through to the dynamic and dramatic Hindu figures.

These reached their culmination in the period when sculpture became an integral part of architecture; it is impossible to tell where building ends and sculpture begins. The architecture competes valiantly with the artwork, which manages to combine high quality with quite awesome quantity. An interesting common element is the highly detailed erotic scenes. The heavenly maidens of an earlier period blossomed into scenes, positions and possibilities that left little to the imagination. Art of this period was not purely a representation of gods and goddesses. Every aspect of human life appeared in the sculptures and obviously in India sex was considered a fairly important aspect!

The arrival of the Muslims with their intolerance of other religions and 'idols' caused enormous damage to India's artistic relics. The early invaders' art was chiefly confined to paintings, but with the Mughals, Indian art went through yet another golden period. Best known of the art forms they encouraged was the miniature painting. These delightfully detailed and brightly coloured paintings showed the events and activities of the Mughals in their magnificent palaces. Other paintings included portraits or studies of wildlife and plants.

At the same time there was a massive revival of folk art; some of these developments embraced the Mughal miniature concepts but combined them with Indian religious arts. The popular Rajasthan or Mewar schools often included scenes from Krishna's life and escapades – Krishna is usually painted blue. Interestingly, this school followed the Persian-influenced Mughal school in its miniaturised and highly detailed approach, but made no use of the Persian-developed sense of perspective, and works are generally almost two dimensional.

The Mughals' greatest achievements were, however, in the architectural field; it is chiefly for their magnificent buildings that they are remembered. After the Mughals there has not been another major artistic period of purely Indian background. During the British period art became imitative of Western trends and ideals. Although there was much British painting in India it is interesting primarily as an historical record rather than as art itself.

SOCIETY & CULTURE

Castes

The caste system is one of India's more confusing mysteries; how it came about, how it has managed to survive for so long and how much harm it causes are all topics of discussion for visitors to India. Its origins are hazy but basically it seems to have been developed by the Brahmins, or priest class, in order to make their own superior position more permanent. Later it was probably extended by the invading Aryans who felt themselves superior to the indigenous pre-Aryan Indians. Eventually the caste system became formalised into four distinct classes, each with rules of conduct and behaviour. At the top are the Brahmins, who are the priests and the arbiters of what is right and wrong in matters of religion and caste. Next come the Kshatriyas,

who are soldiers and administrators. The Vaisyas are the
artisan and commercial class, and finally the Sudras are
the farmers and the peasant class. These four castes are
said to have come from Brahma's mouth (Brahmins),
arms (Kshatriyas), thighs (Vaisyas) and feet (Sudras).

Beneath the four main castes is a fifth group, the
untouchables. These people, members of the so-called
Scheduled Castes, literally have no caste. They perform
the most menial and degrading jobs. At one time, if a
high-caste Hindu used the same temple as an untouchable, was touched by one, or even had an untouchable's
shadow cast across them, they were polluted and had to
go through a rigorous series of rituals to be cleansed.

Today the caste system has been much weakened but
it still has considerable power, particularly among the
less educated people. Gandhi put great effort into bringing the untouchables into society, including renaming
them the Harijans, or Children of God. But an untouchable by any other name...Recently the word Harijan has
lost favour, and the use of it in official business has
actually been banned in Madhya Pradesh. The term the
members of these groups themselves prefer is Dalit,
meaning Oppressed or Downtrodden.

It must be remembered that being born into a certain
caste does not limit you strictly to one occupation or
position in life, just as being black in the USA does not
mean you are poverty-stricken and live in Harlem.
Many Brahmins are poor peasants, for example, and
hundreds of years ago the great Maratha leader Shivaji
was a Sudra. None of the later Marathas, who controlled
much of India after the demise of the Mughals, were
Brahmins. Nevertheless you can generalise that the
better off Indians will be higher caste and that the
'sweeper' you see desultorily cleaning the toilet in your
hotel will be a Dalit. In fact when Indian Airlines
appointed its first Dalit flight attendant it was front-page
news in Indian newspapers.

How can you tell which caste a Hindu belongs to?
Well, if you know that their job is a menial one such as
cleaning streets or in some way defiling, such as working
with leather, they are a Dalit. But for most Hindus you
can't really tell which caste they belong to. However, if
you see a man with his shirt off and he has the sacred
thread (*janeu*) looped round one shoulder he belongs to
one of the higher castes - but then Parsis also wear a
sacred thread. Of course the Sikhs, Muslims and Christians do not have caste.

In many ways the caste system also functions as an
enormous unofficial trade union with strict rules to
avoid demarcation disputes. Each caste has many sub-

A worker taking a break (RI)

divisions so that the servants who polish the brass cannot, due to their caste, also polish silver. Many of the old caste rules have been considerably relaxed, although less educated or more isolated Hindus may still avoid having a lower-caste person prepare their food for fear of becoming polluted. Better educated people are demonstrably none too worried about shaking hands with a caste-less Westerner though! Nor does the thought of going overseas, and thus losing caste completely, carry much weight these days. Often, quite the opposite, particularly if they return with a degree from an overseas university.

The caste system still produces enormous burdens for India, however. During the last few years there have been frequent outbreaks of violence towards members of the Scheduled Castes and so-called Backward classes ('tribals' and those who are poor or poorly educated for reasons other than caste). In an effort to improve the lot of these people, the government reserves huge numbers of public sector jobs, parliamentary seats and university places for them. With nearly 60% of the jobs reserved, many well-educated people are missing out on jobs which they would easily get on merit.

In 1994 some state governments, such as Karnataka, raised the reservation level even higher in an effort to win mass support. In 1991, and again in 1994, there were serious protests against the raising of the quotas. These protests were most violent in Gujarat, Uttar Pradesh, Delhi and Haryana, and at least 100 people died or were seriously injured in self-immolation incidents in the 1991 protests.

Going far back into Western history, it's important to remember that the medieval ideal of heaven was developed in part to keep the peasants in their place – behave yourself, work hard, put up with your lot and you'll go to heaven. Probably caste developed in a similar fashion – your life may be pretty miserable but that's your *karma*; behave yourself and you may be born into a better one next time around.

Marriage

One place where the caste system is still well entrenched is the choosing of marriage partners. You only need to read a few of the 'matrimonial' advertisements that appear in many places, including the national Sunday newspapers (and even these days on the Internet!) to realise that marriage across the 'caste bar', even among wealthy, well-educated or higher caste people, is basically not on. The majority of marriages are still arranged by the parents, although 'love marriages' are becoming more common, particularly in relatively liberal-minded places such as Delhi. When a couple are choosing a partner for their son or daughter, a number of factors are taken into consideration: caste of course is pre-eminent, but other considerations are beauty and physical flaws – the matrimonial ads can seem brutally frank in this regard – and a horoscope for the would-be partner is often called for. Many potential matches are rejected simply because the astrological signs are not propitious. The financial status of the prospective partner's family is also taken into account.

Another facet of marriage is the pernicious dowry. A dowry was originally a gift to the bride from her parents, so she would have something of her own and would in turn be able to provide a dowry to her own daughters. These days, however, the dowry is a matter of status for the bride's family – the bigger the dowry and grander the ceremony, the greater the prestige to the family.

Although the practice is officially outlawed, a dowry is still expected in the majority of cases. For poorer families the marriage can become a huge financial burden. Many men have to borrow the money, either for their daughter's dowry or to stage a lavish ceremony and feast (or both), usually at outrageous rates of interest. The end result is that for the rest of their lives they are indebted to the feared moneylenders, or become bonded labourers.

The amount of an expected dowry varies, but it is never small. The main determining factor is the level of education and social standing of the young man; a dowry of at least US$20,000 would be expected from the family of a young woman hoping to marry a graduate of a foreign university, a doctor or other highly paid professional. A 'Green Card' (American residence card) is also highly desirable, and the holder of one can command a high price.

The official age for marriage is 18 years for women and 21 for men, but this is widely ignored – 8% of girls aged between 10 and 14 are married, and nearly 50% of females aged between 15 and 19 are married, although the average age for marriage is 18.3 for women and 23.3 for men. Virginity is also of vital importance, and it is often listed among the woman's attributes in the matrimonial columns.

Women in Society

India is a country of great fascination and colour; it is also a country of great hardship, and the people who face the worst of it are generally the women. It is also a cruel paradox that at a time when India's prime minister was arguably the world's most powerful woman, 75% of the country's women were living in villages with little education, few rights, strenuous and poorly paid jobs, and little prospect of anything better.

Problems for Indian women begin at birth. Even now boys are considered more desirable than girls for they offer the parents security in old age – traditionally, the sons remain in their parents' house even after marriage. Girls are often seen as a burden on the family, as not only will they leave the family when married, but also an adequate dowry must be supplied. Consequently girls may often be fed less if there is inadequate food, and their education neglected. Such is the desire for boys that clinics in India used to advertise pregnancy testing to determine the sex of the foetus; in many instances abortions were performed if it was female. Although such practices are now illegal, it is believed they still occur.

Arranged marriages are still the norm rather than the exception. A village girl may well find herself married

off while still in her early teens to a man she has never
met. She would have no property rights should her
husband own land, and domestic violence is common;
indeed, a man often feels it is his right to beat his wife.
In many ways her status is little better than that of a
slave.

For the urban, middle-class woman in cities such as
Delhi, life is materially much more comfortable but the
pressures still exist. She is much more likely to be given
an education, simply because this will make her marriage prospects better. Once married, however, she is still
largely expected to be mother and home maker above
all else. Like her village counterpart, if she fails to live
up to expectations – even if it is just not being able to give
her in-laws a grandson – the consequences can be dire;
the practice of 'bride burning' is not uncommon. There
are daily newspaper reports of women burning to death
in kitchen fires, usually from 'spilt' kerosene. The majority of these cases, however, are either suicides –
desperate women who could no longer cope with the
pressure from their parents-in-law – or outright murders
by in-laws who want their son to remarry someone they
consider to be a better prospect.

A married woman faces even greater pressure if she
wants to divorce her husband. Although the constitution
allows for divorcees (and widows) to remarry, few are
in a position to do this simply because they are basically
outcasts from society; even her own family will turn
their backs on a woman who seeks divorce, and there is
no social security net to provide for her. A marriage in
India is not so much a union based on love between two
individuals as a social contract joining two people and
their families. It is then the responsibility of the couple
to make the marriage work, whatever the obstacles; if
the marriage fails both husband and wife are tainted, but
the fall-out for the woman is far worse. Divorce rates are,
not surprisingly, low.

While all this is the downside of being a woman in
India, the picture is not completely gloomy. In the past
decade or so the women's movement has had some
successes in improving the status of women. Although
the professions are still very much male dominated,
women are making inroads – in 1993 the first women
were inducted into the armed forces, and they account
for around 10% of all parliamentarians. Two high-profile
professional women of recent times are, of course,
former Prime Minister Indira Gandhi, and Kiran Bedi,
India's first female police officer, then deputy commissioner of police in Delhi and now head of Delhi's main
prison, Tihar Jail.

For the village women it's much more difficult to get ahead, but groups such as SEWA (Self Employed Women's Association) in Ahmedabad have shown what can be achieved. Here poor or low caste women, many of whom work only on the fringes of the economy, such as scavenging for waste-paper at the dump, have been organised into unions, giving them at least some lobbying power against discriminatory and exploitative work practices. SEWA has also set up a bank, giving many poor women their first access to a savings or lending body, as conventional banks were unwilling to deal with people of such limited means.

Although the attitudes towards women are slowly changing, it will be a long time before they gain even a measure of equality with men. For the moment their power lies in their considerable influence over family affairs and so remains largely invisible.

Indian Clothing

The most well known item of Indian clothing is the *sari*. It is also the one piece of clothing which is very difficult for Western women to carry off properly. This supremely graceful attire is simply one length of material, a bit over a metre in width and five to nine metres long (usually around six metres). It's worn without any pins, buttons or fastenings to hold it in place so in part its graceful appearance is a necessity. The tightly fitted, short blouse worn under a sari is a *choli*. The final length of the sari, which is draped over the wearer's shoulder, is known as the *pallav* or *palloo*.

There are a number of variations in types of saris and styles of wearing them, but there are also other styles of women's costume in India. Kashmiri and Sikh women wear pyjama-like trousers drawn tightly in at the waist and gathered at the ankles. Over these trousers, known as *salwars*, they wear a long, loose tunic known as a *kameez*. This attire is comfortable and 'respectable'. A *churidhar* is similar to the salwar but tighter fitting at the hips. Over this goes a mandarin-collar *kurta* – an item of clothing just as popular in the West, where it is worn by men as much as women, as in India.

Although the overwhelming majority of Indian women wear traditional costume, many Indian men wear quite conventional Western clothing. Indeed a large proportion of India's consumer advertising appears to be devoted to 'suitings & shirtings' the material made for tailor-made, Western-style business suits and shirts. You can easily get a suit made to measure, although the styling is likely to be somewhat dated. The

A flower seller wearing a sari at the market (GE)

collarless jacket, known as a *bandgala* or jodhpuri (or
Nehru) jacket, is a popular buy among travellers. These
khadi (homespun cloth) coats are best bought at the
government Khadi Gramodyog Bhavan in Connaught
Place.

Muslim women, of course, wear more staid and all-
covering attire than their Hindu sisters. In Old Delhi
you'll see many Muslim women wearing the all-envel-
oping, tent-like *burkha*.

Sport

Indians follow a variety of sports including field hockey,
soccer and cricket. In hockey they are one of the world's
leaders with several Olympic golds to their credit.
Soccer has a keen following in a number of big cities,
including Delhi.

India's national sport (obsession almost) has to be
cricket. There's something about a game with as many
idiosyncrasies and peculiarities as cricket which appeals
to the Indian temperament. During the cricket season, if
an international side is touring India and there is a Test
match on, you'll see crowds outside the many shops
which have a TV, and people walking down the street

with a pocket radio pressed to their ear. Test matches with Pakistan have a particularly strong following as the rivalry is intense. One thing you can count on is that most Indians will know the names of the entire touring cricket team and, if you come from the same country but don't know their names, then you may well be regarded as mentally retarded. On the other hand, if you do have an interest in cricket, it can be a great way to start up conversations.

RELIGION

India has a positive kaleidoscope of religions. There is probably more diversity of religions and sects in India than anywhere else on earth. Apart from having nearly all the world's great religions represented, India is the birthplace of Hinduism and Buddhism, an important home to Zoroastrianism, one of the world's oldest religions, and home to Jainism, an ancient religion unique to India.

Hinduism

India's major religion, Hinduism, is practised by approximately 80% of the population, over 670 million people. Only in Nepal, the Indonesian island of Bali, the Indian Ocean island of Mauritius and possibly Fiji, do Hindus also predominate, but it is the largest religion in Asia in terms of number of adherents. It is one of the oldest extant religions, with firm roots extending back to beyond 1000 BC.

The Indus Valley civilisation developed a religion which shows a close relationship to Hinduism in many ways. Later, it further developed through the combined religious practices of the southern Dravidians and the Aryan invaders who arrived in the north of India around 1500 BC. Around 1000 BC, the Vedic scriptures were introduced and gave the first loose framework to the religion.

Hinduism today has a number of holy books, the most important being the four *Vedas* (Divine Knowledge) which are the foundation of Hindu philosophy. The *Upanishads* are contained within the *Vedas* and delve into the metaphysical nature of the universe and soul. The *Mahabharata* (Great War of the Bharatas) is an epic poem containing over 220,000 lines. It describes the battles between the Kauravas and Pandavas, who were descendants of the Lunar race. In it is the story of Rama, and it is probable that the most famous Hindu epic, the *Ramayana*, was based on this. The *Ramayana* is highly revered

by Hindus, perhaps because a verse in the introduction
says 'He who reads and repeats this holy life-giving
Ramayana is liberated from all his sins and exalted with
all his posterity to the highest heaven'. The *Bhagavad Gita*
is a famous episode of the *Mahabharata* where Krishna
relates his philosophies to Arjuna.

Basically the religion postulates that we will all go
through a series of rebirths, or reincarnations, that eventually lead to *moksha*, the spiritual salvation which frees
one from the cycle of rebirths. With each rebirth you can
move closer to or further from eventual moksha; the
deciding factor is your karma, which is literally a law of
cause and effect. Bad actions during your life result in
bad karma, which ends in a lower reincarnation. Con-
versely, if your deeds and actions have been good you
will reincarnate on a higher level and be a step closer to
eventual freedom from rebirth.

Dharma, or the natural law, defines the total social,
ethical and spiritual harmony of your life. There are
three categories of dharma, the first being the eternal
harmony which involves the whole universe. The
second category is the dharma that controls castes and
the relations between castes. The third dharma is the
moral code that an individual should follow.

The Hindu religion has three basic practices. They are
puja (worship), the cremation of the dead, and the rules
and regulations of the caste system (see Society &
Culture). Westerners have trouble understanding
Hinduism principally because of its vast pantheon of
gods. In fact you can look upon all these different gods
simply as pictorial representations of the many attributes of a god. The one omnipresent god usually has
three physical representations. Brahma is the creator,
Vishnu is the preserver and Siva is the destroyer and
reproducer. All three gods are usually shown with four
arms, but Brahma has the added advantage of four
heads to represent his all-seeing presence. The four
Vedas are supposed to have emanated from his mouths.

Each god has an associated animal known as the
'vehicle' on which they ride, as well as a consort with
certain attributes and abilities. Generally each god also
holds a symbol; you can often pick out which god is
represented by the vehicle or symbol. Brahma's consort
is Saraswati, the Goddess of Learning. She rides upon a
white swan and holds the stringed musical instrument
known as a *veena*.

Vishnu, the preserver, is usually shown in one of the
physical forms in which he has visited earth. In all,
Vishnu has paid nine visits and on his 10th he is expected
as Kalki, riding a horse. On earlier visits he appeared in

Sadhus seeking alms at the market (RI)

animal form, as in his boar or man-lion (Narsingh) incarnations, but on visit seven he appeared as Rama, regarded as the personification of the ideal man and the hero of the *Ramayana*. Rama also managed to provide a number of secondary gods including his helpful ally Hanuman, the monkey god. Hanuman's faithful nature is illustrated by his representation being often found guarding fort or palace entrances. Naturally, incarnations can also have consorts and Rama's lady was Sita. On visit eight Vishnu came as Krishna, who was brought up with peasants and thus became a great favourite of the working classes. Krishna is renowned for his exploits with the *gopis*, or shepherdesses, and his consorts are Radha the head of the gopis, Rukmani and Satyabhama. Krishna is often blue in colour and plays a flute. Vishnu's last incarnation was on visit nine, as the Buddha. This was probably a ploy to bring the Buddhist splinter group back into the Hindu fold.

When Vishnu appears as Vishnu, rather than one of his incarnations, he sits on a couch made from the coils of a serpent and in his hands he holds two symbols, the conch shell and the discus. Vishnu's vehicle is the half-man half-eagle known as the Garuda. The Garuda is a firm do-gooder and has a deep dislike of snakes. His consort is the beautiful Lakshmi (Laxmi), who came from the sea and is the goddess of wealth and prosperity.

Siva's creative role is phallically symbolised by his representation as the frequently worshipped *lingam*. Siva rides on the bull Nandi and his matted hair is said to have Ganga, the goddess of the river Ganges, in it. He is supposed to live in the Himalaya and devote much time to smoking dope. He has the third eye in the middle of his forehead and carries a trident. Siva is also known as Nataraj, the cosmic dancer whose dance shook the cosmos and created the world. Siva's consort is Parvati, the beautiful. She, however, has a dark side when she appears as Durga, the terrible. In this role she holds weapons in her 10 hands and rides a tiger. As Kali, the fiercest of the gods, she demands sacrifices and wears a garland of skulls. Kali usually handles the destructive side of Siva's personality.

Siva and Parvati have two children. Ganesh is the elephant-headed god of prosperity and wisdom, and is probably the most popular of all the gods. Ganesh obtained his elephant head due to his father's notorious temper. Coming back from a long trip, Siva discovered Parvati in her room with a young man. Not pausing to think that their son might have grown up a little during his absence, Siva lopped his head off! He was then forced by Parvati to bring his son back to life but could only do so by giving him the head of the first living thing he saw, which happened to be an elephant. Ganesh's vehicle is a rat. Siva and Parvati's other son is Kartikkaya, the god of war.

A variety of lesser gods and goddesses also crowd the scene. Most temples are dedicated to one or other of the gods, but curiously there are very few Brahma temples – perhaps just one in all of India (at Pushkar in Rajasthan). Most Hindus profess to be either Vaishnava-ites (followers of Vishnu) or Shaivites (followers of Siva). The cow is, of course, the holy animal of Hinduism.

Hinduism is not a proselytising religion since you cannot be converted. You're either born a Hindu or you are not; you can never become one. Similarly, once you are a Hindu you cannot change your caste – you're born into it and are stuck with it for the rest of that lifetime. Nevertheless Hinduism has a great attraction to many Westerners and India's 'export gurus' are many and successful.

A *guru* is not so much a teacher as a spiritual guide, somebody who by example or simply by their presence indicates what path you should follow. In a spiritual search one always needs a guru.

A *sadhu* is an individual on a spiritual search. They're an easily recognised group, usually wandering around half-naked, smeared in dust with their hair and beard matted; what clothes they wear are usually saffron coloured. Sadhus following Siva will sometimes carry his symbol, the trident. A sadhu is often someone who has decided that his business and family life have reached their natural conclusions and that it is time to throw everything aside and go out on a spiritual search. He may previously have been the village postman, or a businessman. Sadhus perform various feats of self-mortification and wander all over India, occasionally coming together in great pilgrimages and other religious gatherings. Many sadhus are, of course, simply beggars following a more sophisticated approach to gathering in the paise, but others are completely genuine in their search.

Buddhism

Although there are only about 6.6 million Buddhists in India, the religion is of great importance because it had its birth here and there are many reminders of its historic role. Strictly speaking Buddhism is not a religion, since it is not centred on a god, but a system of philosophy and a code of morality.

Buddhism was founded in northern India about 500 BC when Siddhartha Gautama, born a prince, achieved enlightenment. Gautama Buddha was not the first Buddha but the fourth, and is not expected to be the last 'enlightened one'. Buddhists believe that the achievement of enlightenment is the goal of every being, so eventually we will all reach Buddhahood.

The Buddha never wrote down his dharma, or teachings, and a schism later developed so that today there are two major Buddhist schools. The Theravada (Doctrine of the Elders), or Hinayana (Small Vehicle), holds that the path to *nirvana*, the eventual aim of all Buddhists, is an individual pursuit. In contrast, the Mahayana (Large Vehicle) school holds that the combined belief of its followers will eventually be great enough to encompass all of humanity and bear it to salvation. To some the less austere and ascetic Mahayana school is a 'soft option'. Today it is chiefly practised in Vietnam, Japan and China, while the Hinayana school is followed in Sri Lanka, Burma, Cambodia and Thailand. There are other, sometimes more esoteric, divisions of Buddhism such as the Hindu-Tantric Buddhism of Tibet, which you can see in Ladakh and other parts of north India.

The Buddha renounced his material life to search for enlightenment but, unlike other prophets, found that starvation did not lead to discovery. Therefore he developed his rule of the 'middle way', moderation in everything. The Buddha taught that all life is suffering but that suffering comes from our sensual desires and the illusion that they are important. By following the 'eight-fold path' these desires will be extinguished and a state of nirvana, where we are free from their delusions, will be reached. Following this process requires going through a series of rebirths until the goal is eventually reached and no more rebirths into the world of suffering are necessary. The path that takes you through this cycle of births is karma, but this is not simply fate. Karma is a law of cause and effect; your actions in one life determine the role you will play and what you will have to go through in your next life.

In India, Buddhism developed rapidly when it was embraced by the great Emperor Ashoka. As his empire extended over much of India, so was Buddhism carried forth. He also sent out missions to other lands to preach the Buddha's word, and his own son is said to have carried Buddhism to Sri Lanka. Later, however, Buddhism began to contract in India because it had never really taken a hold on the great mass of people. As Hinduism revived, Buddhism in India was gradually reabsorbed into the older religion.

Today Buddha, to Hindus, is another incarnation of Vishnu. At its peak, however, Buddhism was responsible for magnificent structures erected wherever it held sway. The earlier Theravada form of Buddhism did not believe in the representation of the Buddha in human form. His presence was always alluded to in Buddhist art or architecture through symbols such as the bo tree, under which he was sitting when he attained enlightenment, the elephant, which his mother dreamed of before he was born, or the wheel of life. Today, however, even Theravada Buddhists produce Buddha images.

Islam

Muslims, followers of the Islamic religion, are India's largest religious minority. They number about 105 million in all, almost 10% of the country's population. This makes India one of the largest Islamic nations in the world. India has had two Muslim presidents, several cabinet ministers and state chief ministers since Independence.

The religion's founder, the prophet Muhammad, was born in 570 AD at Mecca, now part of Saudi Arabia. He had his first revelation from Allah (God) in 610 and this and later visions were compiled into the Muslim holy book, the Koran. As his purpose in life was revealed to him, Muhammad began to preach against the idolatry for which Mecca was then the centre. Muslims are strictly monotheistic and believe that to search for God through images is a sin. Muslim teachings correspond closely with the Old Testament of the Bible, and Moses and Jesus are both accepted as Muslim prophets, although Jesus is not the son of God.

Eventually Muhammad's attacks on local business caused him and his followers to be run out of town in 622. They fled to Medina, the 'city of the prophet', and by 630 were strong enough to march back into Mecca and take over. Although Muhammad died in 632, most of Arabia had been converted to Islam within two decades.

The Muslim faith was more than a religion; it called on its followers to spread the word. In succeeding centuries Islam was to expand over three continents. The Arabs, who first propagated the faith, developed a reputation as being ruthless opponents but reasonable masters, so people often found it advisable to surrender to them. In this way the Muslims swept aside the crumbling Byzantine Empire, whose people felt no desire to support their distant Christian emperor.

Islam travelled west for only 100 years before being pushed back at Poitiers, France, in 732, but it continued east for centuries. It regenerated the Persian Empire, which was then declining from its protracted struggles with Byzantium, and in 711, the same year the Arabs landed in Spain, they sent dhows up the Indus River into India. This was more a casual raid than a full-scale invasion, but in the 12th century all of north India fell

A Muslim man reading the Koran (HF)

into Muslim hands. Eventually the Mughal Empire controlled most of the subcontinent. From here it was spread by Indian traders into South-East Asia.

At an early stage Islam suffered a fundamental split that remains to this day. The third caliph, successor to Muhammad, was murdered and followed by Ali, the prophet's son-in-law, in 656. Ali was assassinated in 661 by the governor of Syria, who set himself up as caliph in preference to the descendants of Ali. Most Muslims today are Sunnites, followers of the succession from the caliph, while the others are Shias, or Shi'ites, who follow the descendants of Ali.

Despite its initial vigour, Islam eventually became inert and unchanging, though it remains to be seen what effect the fanatical fundamentalism of recent years will have on the religion world-wide. In India itself, despite Islam's long period of control over the centuries, it never managed to make great inroads into Hindu society and religion. Converts to Islam were principally made from the lowest castes, with the result that at Partition Pakistan found itself with a shortage of the educated clerical workers and government officials with which India is so liberally endowed. Although it did not make great numbers of converts, the visible effects of Muslim influence in India are strong in architecture, art and food. Converts to Islam have only to announce that 'There is no God but Allah and Muhammad is his prophet' and they become Muslims. Friday is the Muslim holy day and the main mosque in each town is known as the Jama Masjid, or Friday Mosque. One of the aims of every Muslim is to make the pilgrimage *(haj)* to Mecca and become a *hajji*.

Sufism Sufism is a branch of Islamic philosophy which has its basis in the belief that abstinence, self-denial and tolerance – even of other religions – are the route to union with God. This religious tolerance sets the Sufis very much apart from conventional Islamic thought, which has led to their persecution in some countries; in India the sect appeals to members of all religions and is growing in popularity.

Sufis also believe that being in a trance-like state of ecstasy brings the believer close to God, and to this end music and dance are used extensively. *Qawwali* music (rhymed, devotional Urdu couplets, usually with harmonium accompaniment) is still performed at the *dargah* (shrine-tomb) of the Sufi saint Shaikh Hazrat Nizam-ud-din Aulia in the suburb of Nizamuddin. It is at such a time that dervishes (Sufi holy men) become so entranced they go into a frenzied whirling.

Sikhism

The Sikhs in India number 18 million and are predominantly located in the Punjab and Delhi, although they are found all over India. They are the most visible of the Indian religious groups because of the five symbols introduced by Guru Gobind Singh so that Sikh men could easily recognise each other. They are known as the five *kakkars* and are: *kesh* – uncut hair; *kangha* the wooden or ivory comb; *kachha* – shorts; *kara* – the steel bracelet; and *kirpan* – the sword. Because of their kesha, Sikh men wear their hair tied up in a bun and hidden by a long turban. Wearing kachha and carrying a kirpan came about because of the Sikhs' military tradition – they didn't want to be tripping over a long dhoti or be caught without a weapon. Normally the sword is simply represented by a tiny image set in the comb. With his beard, turban and upright, military bearing, the 'noble' Sikh is hard to miss! The Sikh religion was founded by Guru Nanak, who was born in 1469. It was originally intended to bring together the best of the Hindu and Islamic religions. Its basic tenets are similar to those of Hinduism with the important modification that the Sikhs are opposed to caste distinctions and pilgrimages to rivers. They are not, however, opposed to pilgrimages to holy sites.

They worship at temples known as *gurdwaras*, baptise their children, when they are old enough to understand the religion, in a ceremony known as *pahul*, and cremate their dead. The holy book of the Sikhs is the *Granth Sahib*, which contains the works of the 10 Sikh gurus together with Hindu and Muslim writings. The last guru died in 1708.

In the 16th century, Guru Gobind Singh introduced military overtones into the religion in an attempt to halt the persecution the Sikhs were then suffering. A brotherhood, known as the *khalsa*, was formed, and entry into it was conditional on a person undergoing baptism *(amrit)*. From that time the majority of Sikhs have borne the surname Singh, which means Lion (although just because a person has the surname Singh doesn't mean he or she is necessarily a Sikh; many Rajputs also have this surname).

Sikhs believe in one god and are opposed to idol worship. They practise tolerance and love of others, and their belief in hospitality extends to offering shelter to anyone who comes to their gurdwaras. Because of their get-on-with-it attitude to life they are one of the better-off groups in Indian society. They have a reputation for mechanical aptitude and specialise in handling machinery of every type, from jumbo jets to auto rickshaws.

Jainism

The Jain religion is an offshoot of Hinduism and was founded around 500 BC by Mahavira, the 24th and last of the Jain prophets, known as *tirthankars*, or Finders of the Path. The Jains now number only about 4.5 million and are found all over India, but predominantly in the west and south-west. They believe that the universe is infinite and was not created by a deity. They also believe in reincarnation and eventual spiritual salvation, or moksha, through following the path of the tirthankars. One factor in the search for salvation is *ahimsa*, or reverence for all life and the avoidance of injury to all living things. Due to this belief Jains are strict vegetarians and some monks actually cover their mouths with a piece of cloth in order to avoid the risk of accidentally swallowing an insect.

The Jains are divided into two sects, the Shvetambara and the Digambara. The Digambaras are the more austere sect and their name literally means Sky Clad since, as a sign of their contempt for material possessions, they do not even wear clothes. Not surprisingly, Digambaras are generally monks who confine their nakedness to the monasteries!

The Jains tend to be commercially successful and have an influence disproportionate to their actual numbers.

Zoroastrianism

This is one of the oldest religions on earth and was founded in Persia by the prophet Zarathustra (Zoroaster) in the 6th or 7th century BC. He was born in Mazar-i-Sharif in what is now Afghanistan. At one time Zoroastrianism stretched all the way from India to the Mediterranean but today is found only around Shiraz in Iran, Karachi in Pakistan, and Bombay in India. The followers of Zoroastrianism are known as Parsis since they originally fled to India to escape persecution in Persia. Zoroastrianism was one of the first religions to postulate an omnipotent and invisible god. Their scripture is the *ZendAvesta*, which describes the continual conflict between the forces of good and evil. Their god is Ahura Mazda, the god of light, who is symbolised by fire. Humanity ensures the victory of good over evil by following the principles of *humata* (good thoughts), *hukta* (good words) and *huvarshta* (good deeds).

Parsis worship in fire temples and wear a *sadra* (sacred shirt) and a *kasti* (sacred thread). Children first wear these sacred items in a ceremony known as Navjote. Flames burn eternally in their fire temples but fire is

Sikhs are the most easily identified of
the religious groups in Delhi. (GE)

worshipped as a symbol of God, not for itself. Because
Parsis believe in the purity of elements they will not
cremate or bury their dead since it would pollute the fire,
earth, air or water. Instead they leave the bodies in
'Towers of Silence' where they are soon cleaned off by
vultures.

Although there are only about 85,000 Parsis, concentrated in Bombay, they are very successful in commerce
and industry, and have become notable philanthropists.
Parsis have influence far greater than their numbers
would indicate and have often acted as a channel of
communication between India and Pakistan when the
two countries were at loggerheads. Because of the strict
requirements that a Parsi must only marry another Parsi
and children must have two Parsi parents to be Parsis,
their numbers are gradually declining.

Christianity

India has around 22 million Christians. There have been
Christian communities in Kerala as long as Christianity
has been in Europe, for St Thomas the Apostle is supposed to have arrived here in 54 AD. The Portuguese,
who unlike the English were as enthusiastic about
spreading their brand of Christianity as making money
from trade, left a large Christian community in Goa.
Generally though, Christianity has not had great success
in India, if success is counted in number of converts. The
first round of Indian converts to Christianity were generally those from the ruling classes and after that the
converts were mainly from the lower castes.

LANGUAGE

There is no 'Indian' language, which is part of the reason why English is still widely spoken over 40 years after the British left India and is still the official language of the judiciary. The country is divided into a great number of local languages and in many cases the state boundaries have been drawn on linguistic lines. In all there are 18 languages officially recognised by the constitution, and these fall into two major groups: Indic, or Indo-Aryan, and Dravidian. Additionally, there are over 1600 minor languages and dialects listed in the 1991 census. The scope for misunderstanding can be easily appreciated!

In Delhi the languages in most common usage after English are Hindi and, in Old Delhi, Urdu.

Major efforts have been made to promote Hindi as the national language of India and to gradually phase out English. For many educated Indians, English is virtually their first language, and for a great number of Indians who speak more than one language it will be their second language. Thus it is very easy to get around Delhi with English – after all, many Indians have to speak English to each other if they wish to communicate. Nevertheless it's always nice to know at least a little of the local language.

The Lonely Planet *Hindi/Urdu Phrasebook* is a handy reference if you want to increase your language skills.

Hindi

yes/no	*han/nahin*
hello, goodbye	*namaste*
excuse me	*maf kijiye*
please	*meharbani se*
big	*bara*
small	*chhota*
today	*aaj*
day	*din*
night	*rat*
week	*haftah*
month	*mahina*
year	*sal*
medicine	*davai*
ice	*baraf*
egg	*anda*
fruit	*phal*
vegetables	*sabzi*
sugar	*chini*

butter	*makkhan*
rice	*chaval*
water	*pani*
tea	*chai*
coffee	*kafi*
milk	*dudh*

Do you speak English?	*Kya ap angrezi samajhte hun?*
I don't understand.	*Meri samajh men nahin aya.*
Where is a hotel?	*Hotal kahan hai?*
How far is...?	*...kitne dur hai?*
How do I get to...?	*...kojane ke liye kaise jana parega?*
How much?	*Kitne paise? Kitne hai?*
This is expensive.	*Yeh bahut mehnga hai.*
Show me the menu.	*Mujhe minu dikhayee.*
The bill please.	*Bill de dijiyee.*
What is your name?	*Apka shubh nam kya hai?*
What is the time?	*Kitne baje hain?*
Come here.	*Idhar aaiyee.*
How are you?	*Ap kaise hain?*
Very well, thank you.	*Bahut achche shukriya.*

Be careful with *acha*, that all-purpose word for 'OK'. It can also mean 'OK, I understand what you mean, but it isn't OK'. As in 'Have you got a room available?' to which the answer *'acha'* means 'I understand you want a room but I haven't got one'.

Numbers

Whereas we count in tens, hundreds, thousands, millions and billions, the Indian numbering system goes tens, hundreds, thousands, hundred thousands, ten millions. A hundred thousand is a *lakh* and 10 million is a *crore*.

These two words are almost always used in place of their English equivalent. Thus you will see 10 lakh rather than one million and one crore rather than 10 million. Furthermore, the numerals are generally written that way too – thus three hundred thousand appears as 3,00,000 not 300,000, and ten million, five hundred thousand would appear numerically as 1,05,00,000 (one crore, five lakh) not 10,500,000. If you say something costs five crore or is worth 10 lakh it always means 'of rupees'.

When counting from 10 to 100 in Hindi, there is no standard formula for compiling numbers – they are all different. Here we've just given you enough to go on with!

1	*ek*	26	*chhabis*
2	*do*	27	*sattais*
3	*tin*	28	*aththais*
4	*char*	29	*unnattis*
5	*panch*	30	*tis*
6	*chhe*	35	*paintis*
7	*sat*	40	*chalis*
8	*ath*	45	*paintalis*
9	*nau*	50	*pachas*
10	*das*	55	*pachpan*
11	*gyarah*	60	*sath*
12	*barah*	65	*painsath*
13	*terah*	70	*sattar*
14	*choda*	75	*pachhattar*
15	*pandrah*	80	*assi*
16	*solah*	85	*pachasi*
17	*satrah*	90	*nabbe*
18	*aththarah*	95	*pachanabbe*
19	*unnis'*	100	*so*
20	*bis*	200	*do so*
21	*ikkis*	300	*tin so*
22	*bais*	1000	*ek hazar*
23	*teis*	2000	*do hazar*
24	*chobis*	100,000	*ek lakh*
25	*pachis*	10,000,000	*ek crore*

Facts for the Visitor

ORIENTATION

Delhi is a relatively easy city to find your way around, although it is very spread out. The section of interest to visitors is on the west bank of the Yamuna River and is divided basically into two parts – Old Delhi and New Delhi. Desh Bandhu Gupta Rd and Asaf Ali Rd mark the boundary between the tightly packed streets of the old city and the spaciously planned areas of the new capital.

Old Delhi is basically the 17th-century walled city of Shahjahanabad, with city gates, narrow alleys, the enormous Red Fort and Jama Masjid, temples, mosques, bazaars and the famous street known as Chandni Chowk. Here you will find the Old Delhi Railway Station and, a little further north, the main interstate bus station near Kashmiri Gate.

To the north of Old Delhi is Civil Lines, where the British used to live and rule from before New Delhi was completed. Today it is really a continuation of Old Delhi, and it still contains a number of interesting Raj-era buildings.

Near New Delhi Railway Station, and acting as a sort of 'buffer zone' between the old and new cities, is Paharganj. This has become the budget travellers' hangout, and there are many popular cheap hotels and restaurants in this area.

New Delhi is a planned city of wide, tree-lined streets, parks and fountains. Its hub is the great circle of Connaught Place and the streets that radiate south from it. Here you will find most of the airline offices, banks, travel agents, the various state tourist offices and the national one, more budget accommodation and several of the big hotels. The Regal Cinema, on the south side of the circle, and the Plaza Cinema, on the north, are two important Connaught Place landmarks and are very useful for telling taxi or auto-rickshaw drivers where you want to go.

Janpath, running off Connaught Place to the south, is one of the most important streets, containing the Government of India tourist office, the Student Travel Information Centre in the Imperial Hotel and a number of other useful addresses.

Rajpath is the old ceremonial Kings Way and the focal point of Lutyens's New Delhi. At its western end is the President's residence, Rashtrapati Bhavan, and the two Secretariat buildings; at its eastern end is the city's answer to the Arc de Triomphe – the All India War Memorial, known these days only by its unofficial name, India Gate.

South of Rajpath and the New Delhi government areas are the city's more expensive residential areas with names like Defence Colony, South Extension, Lodi Colony, Greater Kailash and Hauz Khas. There are a number of excellent shopping centres with upmarket shops and restaurants dotted throughout these suburbs.

A view of densely-packed Delhi (RI)

The Indira Gandhi International Airport is to the south-west of the city, and about halfway between the airport and Connaught Place is Chanakyapuri, the diplomatic enclave. Most of Delhi's embassies are concentrated in this modern area and there is at least one major hotel here.

East of the Yamuna River are the *jhuggis*, or shanty settlements, of the city's poor, many of whom have migrated from the rural areas in the hope of finding work. This is where you really uncover the fact that this city of 10 million is the capital of a country where 75% of the population live in poverty – *New* Delhi seems a million miles away.

The 200-page *A to Z Road Guide for Delhi* includes 60 area maps and is a good reference if you are venturing further into the Delhi environs. It's available at most larger bookshops.

TOURIST OFFICES

Local Tourist Offices

Government of India The Government of India tourist office (☎ 332-0005) at 88 Janpath is open from 9 am to 6 pm Monday to Friday, and 9 am to 2 pm Saturday; it's closed Sunday. The office has a lot of information and brochures on destinations all over India, but none of it is on display – you have to know what you want and ask for it. They usually have a good give-away map of Delhi and can also assist you in finding accommodation, although not in the budget range. This is the most helpful of all the Delhi tourist offices, and you can also have mail sent here.

In the arrivals hall at the international airport terminal there is a tourist counter (☎ 329-4410) open around the clock, but don't expect too much. Here, too, they can help you find accommodation, although like many other Indian tourist offices they may tell you the hotel you choose is 'full' and steer you somewhere else when actually your selected hotel is not full at all. There's also a counter at the domestic terminal (☎ 329-5825).

Delhi Tourism Corporation The Government of India tourist offices are supplemented by those of the Delhi Tourism Corporation, although they have very little in the way of printed information. The main office (☎ 331-5322) is on Middle Circle at N Block, Connaught Place, and is open daily from 7 am to 9 pm.

They also have counters at New Delhi (☎ 373-2374) and (Old) Delhi (☎ 251-1083) railway stations, as well as at the Interstate Bus Terminal (☎ 251-8836) at Kashmiri Gate, and the international (☎ 329-1213) and domestic (☎ 329-5609) terminals at the airport.

Publications A monthly publication called *Genesis*, available for Rs 12 from many hotels and bookstands, gives information on what's happening in Delhi each month. *Delhi Diary* (Rs 6) is a similar booklet.

First City is a monthly society magazine which gives some useless gossip on what the city's social set are up to, but it also has good listings of cultural events and restaurants. It's available from newsstands for Rs 15.

Warning Steer well clear of the dozen or so self-styled 'tourist information centres' across the road from New Delhi Railway Station. None of them are tourist offices as such, despite bold claims to the contrary; they are simply travel agents, and many are simply out to fleece unsuspecting visitors – both foreign and Indian. If you are going to make a train reservation at the foreign tourist booking office at the station you may well be approached by touts from these agencies who will insist the office you want is closed and try to steer you to the shonky travel agents and rake off a commission. Don't be tempted by offers of cheap bus fares or hotels.

Shady characters of similar ilk hang out around Connaught Place, especially around the tourist office on Janpath, and their motives are the same.

Other State Offices Most of the various state governments have information centres in New Delhi. They may be useful if you plan to travel further afield.

The offices for the following states are all on Baba Kharak Singh Marg:

Assam (☎ 34-5897)
Gujarat (☎ 373-2107)
Karnataka (☎ 34-3862)
Maharashtra (☎ 34-3773)
Orissa (☎ 34-4580)
Tamil Nadu (☎ 34-4651)
West Bengal (☎ 373-2840)

In the Chandralok Building at 36 Janpath you'll find the following offices:

Haryana (☎ 332-4911)
Himachal Pradesh (☎ 332-5320)
Uttar Pradesh (☎ 332-2251)

In the Kanishka Shopping Centre between the Yatri Niwas and Kanishka hotels are the offices for:

Bihar (☎ 372-3371)
Jammu & Kashmir (☎ 332-5373)
Kerala (☎ 331-6541)
Madhya Pradesh (☎ 332-1187)

Others offices include:

Andhra Pradesh, 1 Ashok Rd (☎ 38-1293)
Goa, 18 Amrita Shergil Marg (☎ 462-9967)
Meghalaya, 9 Aurangzeb Rd (☎ 301-4417)
Rajasthan, Bikaner House, near India Gate (☎ 38-3837)
Sikkim, New Sikkim Bhavan, 14 Panchsheel Marg,
    Chanakyapuri (☎ 30-5346)

Tourist Offices Abroad

The Government of India Department of Tourism maintains a string of tourist offices in other countries, where you can get brochures, leaflets and some information about India. There are also smaller 'promotion offices' in Osaka (Japan) and in Dallas, Miami, San Francisco and Washington, DC (USA).

Australia
    Level 1, 17 Castlereagh St, Sydney, NSW 2000 (☎ (02) 9232-1600; fax 9223-3003)
Canada
    60 Bloor St West, Suite No 1003, Toronto, Ontario M4W 3B8 (☎ (416) 962-3787; fax 962-6279)
France
    8 Blvd de la Madeleine, 75009 Paris (☎ (01) 42.65.83.86; fax 42.65.01.16)
Germany
    Kaiserstrasse 77-III, D-6000 Frankfurt-am-Main-1 (☎ (069) 23-5423; fax 23-4724)
Italy
    Via Albricci 9, 20122 Milan (☎ (02) 80-4952; fax 7202-1681)
Japan
    Pearl Building, 9-18 Ginza, 7-Chome, Chuo-ku, Tokyo 104 (☎ (03) 571-5062; fax 571-5235)
Malaysia
    Wisma HLA, Lot 203 Jalan Raja Chulan, 50200 Kuala Lumpur (☎ (03) 242-5285; fax 242-5301)
Netherlands
    Rokin 9-15, 1012 KK Amsterdam (☎ (020) 620-8991; fax 38-3059)
Singapore
    United House, 20 Kramat Lane, Singapore 0922 (☎ 235-3800; fax 235-8677)

Sweden
    Sveavagen 9-11, S-III 57, Stockholm 11157 (☎ (08) 21-5081;
    fax 21-0186)
Switzerland
    1-3 Rue de Chantepoulet, 1201 Geneva (☎ (022) 732-1813;
    fax 731-5660)
Thailand
    Kentucky Fried Chicken Building, 3rd Floor, 62/5
    Thaniya Rd, Bangkok 10500 (☎ (02) 235-2585)
UK
    7 Cork St, London W1X 2AB (☎ (0171) 437-3677; fax 494-1048)
USA
    30 Rockefeller Plaza, 15 North Mezzanine, New York, NY
    10112 (☎ (212) 586-4901; fax 582-3274)
    3550 Wilshire Blvd, Suite 204, Los Angeles, CA 90010
    (☎ (213) 380-8855; fax 380-6111)

Glass bangles (HF)

DOCUMENTS

Visas

Virtually everybody needs a visa to visit India. The
application is (in theory) straightforward and the visas
are usually issued with a minimum of fuss.

Tourist visas come in a variety of flavours:

Fifteen-day, single or double-entry transit visas, valid
for 30 days from date of issue. They cost £3 in the UK, A$17
in Australia.

Three-month, *non-extendable*, multiple-entry visas, valid
for a stay of three months *from the date of first entry into
India*, which must be within 30 days of date of issue
(£13/A$40).

Six-month, multiple-entry visas, valid for six months *from
the date of issue of the visa*, not the date you enter India. This
means that if you enter India five months after the visa
was issued, it will be valid for only one more month, not
the full six months. If you enter India the day after it was
issued, you can stay for the full six months. Many travellers get caught out, thinking a six-month visa automati-
cally gives them a six-month stay in India (£26/A$70).

Visa Extensions

Only six-month tourist visas are extendable. If you want to stay in India beyond the 180 days from the date of issue of your visa, *regardless of your date of entry into India*, you're going to have to try to extend your visa. Extensions are not given as a matter of routine. If you have already been in the country for six months, it can be difficult to get an extension, and then you may be given only a month. If you've been in India less than six months, the chances are much better.

Hans Bhavan, near Tilak Bridge, is where you'll find the Foreigners' Registration Office (☎ 331-9489), which can issue 15-day visa extensions if you just need a few extra days before you leave the country. It's as chaotic and confused as ever, with no organisation or plan. The office is open weekdays from 9.30 am to 1.30 pm and 2 to 4 pm.

To apply for a longer visa extension, first collect a form from the Ministry of Home Affairs at Khan Market and take it to the Foreigners' Registration Office (about a Rs 15 rickshaw ride away). A one-month extension costs Rs 800 (four photos required). When (and if) the extension is authorised, the authorisation has to be taken *back* to the Home Affairs office, where the actual visa extension is issued. Also, it is extremely difficult to get an extension; currently, very few are being issued at all.

Tax Clearance Certificates

If you stay in India for more than 120 days, you need a 'tax clearance certificate' to leave the country. This supposedly proves that your time in India was financed with your own money, not by working in India or by selling things or playing the black market.

Certificates are issued by the Foreign Section of the Income Tax Office (☎ 331-7826) in the Central Revenue Building on Vikas Marg, around the corner from Hans Bhavan. Bring exchange certificates with you, though it's quite likely nobody will ask for your clearance certificate when you leave the country. The office is closed from 1 to 2 pm.

Travel Insurance

A travel insurance policy to cover theft, loss and medical problems is a wise idea. There are a wide variety of policies and your travel agent will have recommendations (though not necessarily informed recommendations or personal experience). The international student travel policies handled by student travel organisations are usually good value. Some policies offer lower and higher medical expense options, but the higher one is chiefly for countries like the USA which have extremely high medical costs. Check the small print:

- Some policies specifically exclude 'dangerous activities', which can include motorcycling (definitely a dangerous activity in Delhi!) and even trekking. If such activities are on your agenda, you don't want that sort of policy.
- You may prefer a policy which pays doctors or hospitals directly rather than your having to pay on the spot and claim later. If you have to claim later, make sure you keep all documentation. Some policies ask you to call back (reverse charges) to a centre in your home country, where an immediate assessment of your problem is made.
- Check if the policy covers ambulances or an emergency flight home. If you have to stretch out you will need two seats, and someone has to pay for them.

Driver's Licence

If you plan on driving or motorcycling around you can do this quite legally with your own local licence from home. However, it's not a bad idea to have an International Driving Licence as this is likely to cause you fewer problems.

EMBASSIES

Indian Embassies Abroad

Indian embassies and consulates include:

Australia
   Embassy: 3-5 Moonah Place, Yarralumla, ACT 2600 (☎ (06) 273-3999; fax 273-3328)
   153 Walker St, North Sydney, NSW 2060 (☎ (02) 9955-7055; fax 9929-6058)
   13 Munro St, Coburg, Melbourne, Vic 3058 (☎ (03) 9384-0141; fax 9384-1609)
   195 Adelaide Terrace, East Perth, WA 6004 (☎ (09) 221-1207; fax 221-1206)
Bangladesh
   Embassy: 120 Road 2, Dhanmodi Residential Area, Dhaka (☎ (02) 50-3606; fax 86-3662)
   1253/1256 O R Nizam Rd, Mehdi Bagh, Chittagong (☎ (031) 21-1007; fax 22-5178)
Belgium
   217 Chaussee de Vleurgat, 1050 Brussels (☎ (02) 640-9802; fax 648-9638)
Bhutan
   India House Estate, Thimpu, Bhutan (☎ (0975) 22-162; fax 23-195)

Facts for the Visitor

Burma (Myanmar)
545-547 Merchant St, Rangoon (☎ (01) 82-550; fax 89-562)

Canada
10 Springfield Rd, Ottawa K1M 1C9 (☎ (613) 744-3751; fax 744-0913)

China
1 Ri Tan Dong Lu, Beijing (☎ (01) 532-1908; fax 532-4684)

Denmark
Vangehusvej 15, 2100 Copenhagen (☎ (045) 3118-2888; fax 3927-0218)

Egypt
5 Aziz Ababa St, Zamalek, Cairo 11511 (☎ (02) 341-3051; fax 341-4038)

France
15 Rue Alfred Dehodencq, 75016 Paris (☎ (01) 40.50.70.70; fax 40.50.09.96)

Germany
Adenauerallee 262, 53113 Bonn 1 (☎ (0228) 54-050; fax 54-0514)

Israel
4 Kaufman St, Sharbat House, Tel Aviv 68012 (☎ (03) 58-4585; fax 510-1434)

Italy
Via XX Settembre 5, 00187 Rome (☎ (06) 488-4642; fax 481-9539)

Japan
2-2-11 Kudan Minami, Chiyoda-ku, Tokyo 102 (☎ (03) 3262-2391; fax 3234-4866)

Jordan
1st Circle, Jebel Amman, Amman (☎ (06) 62-2098; fax 65-9540)

Kenya
Jeevan Bharati Building, Harambee Ave, Nairobi (☎ (02) 22-2566; fax 33-4167)

Korea (South)
37-3 Hannam-dong, Yongsan-ku, Seoul 140210 (☎ (02) 798-4257; fax 796-9534)

Malaysia
2 Jalan Taman Dlita, 50480 Kuala Lumpur (☎ (03) 253-3504; fax 253-3507)

Nepal
Lainchaur, GPO Box 292, Kathmandu (☎ (071) 41-1940; fax 41-3132)

Netherlands
Buitenrustweg 2, 252 KD, The Hague (☎ (070) 346-9771; fax 361-7072)

New Zealand
180 Molesworth St, Wellington (☎ (04) 473-6390; fax 499-0665)

Pakistan
Embassy: G-5 Diplomatic Enclave, Islamabad (☎ (051) 81-4371; fax 82-0742)
India House, 3 Fatima Jinnah Rd, Karachi (☎ (021) 52-2275; fax 568-0929)

Russia
      6 Ulitsa Obukha, Moscow (☎ (095) 297-0820; fax 975-2337)
Singapore
      India House, 31 Grange Rd (☎ 737-6777; fax 732-6909)
South Africa
      Sanlam Centre, Johannesburg (☎ (011) 333-1525; fax 333-0690)
Sri Lanka
      36-38 Galla Rd, Colombo 3 (☎ (01) 42-1605; fax 44-6403)
Switzerland
      Effingerstrasse 45, CH-3008 Berne (☎ (031) 382-3111; fax 382-2687)
Sweden
      Adolf Fredriks Kyrkogata 12, 11183 Stockholm (☎ (08) 10-7008; fax 24-8505)
Syria
      40/46 Adnan Malki St, Yassin, Damascus (☎ (011) 71-9581; fax 71-3294)
Tanzania
      NIC Investment House, Samora Ave, Dar-es-Salaam (☎ (051) 28-198; fax 46-747)
Thailand
      Embassy: 46 Soi 23 (Prasarnmitr), Sukhumvit Rd, Bangkok (☎ (02) 258-0300; fax 258-4627)
      113 Bumruangrat Rd, Chiang Mai 50000 (☎ (053) 24-3066; fax 24-7879)
UK
      Embassy: India House, Aldwych, London WC2B 4NA (☎ (0171) 836-8484; fax 836-4331)
      8219 Augusta St, Birmingham B18 6DS (☎ (0121) 212-2782; fax 212-2786)
USA
      Embassy: 2107 Massachusetts Ave NW, Washington, DC 20008 (☎ (202) 939-7000; fax 939-7027)
      3 East 64th St, New York, NY 10021-7097 (☎ (212) 879-7800; fax 988-6423)
      540 Arguello Blvd, San Francisco, CA 94118 (☎ (415) 668-0662; fax 668-2073)

Foreign Embassies in Delhi

Some of the foreign missions in Delhi include:

Afghanistan
      5/50-F Shantipath, Chanakyapuri (☎ 60-3331; fax 687-5439)
Australia
      1/50-G Shantipath, Chanakyapuri (☎ 688-8223; fax 687-4126)
Bangladesh
      56 Ring Rd, Lajpat Nagar III (☎ 683-4668; fax 683-9237)
Belgium
      50-N Shantipath, Chanakyapuri (☎ 60-8295; fax 688-5821)

Bhutan
    Chandragupta Marg, Chanakyapuri (☎ 60-9217; fax 687-6710)
Burma (Myanmar)
    3/50-F Nyaya Marg, Chanakyapuri (☎ 60-0251; fax 687-7942)
Canada
    7/8 Shantipath, Chanakyapuri (☎ 687-6500; fax 687-6579)
China
    50-D Shantipath, Chanakyapuri (☎ 60-0328; fax 688-5486)
Denmark
    11 Aurangzeb Rd (☎ 301-0900; fax 301-0961)
France
    2/50-E Shantipath, Chanakyapuri (☎ 611-8790; fax 687-2305)
Germany
    6/50-G Shantipath, Chanakyapuri (☎ 60-4861; fax 687-3117)
Indonesia
    50-A Chanakyapuri (☎ 611-8642; fax 688-6763)
Iran
    5 Barakhamba Rd (☎ 332-9600; fax 332-5493)
Iraq
    169 Jor Bagh Rd (☎ 461-8011; fax 463-1547)
Ireland
    13 Jor Bagh Rd (☎ 461-7435; fax 469-7053)
Israel
    3 Aurangzeb Rd (☎ 301-3238; fax 301-4298)
Italy
    50-E Chandragupta Marg, Chanakyapuri (☎ 611-4355; fax 687-3889)
Japan
    4-5/50-G Shantipath, Chanakyapuri (☎ 687-6581)
Jordan
    1/21 Shantiniketan (☎ 60-6678; fax 688-3763)
Kenya
    66 Vasant Marg, Vasant Vihar (☎ 687-6540; fax 687-6550)
Malaysia
    50-M Satya Marg, Chanakyapuri (☎ 60-1297; fax 688-1538)
Nepal
    Barakhamba Rd (☎ 332-8191; fax 332-6857)
Netherlands
    6/50-F Shantipath, Chanakyapuri (☎ 688-4951; fax 688-4956)
New Zealand
    50-N Nyaya Marg, Chanakyapuri (☎ 688-3170; fax 687-2317)
Pakistan
    2/50-G Shantipath, Chanakyapuri (☎ 60-0603; fax 687-2339)
Russia
    Shantipath, Chanakyapuri (☎ 687-3799; fax 687-6823)

Singapore
   E-6 Chandragupta Marg, Chanakyapuri (☎ 688-5659; fax
   6886798)
South Africa
   B 18 Vasant Marg, Vasant Vihar (☎ 611-9411, 611-35005)
Spain
   12 Prithviraj Rd (☎ 379-2085; fax 379-3375)
Sri Lanka
   27 Kautilya Marg, Chanakyapuri (☎ 301-0201; fax 301-
   5295)
Sweden
   Nyaya Marg, Chanakyapuri (☎ 687-5760; fax 688-5401)
Syria
   28 Vasant Marg, Vasant Vihar (☎ 67-0233)
Thailand
   56-N Nyaya Marg, Chanakyapuri (☎ 611-8103)
UK
   50 Shantipath, Chanakyapuri (☎ 687-2161; fax 687-2882)
USA
   Shantipath, Chanakyapuri (☎ 60-0651)

CUSTOMS

The usual duty-free regulations apply for India: one litre
of alcohol and 200 cigarettes.

You're allowed to bring in all sorts of Western techno-
logical wonders, but expensive items such as video
cameras and laptop computers are likely to be entered
on a 'Tourist Baggage Re-Export' form to ensure you
take them out with you when you go. It's not necessary
to declare still cameras even if you have more than one.
Your luggage (including hand luggage) may well be
X-rayed on arrival to ascertain whether you have any
items which should be declared.

Export of any object over 100 years old requires a
permit. If in doubt, contact the Director of Antiquities,
Archaeological Survey of India, Janpath (☎ 301-7220).

MONEY

Travellers' Cheques

Although you can change most foreign travellers'
cheques in Delhi, it's best to stick to the well-known
brands – American Express, Visa, Thomas Cook,
Citibank and Barclays – as more obscure ones may cause
problems.

If you want to replace stolen or lost American Express
travellers' cheques, you need a photocopy of the police
report and one photo, as well as the proof of purchase

slip and the numbers of the missing cheques. If you don't have the latter they will insist on telexing the place where you bought them before re-issuing. If you've had the lot stolen, Amex can give you limited funds while all this is going on. For lost or stolen cheques it has a 24-hour number (687-5050) which you should contact as soon as possible.

Credit Cards

Credit cards are widely accepted in Delhi, particularly Diners Club, MasterCard, American Express and Visa.

With American Express, MasterCard or Visa cards you can use your card to obtain cash rupees. With Amex you can also get US dollar or pounds sterling travellers' cheques, or get cash rupees locally from the Amex office, but you must have a personal cheque to cover the amount, although counter cheques are available if you ask for them.

A vendor selling fruit on the streets of New Delhi (TW)

International Transfers

Don't run out of money in India unless you have a credit card against which you can draw travellers' cheques or cash. Having money transferred through the banking system can be time-consuming, although it's usually straightforward if you use one of the foreign banks.

If you do have money sent to you in India, specify the bank, the branch and the address you want it sent to.

Currency

The Indian currency is the rupee (Rs), which is divided into 100 paisa (plural: paise). There are coins of five, 10, 20, 25 and 50 paise and Rs 1, 2 and 5, and notes of Rs 1, 2, 5, 10, 20, 50, 100 and 500.

Officially you are not allowed to bring Indian currency into the country or take it out of the country. You are allowed to bring in unlimited amounts of foreign currency or travellers' cheques, but you are supposed to declare anything over US$10,000 on arrival.

Exchange Rates

A$1	=	Rs 23.5
C$1	=	Rs 23.5
DM1	=	Rs 21.5
FFr1	=	Rs 6.0
¥100	=	Rs 32.5
Nep Rs100	=	Rs 62.5
NZ$1	=	Rs 21
Sin$	=	RS 22
US$1	=	Rs 31.5
UK£1	=	Rs 49

Changing Money

The major offices of all the Indian and foreign banks operating in India can be found in New Delhi. As usual, some branches will change travellers' cheques, some won't. If you need to change money outside regular banking hours, the Central Bank has a 24-hour branch at the Ashok Hotel in Chanakyapuri, although it doesn't accept all currencies. There are also 24-hour branches of the State Bank of India and Thomas Cook in the arrival and departure areas of the international airport.

American Express (☎ 332-4119; fax 332-1706) has its office in A Block, Connaught Place. Although it's usually crowded, service is fairly fast. You don't have to have

Amex cheques to change money here. This office is open every day from 9 am to 7 pm.

Other major banks include:

ANZ Grindlays
    E Block, Connaught Place (☎ 332-0541)
Bank of America
    15 Barakhamba Rd (☎ 372-2332)
Bank of Tokyo
    3 Sansad Marg (☎ 31-0135)
Banque Nationale de Paris
    15 Barakhamba Rd (☎ 331-3294)
Citibank
    Jeevan Bharati Building, Connaught Place (☎ 371-2277)
Deutsche Bank
    15 Tolstoy Marg (☎ 372-1155; fax 331-6237)
Hongkong Bank
    28 Kasturba Gandhi Marg (☎ 331-4355)
Standard Chartered Bank
    17 Sansad Marg (☎ 374-6014)
Thomas Cook
    Imperial Hotel, Janpath (☎ 332-7135; fax 371-5685)

Re-Exchange If you want to change money back into foreign currency, you'll need to produce encashment certificates (see below) which cover the rupee amount and are less than three months old. If you want US dollars cash, you can only re-exchange up to US$500 worth of rupees, and this only within 48 hours of leaving the country and with a plane ticket to prove it. For foreign currency travellers' cheques there is no time or amount limit, but you still need the encashment certificates.

Black Market

The rupee is a fully convertible currency, ie the rate is set by the market not the government. For this reason there's not much of a black market, although you will get a couple of rupees more for your dollars or pounds cash. You will have constant offers to change money, and there's little risk involved although it is officially illegal. If you do decide to change on the black market, do it off the street rather than in the open. US$100 bills fetch the best rates.

Encashment Certificates

All money is supposed to be changed at official banks or moneychangers, and you are supposed to be given an encashment certificate for each transaction. In practice, some people surreptitiously bring rupees into the country with them – they can be bought at a useful discount price in places like Singapore or Bangkok. Indian rupees can be brought in fairly openly from Nepal and again you can get a slightly better rate there.

Banks will usually give you an encashment certificate, but occasionally they don't bother. It is worth getting them, especially if you want to re-exchange excess rupees for hard currency when you leave India.

The other reason for saving encashment certificates is that if you stay in India longer than four months you have to get an income tax clearance. This requires production of a handful of encashment certificates to prove you've been changing money all along and not doing anything naughty.

Costs

By Western standards Delhi is comparatively cheap; by Indian standards it's not. At the bottom end of the scale, if you stay in the cheapest travellers' hotel, eat at *dhabas* (basic restaurants) and use buses to get around, it will cost around US$12 per day. At the other end you could easily spend US$200 on accommodation alone, and as much again on food.

If you are looking for a reasonable level of comfort, eating at moderately priced restaurants and using auto rickshaws to see the sights, you'll be up for around US$25. Of course if you want luxuries like alcohol or get tempted by some of the many excellent souvenirs, daily costs can skyrocket alarmingly.

Baksheesh

In most Asian countries tipping is virtually unknown, but India is an exception to that rule – although tipping has a rather different role in India than in the West. The term *baksheesh*, which encompasses tipping and a lot more besides, aptly describes the concept in India. You tip not so much for good service but to get things done.

Judicious baksheesh will open closed doors, find missing letters and perform other small miracles. Tipping is not necessary for taxis nor for cheaper restaurants, but if you're going to be using something repeatedly, an initial tip will ensure the standards are kept up. Keep things in perspective though. Demands for baksheesh can quickly become never-ending. Ask yourself if it's really necessary or desirable before shelling out.

The colours of tika powder (GE)

In tourist restaurants or hotels, where service is usually tacked on in any case, the normal 10% figure usually applies. In smaller places, where tipping is optional, you need only tip a few rupees, not a percentage of the bill.

Many Westerners find this aspect of visiting India the most trying – the constant demands for baksheesh and the expectations that because you're a foreigner you'll tip. However, from an Indian perspective baksheesh is an integral part of the system – it wasn't invented simply to extract money from foreign tourists. Take some time to observe how Indians (even those who are obviously not excessively wealthy) deal with baksheesh situations. They always give something; it's expected and accepted by both sides.

Although most people think of baksheesh in terms of tipping, it also refers to giving alms to beggars. Wherever you turn you'll be confronted by beggars – many of them (often handicapped or hideously disfigured) genuinely in dire need, others, such as kids hassling for a rupee or a pen, obviously not.

It's a matter of personal choice how you approach the issue of beggars and baksheesh. Some people feel it is best to give nothing to any beggar as it 'only encourages them' and contribute by helping out at Mother Theresa's or similar; others give away loose change when they have it; but others unfortunately insulate themselves entirely and give nothing in any way. It's up to you.

Whether or not you decide to give to beggars on the street, the 'one pen, one pen' brigades should be firmly discouraged.

Taxes

Taxes are something of a minefield. Currently there is a 10% Expenditure Tax levied on accommodation, but if you are staying in a cheaper place (below about Rs 400) this won't apply. Upmarket hotels also add a 7% sales tax on food and 12% sales tax on drinks, but not usually a service charge. In the more expensive restaurants you'll also be charged a 10% service charge on top of the sales taxes added to the food and drink, so be prepared for a total of 27% extra to be slapped on your bill; cheaper restaurants just charge the sales taxes.

Local Bank Accounts

If you are staying in Delhi for a while it may be worth opening a local bank account with one of the major banks. Unfortunately these are heavily regulated (you can't open a foreign currency account, for instance), which makes them cumbersome.

Children enjoying having their picture taken (TW)

Rupee Accounts At banks such as ANZ Grindlays and American Express you can open a Non-Resident Tourist account, but these are only valid for as long as your tourist visa lasts. Any funds transferred into the account from abroad can be repatriated, although you'll lose a bit on the exchange rate as it will have already been converted to rupees. Minimum balance requirements also apply (typically Rs 10,000), but the penalties for dropping below this level are minimal (at ANZ Grindlays it's Rs 50 per quarter, and you don't accrue any interest).

The only other option is what is known as a QA-22 account, which is basically for foreign business people. The same restrictions apply as to the tourist account, but you'll need at least one reference, and the application must be approved by the Reserve Bank. This is a formality, but it does take time.

To open any account you'll need one passport photo and your passport. Some banks, such as the Hongkong Bank, require that you be referred to the bank by an existing customer.

Foreign Currency Accounts The only people eligible to hold foreign currency accounts are Non-Resident Indians (NRIs), and then only fixed-term investment deposits.

COMMUNICATIONS

Post

There is a small post office in A Block at Connaught Place, and another on N Block middle circle, near the Delhi Tourism Corporation office.

The New Delhi GPO is on the traffic circle on Baba Kharak Singh Marg (Radial No 2), one km south-west of Connaught Place. It's open Monday to Saturday from 10 am to 8 pm, and on Sunday to 5 pm.

The Delhi GPO is on Lothian Rd, between the Red Fort and Kashmiri Gate.

Receiving Mail Poste restante mail is held in New Delhi at the Foreign Post Office on Bhai Vir Singh Marg, about 500 metres north of the GPO. The poste restante office is around the back and up the stairs, and is open weekdays from 9 am to 5 pm.

Poste restante mail addressed simply to 'GPO Delhi' will end up at the inconveniently situated *old* Delhi GPO, so ask your correspondents to specify 'GPO New Delhi, 110001'. Some people also send mail to the tourist office on Janpath or the Student Travel Information Centre. Of course American Express has its own clients' mail service.

Postal Rates Aerogrammes and postcards cost Rs 6.50, airmail letters Rs 12.

Posting Parcels Posting a parcel is pretty straightforward, the main consideration being that it should be sewn up in cheap linen. This can be done for a small fee by the guy who sets himself up on the pavement outside the post office in A Block at Connaught Place. He can also tell you what forms you need to fill in.

Parcel post is not all that cheap. Sea mail rates for a parcel of one kg to Australia/UK/USA are Rs 466/-553/349. For five kg the rates are Rs 711/901/917, and for 10 kg it's Rs 976/1181/1561. Maximum parcel weight is 20 kg.

Airmail rates for one kg to the same destinations are Rs 950/775/770, for five kg Rs 3030/1815/2690, and for 10 kg Rs 5630/3115/5290.

If you are just sending books or printed matter, these can go by Bookpost, which is considerably cheaper than parcel post, but the package must be wrapped a certain way: make sure that the package can be opened for inspection along the way, or else is just wrapped in brown paper or cardboard and tied with string, with the two ends exposed so that the contents are visible. No customs declaration form is necessary for such parcels.

Be cautious with places which offer to mail things to your home address after you have bought them. Government emporiums are usually OK, but although most people who buy things from other places get them eventually, some items never turn up (were they ever sent?) or what turns up isn't what they bought.

Sending parcels in the other direction (to you in India) is an extremely hit-and-miss affair. Don't count on anything bigger than a letter getting to you. And don't count on a letter getting to you if there's anything worthwhile inside it.

Couriers & Freight Forwarders For anything larger than 20 kg you'll need a freight agent, and important documents should go by courier. DHL (☎ 686-7090) handles both, and they have an office in the Prakash Deep Building on Tolstoy Marg, near Connaught Place. TNT Express Worldwide (☎ 461-6969) also has an office in the Vandana Building, 11 Tolstoy Marg. Courier charges for documents are typically Rs 935/870 per half kg to Australia/UK-USA.

If you need something professionally packed for shipping, Packwell is a small shop in the tangle of lanes behind the Rivoli Cinema in Connaught Place.

Telephone

You'll come across private 'STD/ISD' call booths everywhere, with direct local, interstate and international dialling. These phones are usually found in shops or other businesses, but are well signposted with large 'STD/ISD' signs advertising the service. A digital meter lets you keep an eye on what the call is costing and gives you a printout at the end. Direct international calls from these phones cost around Rs 70 per minute, depending on the country you are calling.

The international access code from India is 00, so to ring Australia, for example, you dial 00-61, followed by the Australian STD area code and phone number.

Also available is the Home Country Direct service, which gives you access to the international operator in your home country. For the price of a local call (Rs 2) you can then make reverse-charge (collect) or phonecard calls, although you may also have trouble convincing the owner of the telephone you are using that they are not going to get charged for the call. This service is not available from coin-operated public phones. The numbers to dial for Home Country Direct service are:

Australia	000-61-17	
Canada	000-16-7	
Italy	000-39-17	
Germany	000-49-17	
Japan	000-81-17	
Netherlands	000-31-17	
New Zealand	000-64-17	
Singapore	000-65-17	
Spain	000-34-17	
Taiwan	000-886-17	
Thailand	000-66-17	
USA	000-1-17	AT&T
UK	000-44-17	BT
	000-44-27	Mercury

Rooms in more expensive hotels have a direct-dial facility, but hotels usually make quite hefty additional charges for using this.

Fax

Many of the STD/ISD booths also have a fax machine
for public use. The going rate for international faxes is
Rs 160 per page, regardless of what country it is being
sent to. Receiving faxes generally costs Rs 25 per page.

BOOKS

India is one of the world's largest publishers of books in
English: after the USA and the UK, it's up there with
Canada or Australia. You'll find a great number of interesting books on India by Indian publishers, which are
generally not available in the West.

Indian publishers also do cheap reprints of Western
bestsellers at prices far below Western levels. A meaty
Leon Uris or Arthur Hailey novel will often cost less than
US$3. Compare that with your local bookshop prices.
The favourite Western author is probably P G Wode-
house – 'Jeeves must be considered another incarnation
of Vishnu', was one explanation.

Recently published British and American books also
reach Indian bookshops remarkably fast and with very
low mark-ups. If a bestseller in Europe or America has
major appeal for India they'll often rush out a paperback
in India to forestall possible pirates. The novel *City of Joy*
(a European bestseller about Calcutta) was out in paperback in India before the hardback had even reached
Australia.

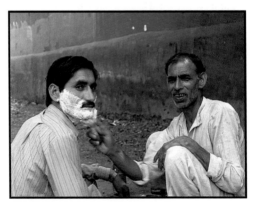

A kerbside close shave need not involve a vehicle! (HF)

Guidebooks

There are a number of useful guidebooks about Delhi which delve into the city's fascinating history and describe the main monuments. Most of these date from the pre-Independence era and were written by British scholars, and therefore have a very unfashionable British slant to them. They also often give conflicting accounts of events and sites of historical interest. Although originally published some years ago, they are currently available as modern reprints.

One of the most comprehensive guides to the city's monuments is *Delhi and Its Neighbourhood* by Y D Sharma (Archaeological Survey of India, 1990, Rs 20).

Also worth getting hold of is the hardback *Delhi, Its Monuments & History* (OUP India, 1994, Rs 275) by Dr Percival Spear, a British historian who taught at St Stephen's College for many years. It was originally written in 1943 as a text book for secondary school students and so is easily accessible, although the author assumes a working knowledge of Persian! The book describes the main sites of interest, and each chapter has been revised and annotated by Laura Sykes and Narayani Gupta to bring them up to date.

The Seven Cities of Delhi by Gordon Risley Hearn (SBW Publishers, 1995, Rs 300) is a recent reprint of this guidebook which was first published in 1906. It is divided into two sections, the first detailing the city's monuments (as they appeared in 1906) and the second dealing with the history.

For those interested in exploring Old Delhi in detail, *Old Delhi, 10 Easy Walks* (Rupa & Co, 1988, Rs 100) by Gaynor Barton & Laurraine Malone is an excellent place to start. The walking routes described take in all the major points of interest, and the authors give some interesting insights into the old city. My only criticism is that specific shop names are used frequently to aid orientation; while this may have been fine when the book was written, many of the shops mentioned have obviously changed hands (and names), which means it's sometimes hard to tell if you're in the right spot.

Mansions at Dusk (Spantech, New Delhi, 1992) is a glossy coffee-table type guide to some of the remaining havelis of old Delhi.

History

Delhi Through the Ages (OUP India, 1993, Rs 145), edited by R E Frykenburg, is an interesting and varied collection of essays about various aspects of Delhi's history from the 13th to the 20th centuries. There are, among other things, accounts of Sufism and the life of the Sufi saint Hazrat Nizam-ud-din Aulia, Shahjahanabad (today's Old Delhi) as it was in the mid-18th century, Colonel James Skinner, the Coronation Durbar of 1911 and the effect the flood of Punjabi refugees following Partition has had on the city.

Twilight in Delhi (Hogarth Press, 1940) by Ahmed Ali is an excellent record of life in Delhi during the so-called 'twilight' era, that time marking the decline of the Mughal empire – which started with Nadir Shah's bloody plunder of the city in 1739 and finally ended with the bloody events of the Mutiny in 1857. Unfortunately this book appears to be unavailable in India.

One of the best accounts of the often lurid events of the Mutiny itself is Christopher Hibbert's *The Great Mutiny* (Penguin, London, 1980). This readable paperback is illustrated with contemporary photographs.

General

Kushwant Singh is one of Delhi's (and India's) most published contemporary authors and journalists, although he seems to have as many detractors as fans. One of his more recent offerings is simply titled *Delhi* (Penguin India, 1990). This novel spans a 600-year time frame and brings to life various periods in Delhi's history through the eyes of poets, princes and emperors. It is ingeniously spiced with short dividing chapters describing the author's peripatetic affair with a *hijda* (hermaphrodite) whore and his own age-induced and overindulgent activities which play havoc with his libido. As the author states: 'History provided me with the skeleton. I covered it with flesh and injected blood and a lot of seminal fluid into it.' A lively and essential read!

Delhi is also the subject of William Dalrymple's very readable *City of Djinns* (Flamingo, 1994). Subtitled 'A Year in Delhi', it delves into this city's fascinating – and in many respects largely overlooked – history. Dalrymple turns up a few surprises in his wanderings around Delhi, and the book is written in a light style which makes it accessible to even hardened non-history readers.

For an assessment of the position of women in Indian society, it is well worth getting hold of *May You Be the Mother of One Hundred Sons* (Penguin, 1991) by Elisabeth Bumiller. The author spent $3\frac{1}{2}$ years in India in the late 1980s and interviewed Indian women from all walks of life. Her book offers some excellent insights into the

plight of women in general and rural women in particular, especially with regard to arranged marriages,
dowry deaths, *sati* and female infanticide.

The Nehrus & the Gandhis (Picador, 1988) by Tariq Ali
is a very readable account of the history of these families
and hence of India this century.

Bookshops

There are a number of excellent bookshops around Con-
naught Place. Some of the better shops include: the New
Book Depot (☎ 332-0020) at 18 B Block; the English Book
Depot; the Piccadilly Book Store (☎ 331-3993), Shankar
Market; the Oxford Book Shop (☎ 331-5896) in N Block;
and Bookworm (☎ 332-2260) in B Block.

Khan Market near the Lodi Garden also has a handful
of bookshops, including the Times Book Gallery (☎ 462-
5066) and Bahri Sons (☎ 461-8637). Prabhu Book Service
in Hauz Khas Village has an interesting selection of
secondhand and rare books, as does R S Books & Prints
(☎ 642-4011) at A-4 South Extension II.

There are plenty of pavement stalls at various places
around Connaught Place, with the major concentration
on Sansad Marg, near the Kwality Restaurant. They have
a good range of cheap paperbacks and will often buy
them back from you if they are returned in a reasonable
condition.

MEDIA

Newspapers & Magazines

A number of daily English-language newspapers are
printed in Delhi, the major ones being the *Times of India*
and the *Hindustan Times*. They are both of the heavy
news variety. A newcomer on the scene is the tabloid *Mid
Day*, which also has a late afternoon edition.

International coverage is generally pretty good. When
it comes to national news, especially politics and eco-
nomics, the copy is invariably strewn with a plethora of
acronyms and Indian words which have no English
equivalent, the majority of which mean nothing to the
uninitiated.

So far all the Indian print media is locally owned,
although there's been much debate recently about the
pros and cons of allowing foreign ownership. Predictably, Rupert Murdoch is reportedly one of a number of
people itching to get a toehold in India.

There's an excellent variety of meaty weekly magazines which cover a whole range of issues in depth and

give good insight into contemporary India. *Frontline* is possibly the best of the lot, but *India Today, The Week, Sunday* and the *Illustrated Weekly of India* are also very good.

There are dozens of other Indian magazines written in English, although many are of very limited interest to Western visitors – it takes a long time to build up an interest in Indian movie stars and their fanzines. Indian women's magazines, so alike yet so unlike their Western counterparts, are definitely worth looking at – *Femina* is probably the most well known. There's also a rash of Indian 'male interest' magazines with some fairly tame photographs of glamorous Indian women in various states of undress.

In keeping with the Indian preoccupation with sport there is an incredible proliferation of sports magazines, but apart from tennis and cricket there is little about what's happening on the international scene.

International newspapers and magazines are available in the Connaught Place bookshops and newsstands, and in the bookshops of the five-star hotels, but they are a number of days old and very expensive.

TV

The revolution in the TV network has been the introduction of satellite TV – millions of viewers each day tune in to, among other things, the BBC, CNN and, broadcasting from Hong Kong, Murdoch's Star TV, Prime Sports and V (an MTV-type music channel). Z TV is a local Hindi cable channel. So now even the Indians can keep up with what's happening on *Neighbours*!

The national broadcaster, Doordarshan, which prior to the coming of satellite TV used to plod along with dry, dull and generally dreadful programmes, has lifted its game and now offers some good viewing.

Most middle-range and all top-end hotels have a TV in every room with a choice of satellite or Doordarshan.

FILM & PHOTOGRAPHY

Colour print film is readily available, and developing and printing facilities are not hard to find. They're usually cheap and the quality is usually (but not always) good. Kodak 100 colour print film costs around Rs 110 for a roll of 36. Developing costs are around Rs 15, plus Rs 6 per photo for printing.

Fujichrome slide film costs around Rs 210 for 36 exposures. Developing costs about Rs 75 unmounted, or Rs 100 with paper mounts.

The Delhi Photo Company at 78 Janpath, close to the tourist office, processes both print and slide film quickly, cheaply and competently.

There are plenty of camera shops which should be able to make minor repairs should you have any mechanical problems.

TIME

India is 5½ hours ahead of GMT (UTC), 4½ hours behind Australian Eastern Standard Time and 10½ hours ahead of US Eastern Standard Time. It is officially known as IST Indian Standard Time, although many Indians prefer to think it stands for Indian Stretchable Time!

Indian Standard Time

It's surprising in a country as vast as India that there is only one time zone. This is a leftover from the days of the Raj. For the sake of simplicity, the British decided to have just the one time zone throughout the whole country.

The base point used was Allahabad in Uttar Pradesh. This is fine if you live in or near Allahabad, but it's a daylight nightmare if you live in the far east of the country. In summer in Assam or the Andaman Islands, for instance, sunrise is around 4 am, and it's dark by around 5 pm! This means that the average office worker who might start work at 10 am has already been up for half the day before he or she even gets to work, and is ready for an afternoon nap!

The issue of splitting the country into two or more time zones has been raised in parliament recently, but it seems to have gone into the 'too hard' basket for the moment. This may not be such a bad thing - the scope for chaos is great enough as it is! ∎

ELECTRICITY

The electric current is 230-240 volts AC, 50 Hz. The supply is generally pretty reliable in Delhi, except during the hotter months when everyone has air-conditioners running. At this time breakdowns and blackouts ('load shedding') lasting from five minutes to a couple of hours are common.

Sockets are of a three round-pin variety, similar (but not identical) to European sockets. European round-pin plugs will go into the sockets, but as the pins on Indian plugs are somewhat thicker, the fit is loose and connection is not always guaranteed.

You can buy small immersion elements, perfect for boiling water for tea or coffee, for Rs 30. For about Rs 70 you can buy electric mosquito zappers. These are the type that take chemical tablets which melt and give off deadly vapours (deadly for the mosquito, that is). There are many different brands and they are widely available – they come with quaint names such as Good Knight.

LAUNDRY

Getting your laundry done is one of the simplest tasks imaginable, even though washing machines are in short supply. At even the smallest hotel you'll be able to hand in your dirty clothes in the morning and have them back freshly laundered and pressed in the evening. The secret lies in the *dhobi-wallahs*, the washermen who still do this enormous task by hand.

The upmarket hotels do it all 'in-house' and charge upmarket prices, but if your laundry is done by a dhobi-wallah the charge is generally no more than about Rs 10 per item.

HEALTH

While there are certainly places in India where just opening your mouth can be a health hazard, Delhi isn't one of them. The general standard of hygiene is on the whole very good, and as long as you are meticulous with your personal hygiene you should experience few problems.

Make sure you're healthy before you arrive. If you are embarking on a long trip ensure your teeth are OK. If you wear glasses take a spare pair and your prescription. Even if you don't lose your glasses, you might like to take advantage of the cheap ones available in Delhi at prices far below what you'd pay at home. Prescription lenses can normally be made up in 24 hours, and prices start at around Rs 500.

If you require a particular medication take an adequate supply, as it may not be available locally. Take the prescription, with the generic rather than the brand name (which may not be locally available), as it will make getting replacements easier.

Even if you're not travelling further afield, it's still a good idea to make sure your vaccinations are current. In the wet season especially there are occasional outbreaks of infectious diseases, and while these are inevitably concentrated in the jhuggis there's still a risk of infection elsewhere. Vaccination as an entry requirement is

Dhobi-Wallahs

In India there's hardly any need for more than one change of clothes. Every day there will be a knock on your hotel door and the laundry boy will collect all those dusty, sweaty clothes you wore yesterday, and every evening those same clothes will re-appear - washed and ironed with more loving care than any washing-powder-ad mum ever lavished upon anything. And all for a few rupees per item. But what happened to your clothes between their departure and their like-new return?

Well, they certainly did not get anywhere near a washing machine. First of all they're collected and taken to the *dhobi ghat*. A ghat is a place with water and a dhobi-wallah is a washerperson, so the dhobi ghat is where the dhobi-wallahs ply their trade and wash clothes. In big cities, dhobi ghats are huge places with hundreds of dhobi-wallahs doing their thing with thousands of articles of clothing.

Then the clothes are separated - all the white shirts are washed together, all the grey trousers, all the red skirts, all the blue jeans. By now, if this was the West, your clothes would either be hopelessly lost or you'd need a computer to keep track of them all. Your clothes are soaked in soapy water for a few hours, following which the dirt is literally beaten out of them. No multiprogrammed miracle of technology can wash as clean as a determined dhobi-wallah, although admittedly after a few visits to the Indian laundry your clothes do begin to look distinctly thinner. Buttons also tend to get shattered, so bring some spares. Zips sometimes fare likewise.

Once clean, the clothes are strung out on miles of clothesline to quickly dry in the Indian sun. They're then taken to the ironing sheds where hundreds of ironers wielding primitive irons press your jeans like they've never been pressed before. Not just your jeans - your socks, your T-shirts, even your underwear will come back with knife-edge creases. Then the Indian miracle takes place. Out of the thousands upon thousands of items washed that day, somehow your very own brown socks, blue jeans, yellow T-shirt and red underwear all find their way back together and head for your hotel room. A system of marking clothes, known only to the dhobis, is the real reason behind this feat. They say criminals have been tracked down simply by those telltale 'dhobi marks'. ■

usually only enforced when you are coming from an infected area – yellow fever and cholera are the two most likely requirements.

Malaria is a problem during the monsoon (July to September), although mosquitoes are a problem year round.

Many health problems can be avoided by taking care of yourself. Wash your hands frequently – it's quite easy to contaminate your own food. Clean your teeth with purified water rather than straight from the tap. Avoid climatic extremes: keep out of the sun when it's hot, dress warmly when it's cold. Avoid potential diseases by dressing sensibly – you can get worm infections through walking barefoot. Avoid insect bites by covering bare skin when insects are around, by screening windows or beds or by using insect repellents. Seek local advice; and in situations where there is no information, discretion is the better part of valour.

Food & Drink

Care in what you eat and drink is the most important health rule; stomach upsets are the most likely travel health problem but the majority of these upsets will be relatively minor. Don't become paranoid – trying the local food is part of the experience of travel, after all.

Food There is an old colonial adage which says: 'If you can cook it, boil it or peel it you can eat it...otherwise forget it'. Salads and fruit should be washed with purified water or peeled where possible. Ice cream is usually OK if it is a reputable brand name, but beware of street vendors and of ice cream that has melted and been refrozen.

Thoroughly cooked food is safest but not if it has been left to cool or if it has been reheated. Take great care with shellfish or fish and avoid undercooked meat. If a place looks clean and well run and if the vendor also looks clean and healthy, then the food is probably safe. In general, places that are packed with travellers or locals will be fine, while empty restaurants are suspect. Busy restaurants mean the food is being cooked and eaten quite quickly rather than being left standing around, and is probably not being reheated.

Water Delhi tap water is safe to drink, although your system may rebel for a day or two until it adjusts. Most short-term visitors to India avoid tap water altogether and stick to bottled mineral water. It is available virtually everywhere and comes in one-litre plastic bottles. The price ranges from Rs 12 to Rs 30, with Rs 18 being about the average. Brand names include Bisleri, India King, Officer's Choice, Honeydew and Aqua Safe.

Virtually all the so-called mineral water available is actually treated tap water. A recent reliable survey found that 65% of the available mineral waters were less than totally pure, and in some cases were worse than what comes out of the tap! Generally, though, if you stick to bottled water any gut problems you might have will be from other sources – contaminated food, dirty utensils, dirty hands, etc.

In hot weather make sure you drink enough – don't rely on feeling thirsty to indicate when you should drink. Not needing to urinate or very dark yellow urine is a danger sign of dehydration. Always carry a water bottle with you on excursions. Excessive sweating can lead to loss of salt and therefore muscle cramping. Salt tablets are not a good idea as a preventative, but in places where salt is not used much, adding salt to food can help.

Medical Services

If you need medical attention in Delhi, the East West Medical Centre (☎ 69-9229, 62-3738), 38 Golf Links Rd, has been recommended by many travellers, diplomats and other expatriates. It's well equipped and the staff know what they're doing. Charges are high by Indian standards, but if you want good treatment...

For 24-hour emergency service, try the All India Institute of Medical Sciences (☎ 66-1123) on Aurobindo Marg, near the Ring Rd in south Delhi. Other reliable places include the Dr Ram Manohar Lohia Hospital (☎ 331-1621) on Baba Kharak Singh Marg and the Ashlok Hospital (☎ 60-8407) at 25A Block AB, Safdarjang Enclave.

Vaccinations are available cheaply at the New Delhi Municipal Corporation's Inoculation Centre on Jai Singh Rd, near the YMCA.

Ambulance service is available by phoning 102, but don't hold your breath.

24-Hour Pharmacies

The various branches of the government-run Super Bazar stores stock subsidised basic necessities, but they also have 24-hour pharmacies. There's one Super Bazar opposite K Block on the outer circle of Connaught Place, and others at the All India Institute of Medical Sciences and the Dr Ram Manohar Lohia Hospital mentioned above.

WOMEN TRAVELLERS

By Indian standards Delhi is a modern, liberal city with modern, liberal views towards women. Certainly in the streets of New Delhi, women in jeans and T-shirts seem

to outnumber those in saris or *salwar kameez*, and the chic
designer boutiques in southern Delhi are chock-full of
haute couture. In Old Delhi, however, it's a very different story and women need to dress fairly conservatively
to avoid causing offence.

Getting stared at is something which you'll have to
get used to. Don't return male stares, as this will be
considered a come-on; just ignore them. Dark glasses
can help. Other harassment likely to be encountered
includes obscene comments, touching-up and jeering.

Getting involved in inane conversations with men is
also considered a turn-on. Keep discussions down to a
necessary minimum unless you're interested in getting
hassled. If you get the uncomfortable feeling he's
encroaching on your space, the chances are that he is. A
firm request to keep away is usually enough. Firmly
return any errant limbs, put an item of luggage between
you and him and, if all else fails, find a new spot. You're
also within your rights to tell him to shove off!

Emergencies

The Delhi police operate a Crimes Against Women unit
(☎ 332-5741).

Women's Organisations

All India Women's Conference
    6 Bhagwan Dass Rd, New Delhi 110001 (☎ 38-9680)
Indian Women's Welfare Association
    N-44 Kirti Nagar, New Delhi 110015, (☎ 53-8115)
Legal Aid Centre for Women
    C-160 Daya Nand Colony, Lajpat Nagar V, New Delhi
    110024 (☎ 641-5071)

DISABLED TRAVELLERS

Very little provision is made for the disabled, as thousands of local inhabitants could attest to. Indeed, even
for the able-bodied, negotiating the average Delhi footpath can be something of an obstacle course – pools of
water, open drains, gaping cracks and mounds of broken
concrete are just a few of the hazards.

Organisations for the Disabled

Handicapped Welfare Federation
    14 Tansen Marg, New Delhi 110001 (☎ 371-0791)

DELHI FOR CHILDREN

Apart from the attractions in the Things to See & Do chapter, which may appeal to children (such as the Nehru planetarium, zoo, dolls museum, natural history museum, science museum and rail transport museum), there are a couple of other places which may be useful distractions.

Appu Ghar

This is Delhi's Luna Park, with various amusement park rides so like yet so unlike those foreigners may be familiar with. The dodgem cars are a scream – anywhere else it's a chance to let your hair down and drive like a maniac; here it's simply practice for the real thing! And it's probably the only place in the country you're likely to see seat belts being used! The ghost train goes by the name of Shoot the Bhoot (ghost), and thankfully it stops a little less often than the average Indian train. The other rides are mostly of the fast-spinning variety, but the safety aspect is a worry.

There's also a cable car which connects Appu Ghar with Pragati Maidan, but this seems to be purely decorative these days.

Appu Ghar is at the northern end of Pragati Maidan, on Mathura Rd close to Tilak Bridge. It is open daily from 12.45 to 8.30 pm; entry is Rs 10 for adults and Rs 5 for children, and there's a small charge for each ride.

India Gate Children's Park

In the gardens which surround India Gate there's a popular little children's park, with swings, monkey bars and other bits and pieces of play equipment.

USEFUL ORGANISATIONS

Libraries & Cultural Centres

The American Center Library (☎ 331-6841) is at 24 Kasturba Gandhi Marg and is open from 11 am to 6 pm Monday to Saturday. It has an extensive range of books.

The British Council Library (☎ 371-0111) is open from 10 am to 6 pm Tuesday to Saturday and is at 17 Kasturba Gandhi Marg. It's much better than the US equivalent, but officially you have to join to get in.

The India International Centre (☎ 61-9431) at 40 Lodi Estate next to the Lodi Garden has a good library and often hosts concerts, lectures and seminars.

A street hawker at Delhi Gate (HF)

The Delhi Public Library is opposite the (Old) Delhi Railway Station on SP Mukherjee Marg. It is open from 8.30 am to 8 pm daily except Sunday.

Other cultural centres include:

Alliance Française
    D-13 South Extension Part II (☎ 644-0128)
Italian Cultural Centre
    Golf Links Rd (☎ 644-9193)
Japan Cultural Centre
    32 Ferozshah Rd (☎ 332-9803)
Max Mueller Bhavan (German cultural centre)
    3 Kasturba Gandhi Marg (☎ 332-9506)
Russian Cultural Centre
    24 Ferozshah Rd (☎ 332-9102)

Trade & Industry Bodies

All India Manufacturers' Association
AIMO House, E1/11 Jhandewalan Extension, New Delhi
110055 (☎ 528-8488)
Associated Chamber of Commerce & Industry
Allahabad Bank Building, 17 Sansad Marg, New Delhi
110001 (☎ 34-4202; fax 31-2193)
Confederation of Indian Industry
23-26 Institutional Area, Lodi Rd, New Delhi 110003
(☎ 462-9994; fax 462-6149)
Federation of Indian Export Organisations
PHD House, opposite the Asian Games Village, New
Delhi 110016 (☎ 685-1310; fax 686-3087)

Export Promotion Councils

Carpet Export Promotion Council
110-A/1 Krishna Nagar, Gali 5, Safdarjang Enclave, New
Delhi 110029 (☎ 60-2742; fax 60-1024)
Council for Leather Export
6G-H Gopala Towers, Rajendra Place, New Delhi 110008
(☎ 571-8516; fax 575-2760)
Gem & Jewellery Export Promotion Council
F-33 Jhandewalan Complex, Rani Jhansi Rd, New Delhi
110055 (☎ 751-4197; fax 777-5274)
Handloom Export Promotion Council
XVI/784-85 Deshbandu Gupta Rd, Karol Bagh, New
Delhi 110005 (☎ 777-0697)

DANGERS & ANNOYANCES

Theft

Having things stolen is a problem in Delhi, not so much
because it's a theft-prone place – it isn't – but because
you can become involved in a lot of hassles getting the
items replaced. Always lock your room, preferably with
your own padlock in cheaper hotels. Lock it at night as
well; countless people have had things stolen from their
rooms when they've actually been in them.

Never leave those most important valuables (passport, tickets, health certificates, money, travellers'
cheques) in your room; they should be with you at all
times or left in your hotel's safe. Have a stout leather
passport wallet on your belt, or a passport pouch under
your shirt, or simply extra internal pockets in your clothing. Never walk around with valuables casually slung
over your shoulder.

Thieves are particularly prevalent on train routes
where there are lots of tourists. The Delhi to Agra
Shatabdi Express service is notorious.

If you do have something stolen, you're going to have to report it to the police. You'll also need a statement proving you have done so if you want to claim on insurance. Unfortunately the police are generally less than helpful, and at times are downright unhelpful, unsympathetic and even disbelieving, implying that you are making a false claim in order to defraud your insurance company. It's also tempting to think that in some cases the police are actually operating in collusion with the thieves.

American Express has a 24-hour number in Delhi (☎ 687-5050) which you must ring within 24 hours of having Amex cheques stolen.

Drugs

For a long time India was a place where you could indulge in all sorts of illegal drugs (mostly grass and hashish) with relative ease – they were cheap and readily available, and the risks were minimal. Although dope is still widely available, the risks have certainly increased.

In the Indian justice system it seems the burden of proof is on the accused, and proving one's innocence is virtually impossible. The police forces are often corrupt and will pay 'witnesses' to give evidence. A conviction for a drugs-related charge will result in a long sentence (*minimum* of 10 years), even for a minor offence, and there is no remission or parole.

Pollution

Air pollution is a real and increasing problem. Each year thousands more vehicles hit the roads, each year the traffic congestion and the pollution become worse. While it has not reached alarming proportions yet, it seems there's little being done to make sure Delhi doesn't become another Calcutta, where you can cut the air with a knife and traffic stops more than it goes.

BUSINESS HOURS

Indian shops, offices and post offices are not early starters. Generally shops are open from 10 am to 5 pm Monday to Saturday. Some government offices open on alternate Saturdays and some commercial offices are open on Saturday morning. Post offices are open from 10 am to 5 pm weekdays, and on Saturday morning.

Banks are open for business between 10 am and 2 pm on weekdays. Shops and offices are usually closed on Sunday.

Calendars

Hindu The Hindu calendar is divided into 12 lunar-solar months and remains constant with the Gregorian calendar. Each month has 30 or 31 days, and the year begins with 1 Chaitra, which corresponds with 22 March (21 March during a Gregorian leap year). The calendar was officially introduced as the definitive all-India calendar by the central government in 1957 and is based on the calendar used by the Saka kings of Ujjain around the time of Christ. Thus 1996 AD is Saka 1917-18.

The Saka months and their Gregorian equivalents are as follows:

Saka Month	Days	Gregorian Month
Chaitra	30 (31)	22 March – 20 April
Vaishaka	31	21 April – 21 May
Jyaistha	31	22 May – 21 June
Asadha	31	22 June – 22 July
Sravana	31	23 July – 22 August
Bhadra	31	23 August – 22 September
Asvina	30	23 September – 22 October
Kartika	30	23 October – 21 November
Aghan	30	22 November – 21 December
Pausa	30	22 December – 20 January
Magha	30	21 January – 19 February
Phalguna	30	20 February – 21 March

The various markets and shopping centres are closed one day a week, and this is not necessarily Sunday. The weekly holiday at the main centres is:

Sunday Closed
> Connaught Place area, Khan Market, Nehru Place, Sunder Nagar Market, Chandni Chowk and Hauz Khas Village.

Monday Closed
> Defence Colony Market, Karol Bagh, Lajpat Nagar, South Extension Part I, INA Market.

PUBLIC HOLIDAYS

Many of the gazetted public holidays revolve around various religious festivals, which are described in the Festivals section.

The following days are observed as public holidays in Delhi:

Muslim The Muslim (Hijra) calendar is also lunar and starts from 622 AD, the date of the Prophet Muhammad's flight *(hijra)* from the city of Medina. It has 12 lunar months which total 354 days, which means events fall 11 days earlier each year according to the Gregorian calendar. The Gregorian year 1996 corresponds with 1416-1417 AH *(anno hejirae)*, with the Hijra New Year's Day (1 Muharram) being 19 May.

The 12 Hijra months, and the corresponding Gregorian period for 1996, are as follows:

Hijra Month	1996 Gregorian Period
Muharram	May – June
Safar	June – July
Rabi' al-Awal	July – August
Rabei ath-Thani	August – September
Jumada al-Awal	September – October
Jumada ath-Thani	October – November
Rajab	November – December
Shaaban	December – January
Ramadan	January – February
Shawwal	February – March

Other Calendars The Jain calendar starts at 527 BC, when Lord Mahavira, the founder of the religion, attained nirvana, which makes 1996 AD the year 2522 in Jain terms.

Fixed Dates

26 January

> *Republic Day* This day celebrates the anniversary of India's establishment as a republic in 1950. This date was chosen for the republic celebration as it was on this day in 1930 that Mahatma Gandhi called for people to work towards independence from Britain. An enormously colourful parade along Rajpath attracts a crowd of millions. Three days later the much less crowded Beating of the Retreat ceremony takes place at Vijay Chowk near Rashtrapati Bhavan.

30 January

> *Martyrs' Day* Remembrance of Mahatma Gandhi and others who died fighting for Independence. Songs and prayers at Raj Ghat.

13 April

> *Mahavir Jayanti* Commemorates the birth of Mahavira, the founder of Jainism.

14 May

> *Buddha Purnima* Celebrates Buddha's enlightenment and attainment of nirvana. Prayers are held at the Buddha

Vihara on Mandir Marg, next to the Laxmi Narayan Temple.

15 August

Independence Day Independence Day celebrates the anniversary of India's independence from Britain in 1947. The prime minister delivers an address from the ramparts of the Red Fort, and the tricolour is raised.

2 October

Gandhi Jayanti This is a solemn celebration of Gandhi's birthday on 2 October, with prayer meetings at Raj Ghat, where he was cremated.

7 November

Guru Nanak's Birthday This day celebrates the birth of Guru Nanak, the founder of Sikhism.

25 December

Christmas Day

Movable Dates

January-February

Id-ul-Fitr, Muslim holiday

March

Holi, Hindu festival

March-April

Good Friday

April

Id-ul-Zuhara, Muslim holiday

May

Muharram, Muslim holiday

July

Milad-un-Nabi, Muslim holiday

September

Ram Lila (Dussehra), Hindu festival

October

Diwali, Hindu festival

FESTIVALS

Because of its religious and regional variations India has a great number of holidays and festivals. Most of them follow the Indian lunar calendar and therefore change from year to year according to the Gregorian calendar, particularly the Muslim holidays and festivals, which are listed at the end of this section.

Apart from the holidays and festivals celebrated nationally there are many local and regional events. In the following lists, public holidays are indicated by 'PH'.

January

Basant Panchami

The most notable feature of this spring festival, held on the 5th of Magha, is that many people wear yellow clothes. In some places, however, Saraswati, the goddess of learning, is honoured. Books, musical instruments and other objects related to the arts and learning are placed in front of the goddess to receive her blessing. It also marks the opening day of the Mughal Garden behind Rashtrapati Bhavan, which is opened to the public for a month.

February-March

Sivaratri

This day of fasting is dedicated to Lord Siva – his followers believe that it was on this day he danced the *tandav*. Processions to the temples are followed by the chanting of mantras and anointing of lingams.

Holi

This is one of the most exuberant Hindu festivals, with people marking the end of winter by throwing coloured water and powder at one another. Unfortunately in tourist places it is seen by some as an opportunity to take liberties with foreigners, especially women; don't wear good clothes on this day, and be prepared to duck. Many travellers find it is much less hassle just to keep off the streets until after the 'ceasefire' at midday. On the night before Holi, bonfires are built to symbolise the destruction of the evil demon Holika.

March-April

Ramanavami

In temples all over India the birth of Rama, an incarnation of Vishnu, is celebrated on this day. In the week leading up to Ramanavami, the *Ramayana* is widely read and performed.

April-May

Baisakhi

This Punjabi festival commemorates the day that Guru Gobind Singh founded the Khalsa, the Sikh brotherhood, which adopted the 'five kakkars' as part of their code of behaviour. The *Granth Sahib* is read right through at *gurdwaras* and is then put in a procession. Feasting and dancing follow in the evening.

July-August

International Mango Festival

Delhi Tourism organises this curious festival, held in the Talkatora Stadium, where hundreds of mango varieties go on show.

Naag Panchami

This festival is dedicated to Ananta, the serpent upon whose coils Vishnu rested between universes. Offerings

A Jain temple illuminated for Mahavir Jayanti festival (HF)

are made to snake images, and snake charmers do a
roaring trade. Snakes are supposed to have power over
the monsoon rainfall and keep evil from homes.

Raksha Bandhan (Narial Purnima)

On the full-moon day of the Hindu month of Sravana,
girls fix amulets known as *rakhis* to their brothers' wrists
to protect them in the coming year. The brothers give their
sisters gifts. Some people also worship the Vedic sea-god
deity, Varuna, on this day.

August-September

Ganesh Chaturthi

This festival, held on the fourth day of the Hindu month
Bhadra, is dedicated to the popular elephant-headed god
Ganesh. It is widely celebrated all over India. Shrines are
erected and a clay Ganesh idol is installed. Firecrackers
are let off at all hours. Each family also buys a clay idol,
and on the day of the festival it is brought into the house
where it is kept and worshipped for a specified period
before being ceremoniously immersed in a river or tank.
As Ganesh is the god of wisdom and prosperity, Ganesh
Chaturthi is considered to be the most auspicious day of
the year. It is considered unlucky to look at the moon on
this day.

Janmashtami

The anniversary of Krishna's birth is celebrated with
happy abandon – in tune with Krishna's own mischie-
vous moods. The Lakshmi Narayan Temple is especially
busy. Devotees fast all day until midnight.

Shravan Purnima

After a day-long fast, high-caste Hindus replace the
sacred thread which they always wear looped over their
left shoulder.

Pateti

This is the day on which Parsis celebrate their new year. A
week later *Khordad Sal* celebrates the birth of Zarathustra.

September-October

Ram Lila (Dussehra)

This is the most popular of all the Indian festivals and takes place over 10 days, beginning on the first day of the Hindu month of Asvina. It celebrates Durga's victory over the buffalo-headed demon Mahishasura. In many places it culminates with the burning of huge images of the demon king Ravana and his accomplices in effigy, symbolic of the triumph of good over evil. In Delhi it is known as Ram Lila (Life-story of Rama) and there are re-enactments of the *Ramayana* and performances of the ballet *Ramlila* at the Ram Lila Grounds near Turkman Gate. (PH – two days)

October-November

Phulwalon ki Sair (Procession of the Flower Sellers)

A festival held in Mehrauli, dating back to the time of the Mughal ruler Bahadur Shah when the flower sellers of Mehrauli honoured the emperor with fans decorated with flowers. This gives rise to the festival's other name, the Punkah (Fan) Festival. After many years' absence, the festival was revived after Independence and is held in early October.

Diwali (or Deepavali)

This is the happiest festival of the Hindu calendar, celebrated on the 15th day of Kartika. At night countless oil lamps are lit to show Rama the way home from his period of exile. Today the festival is also dedicated to Lakshmi

Flowers are symbolic in many celebrations (GE)

and lasts five days. On the first day, houses are thoroughly cleaned and doorsteps are decorated with intricate *rangolis* (chalk designs). Day two is dedicated to Krishna's victory over Narakasura, a tyrant. In the south, new clothes are worn on this day following a predawn oil bath. Day three is spent worshipping Lakshmi, the goddess of fortune. Traditionally, this is the beginning of the new financial year for companies. Day four commemorates the visit of the friendly demon Bali, whom Vishnu put in his place. On the fifth day men visit their sisters to have a *tika* put on their forehead. Diwali has also become the 'festival of sweets' and families give and receive sweets. This has become as much a part of the tradition as the lighting of oil-lamps and firecrackers. Diwali is also celebrated by the Jains as their New Year's Day. (PH)

Govardhana Puja

This is a Hindu festival dedicated to that holiest of animals, the cow.

Muslim Holidays

The dates of the Muslim festivals are not fixed, as they fall about 11 days earlier each year.

Ramadan

The most important Muslim festival is a 30-day dawn-to-dusk fast. It was during this month that the prophet Muhammad had the Koran revealed to him in Mecca. In Muslim countries this can be a difficult time for travellers since restaurants are closed and tempers tend to run short. Fortunately, despite Delhi's large Muslim minority, it causes few difficulties for visitors. For the next two years Ramadan starts around 10 January 1997 and 30 December 1997.

Id-ul-Fitr

This is a day of feasting to celebrate the end of Ramadan. Vast crowds gather for prayers at the Jama Masjid. (PH; 8 February 1997, 29 January 1998)

Id-ul-Zuhara

This is a Muslim festival commemorating Abraham's attempt to sacrifice his son. It is celebrated with prayers and feasts. (PH; 20 April 1996, 9 April 1997, 30 March 1998)

Muharram

Muharram is a 10-day festival commemorating the martyrdom of Muhammad's grandson, Imam Husain. (PH; 19 May 1996, 9 May 1997, 29 April 1998)

Milad-un-Nabi

Festival celebrating the birth of Muhammad (PH; 29 July 1996, 18 July 1997, 7 July 1998)

VOLUNTARY WORK

Numerous charities and international aid agencies have branches in Delhi. Although they're mostly staffed by locals, there are some opportunities for foreigners. Though it may be possible to find temporary volunteer work when you are in Delhi, you'll probably be of more use to the charity concerned if you write in advance and, if they need you, stay for long enough to be of help. A week on a hospital ward may go a little way towards salving your own conscience but you may actually do not much more than get in the way of the people who work there long-term.

Some areas of voluntary work seem to be more attractive to volunteers than others. One traveller commented that there was no difficulty getting foreign volunteers to help with the babies in the orphanage where he was working but few came forward to work with the severely mentally handicapped adults.

For information on specific charities in India contact the main branches in your own country. For long-term posts, the following organisations may be able to help or offer advice and further contacts:

Local Organisations

Mother Theresa's Sisters of Charity organisation runs six centres in and around Delhi, and volunteers are always welcome. The children's orphanage is on Commissioners Lane (Raj Narain Rd) in Civil Lines, or there's Nirmal Hriday at 1 Magazine Rd, north of the Oberoi Maidens Hotel.

International Aid Organisations in Delhi

International Committee of the Red Cross
    84 Golf Links Rd, New Delhi 110003 (☎ 469-8385; fax 463-1723)
UNDP
    55 Lodi Estate, New Delhi 110003 (☎ 462-8877; fax 462-7612)
UNICEF
    73 Lodi Estate, New Delhi 110003 (☎ 469-0401; fax 462-7521)
World Health Organisation
    Indraprastha Estate, New Delhi 110002 (☎ 331-7804; fax 331-8607)

Overseas Addresses

Australian Volunteers Abroad: Overseas Service Bureau Programme
PO Box 350, Fitzroy Vic 3065, Australia (☎ (03) 9279-1788; fax (03) 9416-1619)

Co-ordinating Committee for International Voluntary Service
c/o UNESCO, 1 rue Miollis, F-75015 Paris, France (☎ (01) 45.68.27.31)

Council of International Programs (CIP)
1101 Wilson Blvd Sth 1708, Arlington, VA 22209, USA (☎ (703) 527-1160)

International Voluntary Service (IVS)
St John's Church Centre, Edinburgh EH2 4BJ, UK (☎ (0131) 226-6722)

Peace Corps of the USA
1990 K St NW, Washington, DC 20526, USA (☎ (202) 606-3970; fax (202) 606-3110)

Voluntary Service Overseas (VSO)
317 Putney Bridge Rd, London SW15 2PN, UK (☎ (0181) 780-2266; fax 780-1326)

Getting There & Away

AIR

International

Delhi is a major international gateway to India. At certain times of the year international flights out of Delhi can be heavily booked, so it's wise to make reservations as early as possible. This applies particularly to some of the heavily discounted airlines out of Europe – check and double-check your reservations and be sure to reconfirm your flight.

Airline Offices The Delhi addresses of international airlines that fly to Delhi include the following:

Aeroflot
    Cozy Travels, BMC House, 1st Floor, 1N Block, Connaught Place (☎ 331-2916)
Air France
    7 Atma Ram Mansion, Connaught Circus (☎ 331-0407)
Air India
    Jeevan Bharati Building, Connaught Place (☎ 331-1225)
Air Lanka
    Student Travel Information Centre, Imperial Hotel, Janpath (☎ 332-4789)
Alitalia Airlines
    19 Kasturba Gandhi Marg (☎ 331-1019)
British Airways
    DLF Building, Sansad Marg (Parliament St) (☎ 332-7428)
Gulf Air
    G Block, Connaught Place (☎ 332-2018)
Iran Air
    Ashok Hotel, Chanakyapuri (☎ 60-4397)
Iraqi Airways
    Ansal Bhawan (☎ 331-8632)
Japan Airlines
    Chandralok Building, 36 Janpath (☎ 332-3409)
KLM
    Tolstoy Marg (☎ 331-5841)
Lot Polish Airlines
    G Block Connaught Place (☎ 332-4308)
Lufthansa
    56 Janpath (☎ 332-3206)

Malaysia Airlines (MAS)
   G Block, Connaught Place (☎ 332-5786)
Pakistan International Airlines (PIA)
   Kailash Building, 26 Kasturba Gandhi Marg (☎ 331-6121)
Royal Nepal Airlines
   44 Janpath (☎ 332-0817)
SAS
   B Block, Connaught Place (☎ 332-7503)
Singapore Airlines
   Marina Arcade, G11, Connaught Place (☎ 332-6373)
Syrian Arab Airlines
   GSA Delhi Express Travels, 13/90 Connaught Place (☎ 34-3218)
Tarom
   Antriksh Bhavan, Barakhamba Rd (☎ 335-5248)
Thai Airways International
   Amba Deep Building, Kasturba Gandhi Marg (☎ 332-3608)

To/From Africa Aeroflot operates a service between Delhi and Cairo (via Moscow), and South African Airways has connections to Johannesburg (Rs 21,600).

To/From Australia & New Zealand Advance-purchase return fares from the east coast of Australia to India range from A$1300 to A$1650 depending on the season. From Australia, fares are cheaper from Darwin or Perth than from the east coast. The low travel period is from March to September; the peak is from October to February.

Tickets from Australia to London or other European capitals with a Delhi stopover range from A$1890 to A$2500 return, again depending on the season.

Return advance-purchase fares from New Zealand to India range from NZ$1799 to NZ$1889 depending on the season.

STA and Flight Centres International are major dealers in cheap airfares in both Australia and New Zealand. Check the travel agents' ads in the newspapers and the Yellow Pages and ring around.

To/From Europe Fares from continental Europe are mostly far more expensive than from London; see the To/From the UK section for a comparison. As the following rates show, it's much cheaper to go to London and buy a flight ticket from there.

From Amsterdam to Delhi, return excursion fares are about DFL2400 (UK£900). To Calcutta, expect to pay around DFL2665 (UK£1000).

From Paris to Delhi, return excursion fares range upwards from FFr7880 (UK£980; about a third off the standard return economy fare).

To/From Malaysia Not many travellers fly between Malaysia and India because it is so much cheaper from Thailand, but there are Malaysia Airlines (MAS) flights between Kuala Lumpur and Delhi.

To/From Nepal Royal Nepal Airlines Corporation (RNAC) and Indian Airlines share the route between Delhi and Kathmandu. Both airlines give a 25% discount to those under 30 years of age; no student card is needed.

The daily one-hour Delhi to Kathmandu flight costs US$142. If you want to see the mountains as you fly into Kathmandu from Delhi, you must sit on the left side.

To/From Pakistan Pakistan International Airlines (PIA) and Air India operate flights from Karachi to Delhi for US$75 and from Lahore to Delhi for about US$140.

To/From Singapore Singapore is a great cheap-ticket centre and you can pick up Singapore/Delhi tickets for about S$900 return.

To/From Thailand Bangkok is the most popular departure point from South-East Asia into Asia proper because of the cheap flights from there to Calcutta, Rangoon in Burma, Dhaka in Bangladesh or Kathmandu in Nepal, but there are also direct flights to Delhi.

To/From the UK Various excursion fares are available from London to Delhi, but you can get better prices through London's many cheap-ticket specialists. Check the travel page ads in *The Times, Business Traveller* and the weekly 'what's on' magazine *Time Out*; or check give-away papers like *TNT*. Two reliable London shops are Trailfinders (☎ (0171) 938-3939), 194 High Street Kensington, London W8 7RG, or (☎ (0171) 938-3366) 46 Earls Court Rd, London W8; and STA (☎ (0171) 937-9962), 74 Old Brompton Rd, London SW7, or 117 Euston Rd, London NW1. Also worth trying are Quest Worldwide (☎ (0181) 547-3322) at 29 Castle St, Kingston, Surrey KT11ST and Bridge the World (☎ (0171)911-0900) at 1-3 Ferdinand St, Camden Town, London NW1.

Fares range from around UK£198 one way or UK-£325/460 return in the low/high season. The cheapest

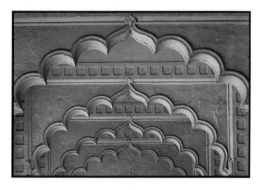

Arch detail of the Rang Mahal pavilion at the Red Fort (HF)

fares are usually with Middle Eastern or Eastern European airlines.

If you want to stop in Delhi en route to Australia expect to pay around UK£500 to UK£600.

Most British travel agents are registered with ABTA (Association of British Travel Agents). If you have paid for your flight to an ABTA-registered agent who then goes out of business, ABTA will guarantee a refund or an alternative. Unregistered bucket shops are riskier but are also sometimes cheaper.

To/From the USA & Canada The cheapest return air fares from the US west coast to Delhi are around US$1200. Another way of getting there is to fly to Hong Kong and get a ticket from there. Tickets to Hong Kong cost about US$500 one way and just under US$800 return from San Francisco or Los Angeles; in Hong Kong you can find one-way tickets to Delhi for US$300 depending on the carrier. Alternatively, fly to Singapore for around US$535/835 one way/return, or to Bangkok for US$535/865.

From the east coast you can find return tickets to Delhi for around US$1100. The cheapest one-way tickets will be around US$550 to US$600. An alternative way of getting to Delhi from New York is to fly to London and buy a cheap fare from there.

Check the Sunday travel sections of papers like the *New York Times, San Francisco Chronicle/Examiner* or *Los Angeles Times* for cheap fares. Good budget travel agents include STA and the student travel chain CIEE. The magazine *Travel Unlimited* (PO Box 1058, Allston, MA 02134, USA) publishes details of the cheapest air fares and courier possibilities for destinations all over the world from the USA.

Fares from Canada are similar to US fares. From Vancouver the route is like that from the US west coast, with the option of going via Hong Kong. From Toronto it is easier to travel via London.

The *Toronto Globe & Mail* and the *Vancouver Sun* carry travel agents' ads. The magazine *Great Expeditions* (PO Box 8000-411, Abbotsford BC V2S 6H1, Canada) is useful.

Cheap Tickets in Delhi Delhi is a good place for cheap airfares. There are a number of 'bucket shops' around Connaught Place, but find out about their current trustworthiness from other travellers.

Fares from Delhi to various European capitals cost around Rs 9400. The cheapest flights to Europe are with airlines like Aeroflot, Tarom, LOT, Kuwait Airways, Syrian Arab Airways or Iraqi Airways. Delhi to east coast Australia costs around Rs 25,000; to South Africa Rs 21,600.

Leaving Delhi

When leaving Delhi with Air India (whether to an international or domestic destination), all baggage must be X-rayed and sealed, so do this at the machine just inside the departure hall before you queue to check in. For international flights the departure tax (Rs 300, payable in rupees) must be paid at the State Bank counter in the departures hall, also before check-in.

Facilities at the international terminal include a dreadful snack bar, a bookshop and a bank. Once inside

Marble inlay detail (RE)

the departure lounge there are a few duty-free shops with the usual inflated prices, and another terrible snack bar where you have the privilege of paying in US dollars. Upstairs in the transit lounge is the Ashok Restaurant, which has probably some of the worst food you'll find anywhere in Delhi.

Domestic

Indian Airlines Indian Airlines, the state-owned domestic carrier, has a number of offices. The Malhotra Building office (☎ 331-0517) in F Block, Connaught Place, is probably the most convenient. It is, however, fairly busy at most times. It's open from 10 am to 5 pm daily except Sunday.

There's another office in the PTI Building (☎ 371-9168) on Sansad Marg, open from 10 am to 5 pm daily except Sunday. At the old Safdarjang Airport, on Aurobindo Marg south of Rajpath, there's a 24-hour office (☎ 462-4332), and this can be a very quick place to make bookings. Business-class passengers can check in by telephone on ☎ 329-5166. Telephone ☎ 140 for general enquiries , ☎ 141 for reservations, ☎ 142 for prerecorded flight arrival information and ☎ 143 for departures.

Indian Airlines flights depart from Delhi to all the major Indian centres. Check-in at the airport is 75 minutes before departure. Note that if you have just arrived and have an onward connection to another city in India, it may be with Air India, the country's international carrier, rather than the domestic carrier, Indian Airlines. If that is the case, you must check in at the international terminal (Terminal II) rather than the domestic terminal. India must be one of the few countries in the world where they can fill 747s on domestic routes!

Other Domestic Airline Offices In addition to Indian Airlines there are half a dozen or so private airlines. These have started operating only in the last few years, and so their route networks are not as well developed as that of Indian Airlines, but new sectors are being added all the time.

As well as the offices listed below, all the private airlines also have offices at the airport's domestic terminal.

Archana Airways
    41-A Friends Colony East, Mathura Rd (☎ 684-1690)
Damania Airways
    UG 26A Somdutt Chambers, 5 Bhikaji Cama Place (☎ 688-1122, fax 688-6286)

Domestic Flights from Delhi

Destination	Time hrs/min	Airline	Frequency d-daily w-weekly	Fare US$
Agra	0.40	IC	1d	23
Aurangabad	3.30	IC	5w	99
Bangalore	2.40	IC	4w	161
		4S	1d	
		S2	1d	
		M9	1d	
Bombay	1.50	IC	7d	115
		D2	2d	
		9W	4d	
		4S	1d	
		S2	1d	
		M9	2d	
Calcutta	2.05	IC	3d	132
		4S	6w	
		M9	2d	
Goa	2.00	IC	6w	150
		M9	3w	
Jaipur	0.40	IC	2d	28
Jodhpur	1.55	IC	5w	56
Khajuraho	2.00	IC	1d	53
		M9	1d	
Kulu	1.30	JA	6w	123
		AL	2d	
Leh	1.15	IC	6w	86
Madras	2.30	IC	2d	162
		D2	6w	
		M9	6w	
Shimla	1.10	AL	1d	96
Srinagar	1.15	IC	2d	77
Thiruvananthapuram (Trivandrum)	5.10	IC	6w	219
Udaipur	1.55	IC	10w	58
Varanasi	1.15	IC	11w	74
		M9	3w	

Airline abbreviation codes:
IC - Indian Airlines
JA - Jagson Airlines
D2 - Damania Airways
9W - Jet Airways
AL - Archana Airways
4S - East West Airlines
S2 - Sahara Indian Airlines
M9 - ModiLuft

East West Airlines
   DCM Building, Barakhamba Rd (☎ 329-5121, fax 375-5166)
Jagson Airlines
   12E Vandana Building, 12 Tolstoy Marg (☎ 332-1593, fax 332-4693)
Jet Airways
   3E Hanslaya Building, 15 Barakhamba Rd (☎ 372-4727, fax 371-4867)
ModiLuft
   Vandana Building, 11 Tolstoy Marg (☎ 335-4446)
NEPC Airlines
   G-39 4th floor, Pawan House, Connaught Place (☎ 332-2525)
Sahara India Airlines
   Ambadeep Building, Kasturba Gandhi Marg (☎ 332-6851, fax 375-5510)
Vayudoot
   Malhotra Building, F Block, Connaught Place (☎ 331-2587)

BUS

The main bus station is the Interstate Bus Terminal (ISBT) at Kashmiri Gate, north of the (Old) Delhi Railway Station. Facilities here include 24-hour left-luggage, State Bank of India branch, post office, pharmacy, and Delhi Transport's Nagrik Restaurant. City buses depart from here to locations all around Delhi – phone ☎ 252-3145 for details. State government bus companies operating from here are:

Delhi Transport Corporation (☎ 251-8836) – bookings from 8 am to 8 pm.
Haryana Government Roadways (☎ 252-1262) – bookings from 6.15 am to 12.30 pm and 2 to 9.30 pm. Reservations can also be made at the Haryana Emporium at Connaught Place from 10 am to 5 pm.
Himachal Pradesh Roadways (☎ 251-6725) – bookings from 7 am to 7 pm.
Punjab Roadways (☎ 251-7842) – bookings from 8 am to 8 pm.
Rajasthan Roadways (☎ 252-2246) – bookings from 7 am to 9 pm. Bookings can also be made at Bikaner House (☎ 38-3469) just south of Rajpath from 6 am to 7 pm.
Uttar Pradesh Roadways (☎ 251-8709) – bookings from 6 am to 9.30 pm.

Buses popular with travellers include the frequent and fast service to Jaipur for Rs 70. Deluxe buses for Jaipur leave from Bikaner House, take five hours and cost Rs 122, or Rs 210 for the less frequent air-con services.

For the five-hour trip to Chandigarh, from where you can take a bus or the narrow-gauge train up to Shimla, the regular buses cost Rs 70. There are deluxe buses for Rs 100. You can also get buses direct to Shimla (10 hours, Rs 90) and Dharamsala (13 hours, Rs 165 or Rs 240 deluxe), and there's a daily deluxe service to Manali (16 hours, Rs 285). To northern Uttar Pradesh, buses cost Rs 60 for Haridwar and Rs 64 for Dehra Dun.

Other destinations served by bus from Kashmiri Gate ISBT include Bharatpur, Bikaner, Jammu, Lucknow, Mussoorie, Naini Tal and Srinagar (24 hours, Rs 350).

There's also the new Sarai Kale Khan ISBT, close to Hazrat Nizamuddin Railway Station in south Delhi. There are buses from here to Agra (Rs 49 ordinary, Rs 56 express, Rs 71 deluxe and Rs 55 video) from 6 am to midnight, Mathura and Vrindaban (Rs 35/41 ordinary/express), Gwalior (Rs 81/90) and Bharatpur. There's a city bus link between this station and Kashmiri Gate ISBT.

TRAIN

Delhi is an important rail centre and an excellent place to make bookings. There is a special foreign tourist booking office upstairs in New Delhi Railway Station. It's open Monday to Saturday from 7.30 am to 5 pm. This is the place to go if you want a tourist-quota allocation, or if you are the holder of an Indrail Pass or want to buy one. It gets very busy and crowded, and it can take up to an hour to get served. If you make bookings here

Indian rail transport (TW)

tickets must be paid for in foreign currency (US dollars and pounds sterling only, and your change will be given in rupees), or with rupees backed up by bank exchange certificates.

The main ticket office is on Chelmsford Rd, between New Delhi Station and Connaught Place. This place is well organised but incredibly busy. Take a numbered ticket from the counter as you enter the building and then wait at the allotted window. Even with 50 computerised terminals it can take up to an hour to get served. It's best to arrive first thing in the morning or when it reopens after lunch. The office is open from 7.45 am to 1.50 pm and 2 to 9 pm Monday to Saturday. On Sundays it's open only until 1.50 pm.

Remember that there are two main stations in Delhi – Delhi Station in Old Delhi, and New Delhi Station at Paharganj. New Delhi is much closer to Connaught Place, and if you're departing from the (Old) Delhi Station you should allow adequate time to wind your way through the traffic snarls of Old Delhi. Between the (Old) Delhi and New Delhi stations you can take the No 6 bus for just Rs 1.

There's also the Hazrat Nizamuddin Railway Station south of the New Delhi area where some trains, such as the popular *Taj Express* to Agra, start or finish. It's worth getting off here if you are staying in Chanakyapuri or elsewhere south of Rajpath.

Recently, trains between Delhi and Jaipur, Jodhpur and Udaipur have been operating to and from Sarai Rohilla Railway Station rather than (Old) Delhi. It's about 3.5 km north-west of Connaught Place on Guru Govind Singh Marg. They may still be operating from there, so check when you book your ticket. The exception is the air-con *Shatabdi Express* to Jaipur, which operates from New Delhi.

TRAVEL AGENTS

Located in the Imperial Hotel, the Student Travel Information Centre (☎ 332-7582) is used by many travellers and is the place to renew or obtain student cards, although their tickets are not usually as cheap as elsewhere. Aerotrek Travels (☎ 371-5966) in the Mercantile Building in E Block is reportedly reliable. Some of the ticket discounters around Connaught Place and Paharganj are real fly-by-night operations, so take care.

Outbound Travel (☎ 60-3902) at B-2/50 Safdarjang Enclave has been recommended as a reliable place to organise travel within India.

Major Trains from Delhi

Destination	Train Number & Name	Depart. Time & Place	Km	Time hr/min	Fare 2nd/lst Rs
Agra	2180 Taj Exp	7.15 am HN	199	2.35	62/183
	2002 Shatabdi Exp*	6.15 am ND		1.55	235/470
Bombay	2952 Rajdhani Exp*	4.05 pm ND	1384	17.0	840/1370
	1038 Punjab Mail	6 am ND		26.0	264/877
Calcutta	2302 Rajdhani Exp*	5.15 pm ND	1441	18.0	705/865
	2304 Poorva Exp	4.30 pm ND		24.0	259/837
Jaipur	2901 Pink City Exp	6 am SR	308	6.00	90/262
	Shatabdi Exp*	5.50 am ND		4.25	300/600
Shimla	4095 Himalayan Queen	6.10 am ND	364	11.0	103/303
Udaipur	2901 Pink City Exp	6 am SR	739	13.30	172/521
Varanasi	2382 Poorva Exp	4.30 pm ND	764	12.20	179/541

Abbreviations:
ND - New Delhi
HN - Hazrat Nizamuddin
SR - Sarai Rohilla

* air-con only; fare includes meals and drinks

For more upmarket travel arrangements, both within India and for foreign travel, there are a number of places, mostly around Connaught Place. These include Cox & Kings (☎ 332-0067), Sita World Travels (☎ 331-1133) and the Travel Corporation of India (☎ 331-2570).

Getting Around

Distances around Delhi are large and the buses are generally hopelessly crowded. The alternative is a taxi, auto rickshaw or bicycle.

TO/FROM THE AIRPORT

Although there are a number of options, airport-to-city transport is not as straightforward as it should be, because of predatory taxi and auto-rickshaw drivers who take advantage of the unwary – usually first-time visitors who arrive in the middle of the night. Bear in mind that, unless notified in advance, budget hotels are closed from about 11 pm to 6 am, so arriving on the doorstep in the middle of the night is useless.

Around the Airport

The domestic terminal (Terminal I of the Indira Gandhi International Airport) is seven km from the centre, and the newer international terminal (Terminal II) is a further nine km.

You'll find 24-hour State Bank of India and Thomas Cook foreign exchange counters in the arrivals hall at Terminal II, after you go through customs and immigration. The service is fast and efficient. Once you've left the arrivals hall, you won't be allowed back in.

Many international flights to/from Delhi arrive and depart at terrible hours in the early morning. Take special care if this is your first foray into India and you arrive exhausted and jet-lagged. If you're leaving Delhi in the early hours of the morning, book a taxi the afternoon before; they are hard to find in the night. See Places to Stay for information about the retiring rooms at the airport.

There is a free IAAI bus between the two terminals. The EATS bus and the DTC bus will also transport you between the two terminals for a small fee (see below).

Bus

EATS (the Ex-Servicemen's Air Link Transport Service; ☎ 331-6530) has a regular bus service between the airport (both terminals) and the old Vayudoot office in Connaught Place. The fare is Rs 25 and they will drop you off or pick you up at most of the major hotels en route if you ask – although this doesn't include

Paharganj. In Connaught Place it leaves from the Vayudoot office on Janpath, opposite the underground Palika Bazaar, at 5, 7 and 11 am and 2, 4, 6, 7.30, 9, 10.20 and 11.30 pm, and the trip takes up to an hour (more during peak hours). When leaving the international terminal, the counter for the EATS bus is just to the right as you exit the building. This is probably the best, although not the quickest, way into the city if you arrive late at night (see the warning about pre-paid taxis in the Taxi section).

Once at Connaught Place, however, there are sometimes shonky auto-rickshaw drivers around who have a scam set up. You are taken into a side street where a bogus policeman – complete with uniform and *lathi* (stick) – stops the vehicle due to supposed 'Hindu-Muslim problem' at Paharganj or wherever you happen to be going. You'll then end up at a hotel of their choice (usually in Karol Bagh) and pay way over the top, and from there you may be talked into getting out of Delhi as quickly as possible, usually in chartered transport at exorbitant rates.

There is also a regular DTC (Delhi Transport Corporation) bus service that runs from both terminals of the airport to New Delhi Railway Station and the Interstate bus station; it costs Rs 20 and there is a Rs 5 charge for luggage. At New Delhi Railway Station it uses the Ajmeri Gate (east) side. There is also a public bus service to the airport (No 780) from the Super Bazar at Connaught Place, but it can get very crowded. You can also catch this on Sansad Marg, outside the Jantar Mantar.

Taxi

Just outside the international terminal is a pre-paid taxi booth; a taxi to the centre costs Rs 280 when booked here. However, recently we've had reports from a number of travellers who have been given the run-around by the pre-paid taxis in the middle of the night; they get taken to a hotel, told it's full, then on to another hotel (often in Karol Bagh) and intimidated into staying there at vastly inflated prices (up to US$150). This seems to happen only when the driver has established that the person hasn't been to India before, and only in the middle of the night when it's difficult to get your bearings and there are few other vehicles about. If you do take a taxi at this time, make an obvious point of noting down the registration number before getting in; this will greatly decrease the driver's scope for mischief as he knows you have some way of tracking him down. When you pre-pay the fare you should get two copies of the docket, one

---

Sandal on a String

If you spend any amount of time on the roads in Delhi, there is one thing which may have caught your attention and have you guessing: Why do vehicles have a sandal dangling from a string at the back? Look around and you'll see them everywhere – on everything from cycle rickshaws to lumbering Tata trucks. And it's not only sandals, but shoes, thongs or just about anything else which can be worn on the feet.

The answer, predictably, lies with religion. It seems that the feet are considered the least worthy of respect and, by association, the shoe is unclean. So if a shoe or other footwear is hung from a vehicle it will disgust and repel any malevolent spirit which might otherwise bring harm to the vehicle and its occupants. ■

---

of which goes to the driver for him to get paid for the journey. It's worth keeping the driver's copy until you arrive at your destination. Don't believe *any* stories about hotels being full, or 'Hindu-Muslim problem' where you want to go or any other rubbish; firmly insist on being taken to the correct destination. If you do end up at a hotel in Karol Bagh or somewhere else and there's no choice but to stay, be very suspicious if it costs more than about Rs 500, and make sure you get hold of some of the hotel's stationery or a business card with the name and phone number.

Given the above-mentioned problems with getting yourself from the airport to a hotel in the centre in the middle of the night, if this is your first trip to India it is probably best to wait in the terminal building until daylight when there is much less risk of getting led astray and your surroundings are far less intimidating.

At the domestic terminal the taxi booking desk is just inside the terminal and charges Rs 98 to Connaught Place, plus Rs 2 per bag. The taxi-wallahs outside will try for much more.

From Connaught Place to the international terminal a taxi costs around Rs 150. There are pre-paid taxis from the Kashmiri Gate bus station to the international terminal (Rs 153) and the domestic terminal (Rs 103).

BUS

Avoid buses during the rush hours as the situation is hopeless. Whenever possible try to board (and leave) at a starting or finishing point, such as the Regal and Plaza cinemas in Connaught Place, as there is more chance of a seat and less chance of being trampled. There are some seats reserved for women on the left side of the bus.

Until recently all buses were run by the Delhi Transport Corporation, but the system has now been privatised to a large degree and private buses vastly outnumber the DTC buses. While privatisation has led to increased frequency, it has also led to increased danger as the two major private operators, Blue Line and Red Line, try to maximise profits and minimise costs – for the most part their drivers are utter maniacs, as you will soon find if you travel for any distance on the Ring Rd. All buses still follow the old DTC numbered routes. A short bus ride (like Connaught Place to Red Fort) is only about Rs 1. DTC publishes a comprehensive route guide, but it is entirely in Hindi (Rs 7.50).

Useful buses include:

42 - Runs from (Old) Delhi Railway Station to Tughlaqabad via Super Bazar at Connaught Place.

104, 139, and 160 – Run between the Kashmiri Gate Interstate bus station and Connaught Place via the Red Fort. In the opposite direction you can pick them up on Barakhamba Rd, outside the Akash Deep Building.

433 – From outside the Jantar Mantar on Sansad Marg, near Connaught Place, it will bring you to Nehru Place, from where it's a 15-minute walk to the Bahai House of Worship.

505 – Goes to the Qutb Minar and Hauz Khas from the Super Bazar, or from Janpath opposite the Imperial Hotel.

620 – Runs between Connaught Place (from outside the Jantar Mantar) and Chanakyapuri.

TAXI

There are plenty of yellow-and-black taxis, all of which are metered. Invariably, however, the meters are out of date or 'not working', or the drivers will simply refuse to use them. It matters not a jot that they are legally required to do so. A threat to report them to the police results in little more than considerable mirth, so you should negotiate a price before you set out. Naturally, this will always be more than it should be. There are exceptions; occasionally a driver will reset the meter without even a word from you. At places like the New Delhi Railway Station, where there are always plenty of police hanging around, you can generally rely on the meter being used because it's too easy to report a driver. Trips during the rush hour or middle-of-the-night journeys to the airport are the times when meters are least likely to be used.

Top : A local bus in Old Delhi (HF)
Bottom : Bicycles are a popular mode of transport (HF)

At the end of a metered journey you will have to pay according to a scale of revised charges or simply a flat percentage increase. Some drivers display these cards in the cab, others consign them to the oily-rag compartment, still others feed them to the cows. So if you do come across a legible copy it's worth noting down a few of the conversions, paying what you think is the right price and leaving it at that. You may rest assured that no-one is going to be out of pocket except yourself, despite hurt or angry protestations to the contrary. The current adjustment is the meter reading plus 50%.

Once you have a feel for fares it's generally best to negotiate a fee beforehand and forget about the meter. This way you know you'll go via the route that uses the least fuel, ie the quickest way, and not have to worry about where on earth you are being taken. Journeys on the meter will definitely be somewhat cheaper, but you need to have a working knowledge of the city's layout and constantly keep an eye on where you are going.

Connaught Place to the Red Fort should cost about Rs 35 by taxi, depending on the traffic. From 11 pm to 5 am there is a 25% surcharge.

AUTO RICKSHAW

An auto rickshaw is a noisy three-wheel device powered by a two-stroke motorcycle engine, with a driver up front and seats for two passengers behind. They don't have doors and have just a canvas top. They are also known as scooters or autos. They're generally about half the price of a taxi, are metered and follow the same ground rules as taxis.

Because of their size, auto rickshaws are often faster than taxis for short trips and their drivers are decidedly nuttier – hair-raising near-misses are guaranteed and glancing-blow collisions are not infrequent; thrillseekers will love it!

While convenient, however, you'll soon find they are far from comfortable. When stopped at traffic lights, the height you are sitting at is invariably the exact same height of most bus and truck exhaust pipes – copping dirty great lungfuls of diesel fumes is part of the fun of auto-rickshaw travel. Also, their small wheel size and rock-hard suspension make them supremely uncomfortable; even the slightest bump will have you instantly airborne. The speed humps and huge potholes found everywhere are the bane of the rickshaw traveller – pity the poor drivers.

MOTORCYCLE RICKSHAW

There are unusual six-seater motorcycle rickshaws running fixed routes at fixed prices. From Connaught Place their starting point is Palika Bazaar, and drivers chop their way through the traffic as far as the Jama Masjid in Old Delhi. They cost Rs 2 per person and are good value, especially during rush hours. In Old Delhi they start from the south side of the Jama Masjid.

CYCLE RICKSHAW

Cycle rickshaws are banned from the Connaught Place area and New Delhi itself, but they can be handy for travelling between the northern edge of Connaught Place and Paharganj, and around Old Delhi.

BICYCLE

Cycling is an excellent way of getting around, especially in New Delhi, where the roads are wide, in good condition and, by Indian standards, uncrowded. At the large traffic roundabouts you need to take a deep breath and plunge in, but otherwise the traffic is pretty orderly. All the sites of New Delhi are easily reached by bicycle, and even the Qutb Minar and the sites to the south are accessible if you don't mind a bit of exercise, although attempting this in summer might be a bit ambitious.

What is surprising is that there are so few places to hire bikes. In Paharganj the only place seems to be Mehta Electricals in Main Bazaar next to the Kesri Hotel, near Rajguru Rd. The bikes are old but well maintained and cost Rs 20 per day, with a Rs 400 deposit. As with many shops in Main Bazaar, this place is closed on Mondays.

ORGANISED TOURS

Delhi is very spread out, so taking a city tour makes a lot of sense. Even by public transport, getting from, say, the Red Fort to the Qutb Minar is comparatively expensive.

Two major organisations arrange Delhi tours – beware of agents offering cut-price (and sometimes inferior) tours. The ITDC, operating under the name Ashok Travels & Tours (☎ 332-2336), has tours which include guides and a luxury coach. Their office is in L Block, Connaught Place, but you can book at the tourist office on Janpath or at the major hotels. Delhi Tourism (☎ 331-4229), a branch of the city government, arranges similar tours; their office is in N Block, Middle Circle.

Motorcycle rickshaws, powered by Harley Davidson copies, shuttle commuters around Delhi (HF)

A 4½-hour morning tour of New Delhi costs Rs 70 with ITDC. Starting at 8.30 am, the tour includes the Qutb Minar, Humayun's Tomb, India Gate, the Jantar Mantar and the Lakshmi Narayan Temple. The afternoon Old Delhi tour for Rs 60 starts at 2.15 pm and covers the Red Fort, Jama Masjid, Raj Ghat, Shanti Vana and Feroz Shah Kotla. If you take both tours on the same day they cost Rs 120.

'Delhi by Evening' is a Delhi Tourism tour which takes in a number of sights, including the sound & light show at the Red Fort. A minimum of 10 people is required before the tour operates.

Tours further afield include ITDC day tours to Agra for Rs 400.

Things to See & Do

HIGHLIGHTS

Delhi has a wealth of things to see – the Archaeological Survey has something over 1300 monuments listed in the Delhi area! Obviously the vast majority of these hold little interest for the casual visitor, but many of them are well worth visiting, while a handful are simply too good to miss.

The main focus of interest for visitors is the monuments left by the Mughals. Foremost among these are the **Red Fort** and **Jama Masjid** (Friday Mosque), which dominate the skyline of Old Delhi. Equally interesting is the majestic, domed **Humayun's Tomb** south of the city centre, a Mughal monument set in a formal garden.

The **British buildings** of New Delhi are the most obvious reminders that this was the capital of British India at a time when the empire was at its peak, but equally interesting is the area north of the old city, known as **Civil Lines**, where the city's British residents lived and fought while helping to carve out the empire long before New Delhi was even thought about.

A couple of other places worth visiting are the **Qutb Minar Complex** on the city's southern outskirts, with its soaring victory tower dating back to the 13th century, and the **ceremonial gardens** lining the Yamuna River.

Martyr's Memorial, depicting Mahatma Gandhi leading the people to independence (HF)

OLD DELHI

Walls & Gates

When Shah Jahan built his new capital of Shahjahanabad here in the 17th century, one of the key elements was a high red-brick wall, pierced by 14 gates. The British strengthened and repaired it with stone and added a number of bastions for further protection. Only four of the original gates remain today – **Kashmiri Gate** on the north side and **Ajmeri, Turkman** and **Delhi Gates** on the southern side.

The only remaining stretch of wall runs west of Delhi Gate towards Turkman Gate, and it's possible to walk along it.

Kashmiri Gate The Kashmiri Gate was the scene of desperate fighting when the British retook Delhi during the Mutiny. It was the only gate to have two openings. These days it looks surprisingly insignificant, partly because about a metre of it is below the current ground level. Scramble over the rubble to see the mortar damage in the far side of the wall, caused by the heavy British shelling in 1857.

Turkman Gate Turkman Gate (often known locally as Truckman Gate) is on the southern edge of the old walled city. It was named after the Muslim holy man Hazrat Shah Turkman Bayabani, whose *dargah* (tomb) is on the outer eastern side of the gate. The small, well-maintained tomb dates from 1240 and it's possible to enter the shrine (remove shoes).

Just 50 metres from the Turkman tomb along the small side road is the **Holy Trinity Church**, a small, austere building built at the turn of the century.

Chandni Chowk

The main street of Old Delhi is the colourful shopping bazaar known as Chandni Chowk (Silver St). It's hopelessly congested day and night, a very sharp contrast to what it must have been like during Shah Jahan's time, when it was lined with mansions and gardens and had an ornamental canal down the centre. Today the canal has been filled and the mansions and gardens have made way for modern structures. (See Walking Tour 1.)

Fatehpuri Masjid The western end of Chandni Chowk is marked by the Fatehpuri Masjid, which was erected in 1650 by Fatehpuri Begum, one of Shah Jahan's wives. The courtyard surrounding the mosque has changed much over the years, which explains the out-of-character clock above the main gateway.

After the Mutiny, the building ceased to function as a mosque and it wasn't until the British allowed the Muslims back into Old Delhi that it resumed its former role.

In the meantime, however, the courtyard had been sold to a Hindu family, and the British had to buy them out – with four Hindu villages! – in order to return it to the Muslims.

Khari Baoli

Khari Baoli, the street which runs from the Fatehpuri Masjid to the western edge of the old city, is Delhi's bustling **wholesale spice market**. Even if you're not in need of spices, it's well worth a wander simply to take in the sights and smells. Things have changed here very little over the decades – huge sacks of herbs and spices are brought to the wholesalers on long, narrow barrows pushed by wiry labourers. In the mornings the activity is hectic as literally hundreds of barrow-pushers jostle for position. Even though it's the wholesale market, you can buy any quantity of any item, and the choice, quality and price are the best in the city.

Although herbs and spices are the main items in Khari Baoli, there are also a number of shops selling other produce. Each merchant goes to great lengths to make an eye-catching display of produce samples – whether it be a dozen varieties of lentils or rice, giant jars of chutneys and pickles, or nuts, tea or even block soap.

Gadodia Market, on the south side of the street roughly half-way along, is one of a number of wholesalers' stores. The small courtyard is lined with storerooms, each with its own huge beam scale and mountains of sacks. This market was built in the 1920s by a prosperous merchant.

Sadar Bazaar

West of Khari Baoli, just over the railway line, is Sadar Bazaar, the wholesale market for household items. It requires some patience to negotiate this street on foot, simply because it's so incredibly busy; people come here from all over Delhi – Old and New – as the prices are low and the choice extensive. I don't know of anywhere else where you can buy saucepans or thali plates by the kg!

Walking Tour 1: Chandni Chowk
(2 hours; Map 15)

Starting at the eastern (Red Fort) end of Chandni Chowk, and north of the Jama Masjid, is the **Digambar Jain temple**, with a small marble courtyard surrounded by a colonnade. The main devotional room of the temple is on the 1st floor, and it glitters with gilt, lit by butter lamps offered by worshippers. The main image is of the founder of Jainism, Mahavira, while in the shrine to the right is a statue of Lord Parasnath. In the same compound is the **Jain Bird Hospital**, where injured birds (mostly pigeons) are brought for treatment. The entrance to the temple and bird hospital enclosure is actually on the main road, Netaji Subhash Marg, about 50 metres south from Chandni Chowk.

Next door to the Jain Temple along Chandni Chowk is the 800-year-old **Gauri Shankar Temple**, dedicated to the Hindu god Siva. Inside the temple there are shrines to Siva, his wife Parvati and sons Ganesh and Kartik, and his consort Nandi, the bull. There's also a marble chair in the courtyard, and it was here that Bhagwat Swaroop Brachmachari, a Hindu saint, spent more than 50 years. It's his photo and sandals on the chair. Outside the temple are stalls where from early morning until late evening men and women make colourful and fragrant flower garlands, which people buy for the small shrines found in most Hindu homes or to decorate cars and homes for weddings and other festivals.

Continue along Chandni Chowk, crossing the atypically straight Esplanade Rd, and turn left at the next street; there's a Jalebi Wala sweet shop on the corner. This street is **Dariba Kalan** (street of the incomparable pearl) and since the time of Shah Jahan it has been Delhi's gold, silver and jewellery market. You won't find any of the glitzy, high-security shops of Connaught Place here; the tone is much more relaxed. It may come as a surprise to find that jewellery here is sold by weight rather than by the piece – it seems no great value is placed on the craft of the jewellers themselves.

Where Dariba Kalan makes a slight bend to the left at shop No 1658, take the narrow street to the right, **Kinari Bazaar**. From all over the city Delhi-ites come specifically to the glittering shops in this street for wedding ceremony accessories – hair-braids feature prominently, as do amazingly intricate garlands made from tinsel and crisp, new Rs 5 and Rs 10 notes. This area has always been Hindu-dominated, so even during the trauma of Partition there was very little disturbance here.

As you walk along Kinari Bazaar, after a few hundred metres keep an eye on the lanes opening off to the left; down one of these you'll see some colourfully painted house facades, and at the end is the **Jain Svetambara**

temple. The entrance is the last door on the right-hand side, and the devotional rooms and images are on the 1st and 2nd floors. The main feature on the 1st floor is the black carved image of Lord Parasnath, the 23rd Jain Mltirthankar (saint), while on the 2nd floor it's the colourful mosaic tracing the life of Lord Mahavira which catches the eye.

Turn left back onto Kinari Bazaar, take the first lane to the right – there's a red letterbox right by the entrance – and this takes you back to Chandni Chowk. Turn right and after 50 metres you come across another Delhi institution – the **Ghantewala** sweet shop. This shop was established in the late 18th century and satisfied the royal Mughal sweet tooth. It is said the recipes remain unchanged today. It's also said that the shop got its name, which means 'bell ringer', from the fact that during processions the emperor's elephant would stop outside and ring its bell until fed with sweets.

Close by, on the same side of the road, is the 18th-century, triple-domed **Sunehri Masjid** (one of two in the city). In 1739, Nadir Shah, the Persian invader who carried off the Peacock Throne when he sacked Delhi, stood on the roof of this mosque and watched while his soldiers conducted a bloody massacre of the city's inhabitants.

Further along and also on the same side is the Sikh's **Sisganj Gurdwara**, built on the site where the 10th Sikh guru, Guru Tegh Bahadur, was executed on the Mughal emperor Aurangzeb's orders. To visit you must leave your shoes outside and cover your head (scarves are provided for this). The Sikh's holy book, the Guru Granth Sahib, is kept under an amazing gold canopy, and holy men sing hymns there throughout the day.

Across the road here is the Victorian-era **Fountain**, known today as Fountain Chowk. It is near the site of the old police station (kotwali) and it was here that the British, having effectively wiped out the Mughal lineage by murdering the last Mughal emperor's sons and grandsons during the Mutiny in 1857, put their bodies on public display.

Cross over to this side and head back towards the Red Fort. After passing the Kumar Cinema building, turn left along a lane heading towards a group of trees about 100 metres along. There is a small Hindu shrine under the trees, but the main point of interest here is the fine old mansion known as **Begum Samru's Palace**, which is hidden away behind the building directly behind the shrine, although it is now almost unrecognisable behind the bank signs and other hoardings. The owner of the house was Begum Samru, an influential Kashmiri woman who held a high place in society, not least because her private army could be called upon by the Mughal emperor to help out when needed. She married a wealthy European mercenary, Walter Reinhard, who was more commonly known as Sombre, from which the name Samru is derived. ∎

Red Fort

The evocative red sandstone walls and gates of Lal Qila, the Red Fort, are the most impressive sight in Delhi – Old or New. The facade totally dominates the eastern edge of Old Delhi and the area outside the main gate is always alive with tourists and hawkers. Unfortunately, the inside no longer creates such a grand impression, mainly because the British used the fort to house the army and many buildings were demolished after the 1857 Mutiny and the formal, delicately balanced layout altered. Nevertheless, it's still Delhi's number one attraction and shouldn't be missed.

The Red Fort dates from the very peak of Mughal power, when it was known as the Qila-e-Mu'alla (Auspicious Fort). The name Lal Qila dates back to the British era. When the emperor rode out on elephant-back into the streets of Old Delhi it was a display of pomp and power at its most magnificent.

The crenellated walls extend for two km and vary in height from 18 metres on what was the river side to 33 metres on the city side. Shah Jahan started construction of the massive fort in 1638 and it was completed in 1648.

Today, the fort is typically Indian with would-be guides leaping forth to offer their services as soon as you enter. It's still a calm haven of peace if you've just left the frantic streets of Old Delhi, however. The city noise and confusion are light-years away from the fort gardens and pavilions. The Yamuna River used to flow right by the eastern edge of the fort and filled the 10-metre-deep moat. These days the river is over one km to the east and the moat remains empty. Entry to the fort is Rs 0.50, free on Fridays.

Lahore Gate The main gate to the fort takes its name from the fact that it faces towards Lahore, now in Pakistan. The ornate gate itself is obscured by a sandstone bastion which was added at a later date by Aurangzeb. Other more recent modifications include the installation of a sandstone tower which houses a lift, and the blanking off of the gate-tower windows with sandstone during the 1980s; it was thought they would make a great perch for a sniper trying to knock off the prime minister during the Independence Day speech.

If one spot could be said to be the emotional and symbolic heart of the modern Indian nation, the Lahore Gate of the Red Fort is probably it. During the struggle for independence, one of the nationalists' declarations was that they would see the Indian flag flying over the Red Fort in Delhi. After Independence, many important political speeches were given by Nehru and Indira Gandhi to the crowds amassed on the maidan outside, and on Independence Day (15 August) each year, the prime minister addresses a huge crowd.

Chatta Chowk You enter the fort through the Lahore Gate and immediately find yourself in a vaulted arcade, the Chatta Chowk (Covered Bazaar). The shops in this arcade used to sell the upmarket items that the royal household might fancy – silks, jewellery, gold. These days they cater to the tourist trade and the quality of the goods is certainly a little less, although some still carry a royal price tag! This arcade of shops was also known as the Meena Bazaar, the shopping centre for ladies of the court. On Thursdays the gates of the fort were closed to men, women staffed the shops and only women were allowed inside the citadel. Just above some of the shop signs it's still possible to make out the cusped arches of the original shopfronts.

Naubat Khana The Chatta Chowk arcade leads to the Naubat Khana, or Drum House, where musicians used to play for the emperor and the arrival of princes and royalty was heralded. Here visiting nobles had to dismount from their elephants and proceed on foot. The 1st floor now houses a small military museum.

The grassed open courtyard beyond the Naubat Khana formerly had galleries along either side, but these were removed by the British Army when the fort was used as their headquarters. Other intrusive reminders of the British presence are the huge, monumentally ugly, three-storey barrack blocks which lie to the north of this courtyard.

Diwan-i-Am The Hall of Public Audiences was where the emperor would sit to hear complaints or disputes from his subjects. His alcove in the wall was marble-panelled and set with precious stones, many of which were looted following the Mutiny. This elegant hall was restored as a result of a directive by Lord Curzon, the Viceroy of India between 1898 and 1905. The marble panels behind the throne canopy are thought to have been designed in Italy. The marble table below the throne is where the prime minister used to sit; he would listen to the petitioners and relay the complaints to the emperor. Although the hall is in good condition, it would have created a vastly different impression when it was in use. Not only were the walls and pillars completely covered with white plaster, but the floor was

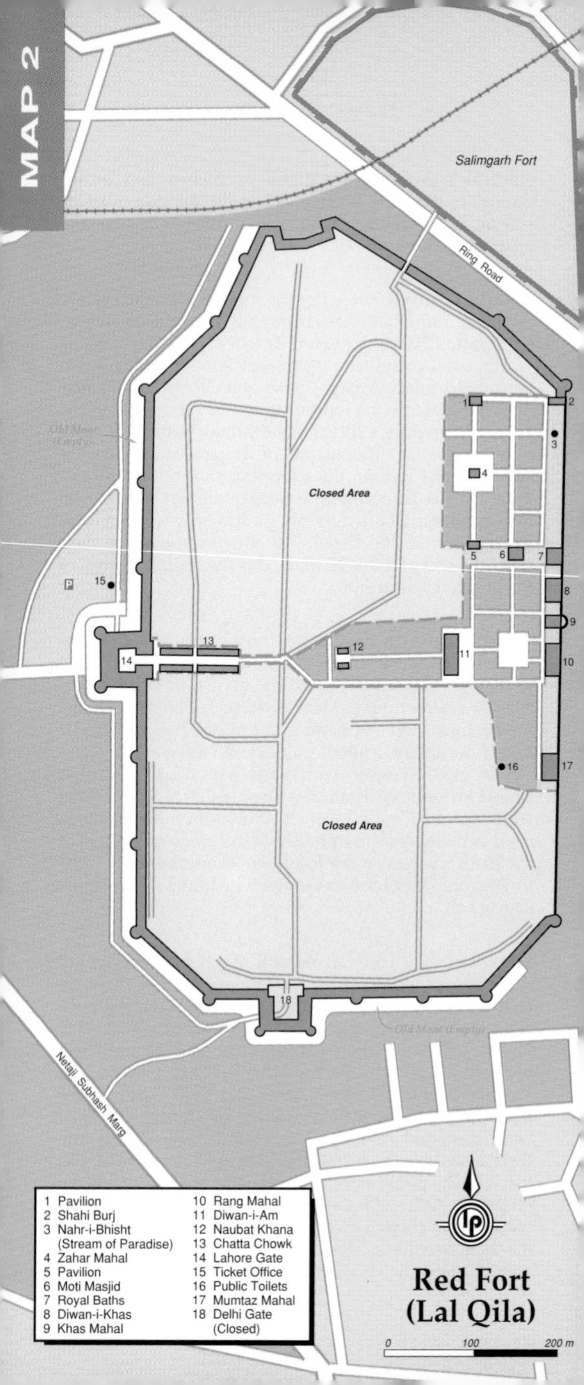

MAP 2

Salimgarh Fort

Ring Road

Old Moat (empty)

Closed Area

P
15

13
14
12
11
16

1
2
3
4
5 6 7
8
9
10
17

Closed Area

18

Old Moat (empty)

Netaji Subhash Marg

1 Pavilion
2 Shahi Burj
3 Nahr-i-Bhisht
  (Stream of Paradise)
4 Zahar Mahal
5 Pavilion
6 Moti Masjid
7 Royal Baths
8 Diwan-i-Khas
9 Khas Mahal
10 Rang Mahal
11 Diwan-i-Am
12 Naubat Khana
13 Chatta Chowk
14 Lahore Gate
15 Ticket Office
16 Public Toilets
17 Mumtaz Mahal
18 Delhi Gate
   (Closed)

Red Fort
(Lal Qila)

0   100   200 m

strewn with rugs and rich crimson awnings shaded the interior.

This was as far into the palace as most nobles could ever hope to go.

Diwan-i-Khas The Hall of Private Audiences, built of white marble, was the luxurious chamber where the emperor would hold private meetings. Centrepiece of the hall was the magnificent Peacock Throne, until Nadir Shah carted it off to Iran in 1739. The solid gold throne had figures of peacocks standing behind it, their beautiful colours resulting from countless inlaid precious

The Lahore Gate, entrance to the Red Fort (HF)

stones. Between them was the figure of a parrot carved out of a single emerald.

This masterpiece in precious metals, sapphires, rubies, emeralds and pearls was broken up, and the so-called Peacock Throne displayed in Teheran simply utilises various bits of the original. The famous Koh-i-Noor Diamond is now set in a crown belonging to the Queen Mother and is on display in the Tower of London. The marble pedestal on which the throne used to sit is all that remains.

In 1760, the Marathas also removed the silver ceiling from the hall; the gilt work on the ceiling today dates back to the time of the Coronation Durbar of 1903. Inscribed on the walls of the Diwan-i-Khas is that famous Persian couplet:

If there is a paradise on earth
it is this, it is this, it is this.

Royal Baths Next to the Diwan-i-Khas are the *hammams*, or baths – three large rooms surmounted by domes, with a fountain in the centre – one of which was set up as a sauna. The floors used to be inlaid with *pietra dura* work, and the rooms were illuminated through panels of coloured glass in the roof. The baths are closed to the public.

Moti Masjid Built in 1659 by Aurangzeb for his personal use, the small and totally enclosed Pearl Mosque, made of marble, is next to the baths. One curious feature of the mosque is that its outer walls are oriented exactly to be in symmetry with the rest of the fort, while the inner walls are slightly askew, so that the mosque has the correct orientation with Mecca.

Shahi Burj This modest, three-storey octagonal tower at the north-eastern edge of the fort was once Shah Jahan's private working area. From here the **Nahr-i-Bhisht** (Stream of Paradise) water channel used to flow through the Royal Baths, the Diwan-i-Khas, the Khas Mahal and the Rang Mahal. The channel is now largely overgrown and it's difficult to imagine what it must have once been. Like the baths, the tower is closed.

Khas Mahal The small Khas Mahal, south of the Diwan-i-Khas, was the emperor's private palace, divided into rooms for worship, sleeping and living. Today its most outstanding feature is the fine marble screen *(jali)* which spans the small water channel.

A small balcony protrudes out over what was the river bank, and from here the emperor used to give a morning audience. If for some reason he didn't appear, nervous speculation rapidly mounted as to his wellbeing.

Below the Khas Mahal is the gate by which the emperor and senior nobles would enter the palace.

Rang Mahal The Rang Mahal pavilion, or Palace of Colour, further south again, took its name from the painted interior, which sadly is now gone. This was once the residence of the emperor's chief wife and is where he ate. On the floor in the centre is a beautifully carved marble lotus, and the water flowing along the channel from the Shahi Burj used to end up here. Originally there was a fountain made of ivory in the centre. In the rooms at either end it is still possible to see beautiful inlaid mirrorwork on the ceilings.

In an effort to alleviate the heat of Delhi's fierce summers many people built underground rooms. This is the case with the Rang Mahal, although you can only peer in through the sandstone grilles that line the building below its floor level.

Mumtaz Mahal Still further south along the eastern wall is the last of the remaining pavilions, the Mumtaz Mahal. It was formerly the residence of one of the Mughal court's greatest ladies, Jahanara Begum, Shah Jahan's favourite daughter and boss of the royal harem. Today this building houses a small and rather tatty Archaeological Museum.

Gardens Between all the exquisite buildings were highly formal Persian gardens, complete with fountains, pools and small pavilions. While the general outline and some of the pavilions are still in place, the gardens were uprooted by the British and replaced with sterile, featureless lawns.

Sound & Light Show Each evening an interesting sound and light show re-creates events of Delhi's history, particularly those connected with the Red Fort. There are shows in English and Hindi, and tickets (Rs 20) are available from the fort. The English sessions are at 7.30 pm from November to January, 8.30 pm February to April and September to October, and at 9 pm from May to August. It's well worth making the effort to see this show as it brings back some of the life and colour so absent during the day, but make sure you are well equipped with mosquito repellent.

Jama Masjid

The great mosque of Old Delhi is both the largest in India and the final architectural extravagance of Shah Jahan. Begun in 1644, the mosque was not completed until 1658. It has three great gateways, four angle towers and two minarets standing 40 metres high and constructed of vertical strips of red sandstone and white marble.

Broad flights of steps lead up to the imposing gateways. The eastern gateway was originally opened only for the emperor. It is open to the public only on Fridays and Muslim festival days. The general public can enter by either the north or south gate (Rs 15). Shoes should be removed and those people considered unsuitably dressed (bare legs for either men or women) can hire robes at the northern gate.

The courtyard of the mosque has a capacity of 25,000 people. For Rs 5 it's possible to climb the southern minaret, and the views in all directions are superb – Old Delhi, the Red Fort and the polluting factories beyond it across the river, and New Delhi to the south. You can also see one of the features that the architect Lutyens incorporated into his design of New Delhi – the Jama Masjid, Connaught Place and Sansad Bhavan (Parliament House) are in a direct line. There's also a fine view of the Red Fort from the east side of the mosque.

The mosque is open to non-Muslims from half an hour after sunrise until half an hour before sunset and is closed on Fridays for two hours during mid-day prayers. There's a Rs 15 fee for cameras inside the mosque, and another Rs 15 to take them up the minaret (Rs 25 for video cameras). (See Walking Tour 2.)

Sunehri Masjid

Outside the Delhi Gate of the Red Fort is this beautiful little mosque, the second with this name in the old city (the other being on Chandni Chowk). Its three domes were originally faced with copper, hence the name, which means Golden Mosque. This one was built by Qudsia Begum, wife of emperor Ahmed Shah, and was repaired in 1852 by Bahadur Shah.

Zinat-ul Masjid

This rarely visited but quite beautiful mosque (its name means Most Beautiful of Mosques) towers over Raj Ghat south of the Red Fort in Darya Ganj. It was built by Zinat-un Nisaa, a daughter of Aurangzeb. Although not as large as the Jama Masjid, it is still a big mosque, with

Walking Tour 2: Old Delhi – Maruti Car Parts, Mosques and Mansions (1½ hours; Map 15)

Jama Masjid to Ajmeri Gate Within the old walled city of Shahjahanabad there are still a number of reminders of the days when the narrow streets of Shah Jahan's city were lined with elegant mansions (havelis). Few exist today, and those that have survived are in a sorry state. The facades are often the only identifying sign of what once was, and even these usually have modern shops at street level.

Any walking trip around the old city requires a good deal of patience – the streets are narrow and crowded – but it's well worth the effort.

From the southern gate of the **Jama Masjid**, the street that leads due south away from the mosque is **Matya Mahal Bazaar**, a busy commercial street with many cheap restaurants and guest houses at its northern end. In fact, a great way to start this walk is to drop into Karims Restaurant, in a small courtyard just 20 metres on the left along Matya Mahal from the Jama Masjid. This place has been serving food to Delhi-ites for over 80 years and is extremely popular. Outside a number of the restaurants you may see destitute people sitting patiently on the ground as they wait for the daily handouts from the restaurants.

Starting from the southern gate of the Jama Masjid, head to the right around towards the rear corner of the mosque, and the first thing you'll notice is that the shops here are chock-a-block with spare car parts, and in fact this corner is known as **Car Parts Bazaar** – if you're in need of anything from a valve spring to a shock absorber, you'll find it here.

Take the small lane that runs parallel to Matya Mahal, between the used-tyre shops, near the large tree decorated with car parts in the centre of the road. This lane

Courtyard of the sandstone and marble Jama Masjid (HF)

takes you on a zigzag route past more car parts – mainly panels, doors and roofs of Marutis – past the Hotel Salam and comes out at the street known as Chitli Qabar.

Go straight across the small intersection, down the lane with a large upright steel post at its entrance blocking the way for anything larger than a pushbike. This lane is known as **Churi Walan**, and is probably the best example of a pre-Partition Old Delhi streetscape – houses with highly decorated ground-floor stone gateways and enclosed upper-floor wooden balconies with some fine woodcarving.

Churi Walan doglegs to the right and then left, and about half-way along the next straight stretch is a fine haveli entrance. It is just past the sign for the JK Happy School and, according to the sign, is currently the office of O P Gupta & Co, Finance Brokers. The pale green building at the end on the left is also very fine and has a small Hindu shrine on its ground floor.

Here you need to turn right, and then take the first left, which is the continuation of Churi Walan. On the right after 50 metres is a relatively recent but very ornate haveli belonging to the Aggarwal family. This house was built about 100 years ago by the same family; the grandson now runs a free medical clinic from the ground floor. The outstanding features of the building are the fine sandstone facade and the intricately carved Burmese teak front doors. At one time such doors would have graced the front of many Old Delhi havelis, but unfortunately few remain these days.

At the end of the lane, a locale of printers and paper merchants, turn right, and after just a few metres the laneway ends, opening out onto one of the old city's larger thoroughfares, **Prem Narain**. At this end of the lane, note the old stone pillar with capital haphazardly buried in the bitumen to block wider vehicles. There is also a small white-tiled shrine on the wall at head height.

Turn left (south) along Prem Narain and after 150 metres it comes to a T-junction with a yet larger street, Sita Ram Bazaar. On the left hand corner here is the remains of one of the old city's finest buildings, the **Bishan Swaroup Haveli** (also known as the Haksar haveli). All that remains today is part of the fine facadê, with its graceful balconies and entrance decorated with carved fish. One look at the rubble inside the locked gate suggests that even the facade would have disappeared if shops hadn't been built into it. Bishan Swaroup was an important finance official who worked in the court of Shah Alam II, the second-last Mughal emperor. The haveli was later occupied by the Haksars, a well-connected Kashmiri family. It's almost impossible to believe now, but it was in this haveli only 70-odd years ago that Jawaharlal Nehru, the country's first prime minister, married his wife Kamla.

It's a tragedy that fine old buildings such as this are today so totally neglected – or have completely disappeared.

Turn left along Sita Ram and after a few minutes of walking (well, dodging and side-stepping) you come to a short right curve in the road, with a small lane heading uphill on the left – this lane takes you on a short detour to the **Tomb of Sultan Raziya**, the only woman ever to have ruled Delhi (see under History in the Facts about Delhi chapter). Take this lane and then head right (uphill) at the next small junction. The lane narrows and darkens, and goes through a number of right-angle turns before finishing at the walled courtyard of the tomb. Raziya was nominated by her father, Iltutmish, to succeed him as sultan, which she in fact did in 1236. After a revolt by the city's nobles she fled to Kaithal in Karnal District northwest of Delhi, where she was killed. The tomb today is just a plain stone slab on a raised platform, and alongside it is the grave of her sister, Saziya. The small courtyard today makes a handy goat-pen for the local city inhabitants.

Retrace your steps to Sita Ram, and turn left onto it. The next point of interest is the **Kalan Masjid**, which actually predates Shahjahanabad. It's just off Sita Ram Bazaar, down a small lane to the right, opposite the Delhi Beads House shop. The mosque is at the top of a small flight of stairs, and although it looks closed non-Muslims are allowed to enter (remove shoes). This mosque was built in the 14th century in the time of Feroz Shah Tughlaq, whose ruined city is Feroz Shah Kotla in present-day New Delhi. The man who built this mosque, Khan Jahan, was a Hindu convert, and other mosques built by him include the Khirki Masjid and the Begumpur Masjid in south Delhi, both of which are worth a visit.

Once again on Sita Ram Bazaar, return the way you came, passing Prem Narain and the Bishan Swaroop haveli. After a few hundred metres, on the left at No 1043, is the finely carved entrance of the **Lala Pearey Lal Madho Ram Dharmsala**. It was built in 1921 by a merchant family and provides free accommodation for pilgrims.

The next big intersection is **Hauz Qazi Chowk**, but about 100 metres before it, on the left-hand side of Sita Ram opposite an arched entrance on the right, is another alley worth exploring, **Kucha Pati Ram**. This street also has a number of fine carved doorways and overhanging wooden balconies, most of which date back to the turn of the century. Follow the road around a few right-angle turns and eventually it comes out at a small open square. Bear right here, following the main flow of pedestrians and before long you come to the main southern access road into the old city, Lala Harichand Rd. Just before you get to the main street, you pass a small shop on the right selling clay pots and a variety of other terracotta items in bulk – including neat little chillums.

The main street is lined with shops selling mainly hand-tools and plumbing supplies and leads to another of the city gates, **Ajmeri Gate**, this one well camouflaged with movie posters and advertising banners.

Across the main road to the right of the gate you can see the red sandstone of the 17th-century **Madrasa of Ghazi-ud-din**, known today as the Delhi Anglo-Arabic School. The ornate, two-storey building is built around three sides of a courtyard, the fourth side being the site of a small mosque, also built of red sandstone. To the left of the mosque is the small white marble tomb of the madrasa's builder, Ghazi-ud-din, which is surrounded by some fine jali screens. The fabric of the building remains largely unchanged, and although now part of the Delhi University, its original function – as a place for the study of Arabic and Persian – remains.

The street running north-west from the college, following the line of the old wall, is Shardhanand Marg, although it's much better known by its old name, **GB Rd**. This is Delhi's infamous **red-light district** – men mill about on the pavement, gazing up at the heavily made-up women who hang over the upstairs balconies trying to entice the punters, while pimps do their best at ground level. It's all very low-key and unthreatening, although it's probably not wise for females to walk here unaccompanied. ■

Car parts displayed on a tree in the middle of the road at the Car Parts Bazaar (HF)

the typical Mughal feature of thin black stripes on the dome. It was also known as the Ghata Masjid, or Cloud Mosque.

Salimgarh Fort

Outside the northern wall of the Red Fort are the ruins of the roughly triangular Salimgarh Fort, although there is very little of it left today and the railway line runs right through the middle. The fort was built by the son of Sher Shah Sur in the mid-16th century.

A branch of the Yamuna River used to flow between the two forts (where the Ring Rd now runs), and the two are connected by a sandstone bridge. During Mughal times the fort was used as a prison, and from the Mutiny until just a few years ago it was in the hands of the army.

Raj Ghat

To the east of the Red Fort, between the noisy Ring Rd and the banks of the Yamuna River are the revered cremation sites of the man known as the Father of the Nation – Mahatma Gandhi – and those of independent India's famous dynasty, the Nehru/Gandhis.

The most southerly of these sites is Raj Ghat, where a simple square platform of black marble marks the spot where Mahatma Gandhi was cremated following his assassination in 1948. A commemorative ceremony takes place each Friday, the day he was killed. The platform lies in a beautiful park, complete with labelled trees planted by a mixed bag of notables including Queen Elizabeth II, Gough Whitlam, Dwight Eisenhower and Ho Chi Minh! It's open during daylight hours. Two museums dedicated to Gandhi are close by (see the later Museums section).

Adjoining Raj Ghat to the north is **Vir Bhumi**, the cremation site of Rajiv Gandhi, who was assassinated in 1991 by suspected Tamil guerrillas.

North again is **Shakti Sthal**, where Rajiv's famous mother, Indira Gandhi, was cremated following her assassination in 1984. Completing the family picture is **Shanti Vana** (Forest of Peace), where India's first prime minister, Jawaharlal Nehru, was cremated in 1964. In 1980 Rajiv's brother, Sanjay, was also cremated here.

The northernmost section of this parkland is **Vijay Ghat**, which commemorates India's second prime minister, Lal Bahadur Shastri. The small artificial lake here is a popular washing place for the poor jhuggi dwellers who live in utter squalor, out of sight over the levee bank, between the park and the river.

CIVIL LINES & BEYOND

The area immediately north of Old Delhi is known as Civil Lines, and this was the British part of Delhi before New Delhi was built. There are a number of interesting old buildings in the area and it's well worth spending a couple of hours wandering around. Walking Tour 3 takes in the major points of interest.

Further afield are two important Mughal gardens and the forlorn Coronation Durbar Site. The only practical way to visit these is by car or auto rickshaw.

Skinner's Horse

James Skinner was one of a number of colourful European adventurers turned mercenaries who, in the latter part of the 18th century, made a name for themselves fighting for the various warring Hindu clans in Rajasthan – among them the Marathas, Jats and Rohillas. Born of an English father and a Rajput mother, Skinner had found there was no room for him in the East India Company due to his mixed blood, and so had to look elsewhere for a career. He was warmly welcomed into the ranks of the Marathas and they soon allowed him to raise his own irregular cavalry unit, which enjoyed great success.

In 1803 Skinner's mixed blood worked against him once again, but this time the other way - when the Marathas decided to take on the British, all European and Anglo-Indians within the Maratha ranks were dismissed. Skinner was later persuaded to fight for the British, not as part of the army but as an irregular unit under the Company flag.

This unit was known as Skinner's Horse. They wore distinctive yellow uniforms and became well known for their courage in battle. Eventually Skinner's Horse became part of the regular army and Skinner himself was made a Lieutenant Colonel.

Although Skinner died in 1841, his unit remained unchanged until 1921 when it became the 1st Duke of York's Skinner's Horse. The regiment changed from horses to vehicles in the 1930s, and it still serves in the Indian Army today.

Skinner himself was a larger-than-life character, who, like a number of other prominent Englishmen of the time, took many of the local customs on board. He had received a title from the Mughal emperor but was known locally as Sikander Sahib, as it seems the local population saw him as the new Alexander the Great. Although Skinner was initially educated at an English school in Calcutta, in later life he wrote in Persian and produced a volume on the castes and tribes of northern India and another on the princes. ■

Walking Tour 3: Memories of the Mutiny (1½ hours; Map 9)

Old Delhi GPO to Qudsia Masjid This short walk takes you to some of the poignant reminders of 1857, when the local population rebelled against the British, who regained control only after a siege lasting some months –, with heavy casualties on both sides.

The tour starts from the GPO on Lothian Rd in Old Delhi. Walk south towards the railway bridge, and just before going under it there's a small sign on a wall on the left indicating the **Lothian Cemetery**. The graves here actually pre-date the Mutiny, but it is worth a quick look, if only to see how the Christian squatters have moved in to stop the land from being overrun by Hindus.

Walk back along Lothian Rd towards the GPO, and in the dividing strip in the middle of the road you'll see the remaining bastions of the former British **Magazine**. The second one is the more interesting; a marble tablet above the gateway describes the scenes which led to the British blowing it up. A second tablet, obviously added at a later date, points out that the 'enemy' described in the first tablet were in fact freedom fighters trying to rid the country of its foreign rulers. Unfortunately, it's difficult to read these inscriptions without taking the suicidal step of standing in the middle of chaotic Lothian Rd.

Fifty metres further on, still in the median strip, is the **Telegraph Memorial**. It was from this spot that the now-famous signal 'We are off' was relayed as the signallers hastily evacuated in the face of the sepoys invading from Meerut. (A copy of this telegram is displayed in the archaeological museum in the Red Fort.)

Cross to the right hand (eastern) side of the road and enter the gates of the Delhi College of Engineering. A sign also announces the Department of Archaeology's **Dara Shikoh Library**. It's the large beige building with the heavy columns and green shutters. This is the former **Residency**, where Sir James Ochterlony lived, and it has recently been converted into a small **Archaeological Museum** (see the Museums section for further details).

Return to Lothian Rd and continue along it, and before long you come to a strange building on the first corner on the right, behind a concrete wall and disused gate. **St Stephen's College** was one of the first in the city, and the old part of this building was the original **college hostel**. The college itself is across the road, hidden by tall trees.

Immediately beyond the old hostel you can see through the trees the elegant cream and white shape of **St James' Church**; with its calm garden it's a haven of peace in one of the city's grubbiest and noisiest areas. The church was built by James Skinner (of Skinner's Horse fame), and the graves of many of the Skinner family are in the garden on

St James' Church on Lothian Road (HF)

the church's north side, while that of James Skinner himself is inside the church. Entry to the church is from the side street, and you may have to hunt around for the caretaker to open it up for you. A small booklet detailing the life of Skinner and giving some details about the church itself is available for a small donation.

On exiting the church, turn left and then left again along a small side street, and on the right after 200 metres you'll see the sign proudly announcing the Office of the Chief Engineer, Northern Railways (Construction). Although it's only possible to look at it from the gate, the building you see at the end of the drive is the former residence of the colourful William Fraser, Assistant to the British Resident in the 1830s. There are a number of modern accretions, including the enormous dome. (Fraser is also buried in the grounds of St James' Church.)

Back on Lothian Rd we continue, all the while dodging the holes in the pavement, stray cows and the goods from the shop that line the road at this point. On the left-hand side of the road, just past the faded sign for the Bengal Club, you'll see the low outline of **Kashmiri Gate**, one of the original gates of Shah Jahan's walled city, and the only one to have two openings.

Continue to the busy intersection, where, on the right, the grey decaying hulk of the interstate bus station is the dominant feature. Cross at the lights (keeping in mind that traffic lights here are part function and part decoration), and turn west along busy Boulevard Rd. After just 50 metres the high gateway of the **Nicholson Cemetery** appears on the right. Although a little overgrown, it's worth wandering around. On a small mound just inside the gate to the right is the grave of Brigadier General John Nicholson, one of the key figures in the British attack on the mutineers in May 1857. He was a larger-than-life character held in high regard, and long after his death there was still a Punjab sect known as the Nikalsini. The inscriptions on many of the graves are a poignant reminder of how hard life was for the early European settlers, such as Charles Corcoran, who died 'leaving a widow and infant daughter to lament his untimely end'.

Return to the intersection, and turn left (north) along Shamnath Marg. On the right the statue of **Rana Pratap Singh** looms above the wall of **Qudsia Bagh**. The garden gate is another 100 metres further on. The gardens were set out in the typical Persian charbagh style by Qudsia Begum, the wife of Muhammad Shah. Much of it is now taken up by the interstate bus terminal, the main remaining features being the monumental gate, and, in the corner by the new flyover, the remains of the **Qudsia Masjid**. ■

The remaining entrance gate to Qudsia Bagh (HF)

The Ridge

The old Civil Lines straddles the Ridge, a small, scrub-covered rise which in pre-Mughal times was a hunting retreat. During the 1857 siege the British camped out on and behind the Ridge, and from here they bombarded the northern walls of the city. Remarkably, the bush has survived the pressures of an increasingly crowded city and provides a welcome respite from the chaos.

Rani Jhansi Rd runs right along the Ridge, and along it are a number of points of interest.

Mutiny Memorial (Ajitgarh) This somewhat bizarre structure, looking like a cross between a church spire and a rocket, was built by the British in 1863 to commemorate their victory over the mutineers and to honour those (on the British side, of course) who died. The original – and now extremely unfashionable – British inscriptions remain, but they are supplemented by one raised since independence which points out that the 'enemy' referred to by the British were 'those who rose against colonial rule and fought bravely for national liberation in 1857'.

Ashokan Pillar Further along the Ridge is an Ashokan pillar, similar to the one at Feroz Shah Kotla in New Delhi, brought here from Meerut by Feroz Shah Tughlaq. This one is in pretty poor condition, as it was blown into five pieces in an explosion in the 18th century. It was re-erected here in 1867, when the bits were brought back from Calcutta, where they had been in the keeping of the Asiatic Society of Bengal.

Hindu Rao's House Almost opposite the Ashokan Pillar is the entrance to the Hindu Rao Hospital. While the hospital itself is not the most riveting place in Delhi, its core building is an expansive old bungalow known as Hindu Rao's House. This house was in fact built by the aforementioned William Fraser at great expense in the 1820s and is located on the spot where Timur had camped roughly 400 years before. For Fraser, the location not only gave him sweeping views but also allowed him to maintain a distance between himself and the European social scene, which he found shallow and unsatisfying.

In 1833 Fraser, after nearly 30 years in Delhi, finally became the city's Resident. He was murdered outside his house soon after, however, by a disgruntled Mughal nobleman.

The house was later lived in for many years by Hindu Rao, the brother of the Rani of Gwalior. During the Mutiny it came under heavy shelling but was later restored and became the Hindu Rao Hospital.

Pir Ghaib Further north along the Ridge, still in the grounds of the hospital but visible from the road, is a dilapidated, two-storey stone building known as Pir Ghaib (Vanishing Saint). Built in the time of Feroz Shah Tughlaq as part of a hunting lodge (Kushk-i-Shikar), it takes its name from the cenotaph of a saint who used to worship here but one day mysteriously disappeared (*ghaib*).

This place is also sometimes called the Observatory, due to holes in the roof which led some scholars to the conclusion that the building was used for astronomy.

About 1.5 km further north again, Rani Jhansi Rd is intersected by Chauburja Marg, and to the right lies the ruins of the **Chauburja Masjid** (Four Domes Mosque), which was also built by Feroz Shah Tughlaq as part of his hunting lodge complex.

Flagstaff Tower On the northern part of the Ridge is this circular tower – minus its flagstaff these days – built by the British to commemorate the spot where English women and children gathered during the Mutiny in 1857, waiting for help which never came. In the end they fled to Karnal.

Metcalfe House

Due east of the Ridge, right by the Ring Rd, is the sprawling mansion of Sir Thomas Metcalfe, a Commissioner of Delhi from 1835 to 1853 and nephew of former Resident, Lord Charles Metcalfe. It was built in the 1830s and was the scene of many social gatherings. The house was sacked by the rebels during the Mutiny and was later sold by Metcalfe's son, Sir Theophilus Metcalfe. It eventually came to be owned by the government and is now the Defence Services Documentation Centre (closed to the public).

Sir Thomas Metcalfe was a great admirer of Napoleon, and one room of the house was given over entirely to Napoleon memorabilia, including a signed portrait. He was also extremely finicky on matters of etiquette – it's said he couldn't stand the sight of women eating cheese – and had tailored clothes and books dispatched regularly from England. His most idiosyncratic habit, however, was the way he reprimanded errant servants: A pair of white kid gloves were brought on a silver platter. Metcalfe would draw these on and then with great ceremony pinch the ear of the offender, a punishment that was, according to Metcalfe's daughter, 'entirely efficacious'.

Such prudish behaviour was in great contrast to that of British administrators such as Ochterlony, who less than half a century earlier adopted many Mughal habits and mores.

Old Secretariat

On Alipur Rd close to Metcalfe House is this sprawling white building with its twin towers, built in 1912 to house the government secretariat until New Delhi was completed. These days it is used by the Delhi administration.

Tomb of Shah Alam

Right at the northern end of Civil Lines, where the Wazirabad Rd heads east from the Ring Rd, is the forlorn rubble-built mosque and tomb of the saint Shah Alam (not the Mughal emperor of the same name), which dates to the time of Feroz Shah Tughlaq (1351-88). The nine-arched bridge across the channel here also dates from the same period.

Roshanara Bagh

A km or so to the west of Civil Lines lies this Mughal garden, designed and laid out by Roshanara, younger daughter of Shah Jahan and staunch supporter of her brother Aurangzeb. The centrepiece of the garden is the finely proportioned pavilion, which also contains the tomb of Roshanara. Unfortunately, it looks fairly shabby these days – the plaster is crumbling, graffiti covers the walls, the *jali* screens have been vandalised and the water channels are long dry – but it's not hard to visualise how beautiful it must once have been.

The gardens themselves have also changed, from a formal Mughal garden to a conventional park with winding paths and open lawns.

Shalimar Bagh

The Shalimar Garden, which lies on the fringes of the city about 10 km north-west of Old Delhi and just off the Grand Trunk Rd, is one of the most important Mughal gardens in the city. This was once the first night staging post for the Mughals on their trips to Kashmir and Lahore. Aurangzeb stayed here while pursuing his brother, Dara Shikoh, and also had himself crowned emperor here in 1658.

Top : Red sandstone chattri in Lutyens's Delhi (HF)
Bottom : Surviving floral paintings on the Shish Mahal in
Shalimar Bagh (HF)

The beautiful central pavilion, the Shish Mahal, was built by Shah Jahan, and although it is in a fairly advanced state of decay, remarkably some of the original painted flower decoration has survived. In later times it was used by Sir David Ochterlony and Lord Metcalfe as a summer house. Despite the condition of the building, this place has bags of atmosphere, due in part to the fact that it still has a largely rural setting.

The Shalimar Bagh can be a task to locate; asking locals for Shalimar Bagh gets you to the new housing development of the same name close by. Once here, ask for the Shish Mahal.

Coronation Durbar Site

This is a must for incurable Raj fans looking for their fix of nostalgia. In open country in Delhi's outer northern suburbs stands a lone obelisk in a desolate field. It was on this site that in 1877 and 1903 the durbars were enacted and that in 1911 King George V was declared Emperor of India.

Close by there's a walled garden complete with a rogues' gallery of marble statues of former Imperial dignitaries, languishing like disgraced schoolboys out of the public eye. Pride of place goes to a 15-metre-high statue of George V which rises ghost-like above the acacia trees. It was placed here after being removed from the canopy midway along Rajpath, between India Gate and Rashtrapati Bhavan, soon after Independence. (The place it was taken from remains empty, supposedly signifying the freedom of India, although a bronze statue of Gandhi was due to be installed in 1995.)

These days this lonely yet historic bit of spare ground lies forgotten on the outskirts of the city, a reminder of really quite recent ceremonies of lavish proportions which today seem distant and irrelevant.

Auto-rickshaw and taxi drivers seem to be unaware of this place (as indeed are most of Delhi's residents). Ask for Radio Colony, a suburb close by, and the site is just north of the radio masts, near the Outer Ring Rd.

NEW DELHI

Connaught Place

At the northern end of New Delhi, Connaught Place is the business and tourist centre. It's a vast traffic circle ringed by an architecturally uniform series of colonnaded buildings around the edge – mainly devoted to shops, banks, restaurants, airline offices and the like. It's spacious but busy, and you're continually approached by people willing to provide you with everything imaginable, from an airline ticket for Timbuktu to having your fortune read.

Jantar Mantar

Only a short stroll down Sansad Marg (Parliament St) from Connaught Place, this strange collection of salmon-coloured structures is one of Maharaja Jai Singh II's observatories. The ruler from Jaipur constructed this observatory in 1710, and it is dominated by a huge sundial, the **Samrat Yantra**, or Supreme Instrument.

Just south of the Samrat Yantra is the **Jai Prakash**, an instrument designed by Jai Singh (hence the name, which means Invention of Jai) consisting of two concave hemispherical structures which together ascertain the position of the sun and other heavenly bodies.

South again are two circular buildings which together form the **Ram Yantra**. Each has a central metal pole, and the shadow cast falls upon markings on the walls and floor, thus making it possible to determine the azimuth and altitude of the sun.

Other instruments include the **Misra Yantra**, or Mixed Instrument, which stands to the right of the garden as you enter. This ingenious device makes it possible to tell the time in four other places in the world when it is noon in Delhi.

The Jantar Mantar is open daily from sunrise to sunset, and there is no entry fee.

Rajpath

The Kingsway is another focus of Lutyens's New Delhi. It is immensely broad and is flanked on either side by ornamental ponds. The Republic Day parade is held here each 26 January, and millions of people gather to enjoy the spectacle.

At the eastern end of Rajpath lies the India Gate while at the western end lies Rashtrapati Bhavan, now the president's residence, but built originally for the viceroy. It is flanked by the two large Secretariat buildings, and these three buildings sit upon a small rise, known as Raisina Hill.

Three days after the Republic Day Parade, the Beating of the Retreat, a much smaller ceremony, takes place at **Vijay Chowk** (Victory Square, originally called the Central Vista), the open intersection at the foot of the Secretariat buildings. During the construction of New Delhi, this was where the narrow-gauge Imperial Delhi

Railway terminated. It was constructed specially to transport the buff sandstone from Dholpur, the red sandstone from Bharatpur and the marble from Rajasthan to the site. In the early '20s there were over 3500 Indian stonemasons working on the site. The names of the architects and builders who worked on the buildings here are inscribed in the sandstone walls which line the rise from here up to the Secretariat buildings.

The Battle of the Gradient

The rise known as Raisina Hill, and the approach road up to it (or, more precisely, the angle of the approach road up to it), were the cause of a trivial yet major dispute, known as the 'battle of the gradient', between Delhi's designer, Lutyens, and his colleague, Herbert Baker. While Baker was charged with designing the Secretariat and parliament buildings, Lutyens made himself responsible for the viceroy's residence and the India Gate. It was Lutyens's intention that the residence should be slightly higher than the Secretariats and visible from a greater distance. Baker wanted all three buildings on the same level, so that the viceroy's residence would majestically come into view as one approached it up the rise. After numerous discussions, and referral to successive viceroys, Baker won, and the two men refused to talk to each other for some years. ■

India Gate The 42-metre-high stone arch of triumph stands at the eastern end of Rajpath. Officially known as the All India War Memorial, it bears the names of 90,000 Indian Army soldiers who died in the campaigns of WW I, the North-West Frontier operations of the same time and the 1919 Afghan fiasco. In the 1970s an eternal flame, flanked by uniformed soldiers, was established in the arch to honour the Unknown Soldier.

The best time to visit India Gate is at sunset, when large numbers of Delhi-ites come out for an evening promenade. The place takes on a real carnival atmosphere, complete with the usual gaggle of hawkers and hangers-on that always seem to materialise whenever there's a crowd about. The monument is illuminated nightly from 7 to 9.30 pm.

Secretariat Buildings Designed by Herbert Baker, the north and south Secretariat buildings lie either side of Rajpath on Raisina Hill. These imposing two-tone

Top : The modern buildings of Connaught Place (TW)
Bottom : The observatory, Jantar Mantar (TW)

sandstone buildings are a skilful blend of Classical and
Mughal styles – the baroque, cathedral-like central
domes are surrounded by Mughal *chhatris*. The two red
sandstone columns at the front of each block together
represent the four dominions of Empire – Australia,
Canada, New Zealand and South Africa – and each is
topped by a tarnished bronze model of a sailing vessel.

On the eastern face of each building are the foundation stones of New Delhi, originally laid down by
George V and Queen Mary at the Coronation Durbar in
1911, when the move from Calcutta to New Delhi was
formally announced. The stones were moved here at a
later date once construction was under way.

The North Block now houses the ministries of Home
Affairs and Finance, the South Block the External Affairs
ministry.

Rashtrapati Bhavan The official residence of the
president of India stands at the opposite end of the
Rajpath from India Gate. It is the centrepiece of New
Delhi, a huge, grandiose building designed and posi-
tioned to assert the dominance of the British Empire,
despite the fact that by the time of its construction the
British were already facing an increasingly effective
Indian Nationalist movement.

Designed by Lutyens and completed in 1929, the
palace-like building, formerly the viceroy's residence,
also combines Mughal and Western architectural styles, the
most obvious Indian feature being the huge copper dome.

In the centre of the forecourt, behind the high railing
fence which now separates Rashtrapati Bhavan from the
Secretariats, is the 44-metre-high **Jaipur Column**.
Although designed by Lutyens, this soaring sandstone
column was a gift to the viceroy by the Maharaja of
Jaipur. It is topped by a bronze lotus flower and a glass
Star of India and bears the following inscription: 'In
thought faith; in word wisdom; in deed courage; in life
service. So may India be great'.

Uniformed guards are posted at the main fence, and
every Saturday at 9.30 am a guard-changing ceremony
takes place.

To the west of the building lie the gardens of the
president's estate, which occupy 130 hectares. The
Mughal Garden here is open to the public in February.
At the time of Mountbatten, India's last viceroy, the
number of servants needed to maintain the 340 rooms
and its extensive gardens was enormous. There were 418
gardeners alone, 50 of them boys whose sole job was to
chase away birds!

Sansad Bhavan Although another large and imposing building, Sansad Bhavan, the Indian parliament building, stands almost hidden and virtually unnoticed at the end of Sansad Marg, just north of Rajpath. The building is a circular colonnaded structure 171 metres in diameter, the foundation stone for which was laid by the Duke of Connaught in 1921. It was opened in 1927. Although an impressive building, its relative physical insignificance in the grand scheme of New Delhi shows how the focus of power has shifted from the viceroy's residence, which was given pride of place during the time of the British Raj when New Delhi was conceived.

Permits to visit the parliament and sit in the public gallery are available from the reception office on Raisina Rd, but you'll need a letter of introduction from your embassy.

Ugrasen-ki-Baoli

Highly decorated *baolis* (step-wells) are a feature of northern India, and while this one is far from being the best of its type, it is certainly the best in Delhi and is therefore worth a look. It's also surprising to find a 14th-century construction right in the heart of 20th-century New Delhi.

The baoli is just off Hailey Rd, a small road which joins Kasturba Gandhi Marg and Barakhamba Rd, about 500 metres south-west of Connaught Place.

Lakshmi Narayan Temple

About 1.5 km due west of Connaught Place, this garish, modern, Orissan-style temple was erected by the industrialist B D Birla in 1938. It's dedicated to Narayan (Vishnu the Preserver) and his wife Lakshmi (The Goddess of Prosperity and Good Fortune). The temple, faced with red sandstone, was inaugurated by Mahatma Gandhi and is commonly known as Birla Mandir.

The main shrine features idols of Narayan and Lakshmi, while secondary shrines hold images of Siva (The Destroyer) and his wife Durga.

Feroz Shah Kotla

Despite the fact that there were already at least three existing palaces in Delhi at the time (Siri, Bijai Mandal and at the Qutb at Mehrauli), Feroz Shah Tughlaq decided to build a new one on the banks of the Yamuna in 1354, and this became Ferozabad, the fifth city of Delhi. The city is thought to have extended from the

The Rashtrapati Bhavan, the president's residence, was designed as the centrepiece of New Delhi. (HF)

Ridge north of Old Delhi to Hauz Khas to the south-west.

The ruins of this city can be found at Feroz Shah Kotla, east of Connaught Place by the Ring Rd, although not a great deal remains of the fortress-palace today as most of the materials were pinched for the construction of Shahjahanabad.

The high stone walls enclose a peaceful garden, in stark contrast to the mayhem of Bahadur Shah Zafar Marg right outside. The main structure is the remains of the royal apartment, atop which is a 13-metre-high sandstone **Ashokan Pillar**, which dates to the 3rd century BC. The pillar was erected by the emperor Ashoka in Ambala and was brought to Delhi by Feroz Shah after he took a liking to it. It is similar to the one now on the Ridge north of Old Delhi but is in much finer condition. The Brahmi-script inscription on the pillar was first deciphered in 1837; it details Ashoka's edicts to his subjects.

Next to the apartment building are the remains of what was once the fine **Jama Masjid**, built on a series of ground floor cells. Only the rear (western) wall remains. It is said that Timur prayed here when he sacked Delhi in 1398. As the mosque is still in use today, you should remove your shoes before entering.

The large circular construction in the middle of the garden is a **baoli**, or step-well, which includes subterranean apartments. Unfortunately, it is fenced off so you can only catch glimpses of the interior through the openings in the stone work.

In the dividing strip on Mathura Rd right outside Feroz Shah Kotla is the **Khuni Darwaza**, or Bloody Gate, a survivor of Sher Shah's 16th-century city some distance to the south. Its popular name dates from the time of the Mutiny, as it was here in 1857 that the sons of the last Mughal emperor, Bahadur Shah, were shot by a British officer, Captain Hodson.

Purana Qila

Just south-east of India Gate and north of Humayun's Tomb and the Hazrat Nizamuddin Railway Station is the old fort, Purana Qila. This is the supposed site of Indraprastha, the original city of Delhi. Although construction was started by Humayun, the Afghan ruler, Sher Shah, who briefly interrupted the Mughal Empire

Inscription on the Ashokan Pillar at Feroz Shah Kotla (HF)

by defeating Humayun, completed the fort during his
reign in 1538-45, before Humayun regained control of
India. The fort has massive walls and three large gateways.

Entering from the south gate you'll see the small
octagonal red sandstone tower, the **Sher Mandal**, later
used by Humayun as a library. It was while descending
the stairs of this tower one day in 1556 that he slipped,
fell and received injuries from which he later died. Just
beyond it is the **Qila-i-Kuhna Masjid**, or Mosque of Sher
Shah, which, unlike the fort itself, is in fairly reasonable
condition. This building is probably Delhi's finest
example of the Lodi style of architecture, which blended
Hindu elements, such as square pillars, with Muslim
arches and domes to create the first genuinely Indian
architectural style.

There's a small archaeological museum just inside the
main gate, and there are good views of New Delhi from
atop the gate.

Just across Mathura Rd is the **Khairu'l Manzil
Masjid**, a 16th-century mosque built by Akbar's influential wet-nurse and mother of Adham Khan, Maham
Anga. The main features are the outstanding sandstone
gate and the double-storeyed cloisters, which were used
as a madrasa (Islamic college).

Next to the mosque is the imposing **Sher Shah's Gate**,
another of the gates into Sher Shah's city which lay to
the west of the Purana Qila.

Delhi Zoo

The extensive Delhi Zoo on the south side of the Purana
Qila is not terribly good, although the animals do at least
have a reasonable amount of space. The cages are poorly
labelled, many of them are empty and in winter many
of the animals are kept inside. The highlight is the white
tigers. In the grounds stands a **kos minar**, one of the
milestones erected by the Mughals along the main
routes, this one being on the Delhi to Agra road (a *kos* is
roughly 3.2 km).

In the centre of the grounds a bored elephant takes
visitors on five-minute rides from 11 am to 1 pm and 2
to 4 pm. The cost is Rs 5 (Rs 2 for children).

The zoo is open from 9 am to 4.30 pm; closed Friday.
Entry is Rs 3.

Humayun's Tomb

Built in the mid-16th century by Haji Begum, senior wife
of Humayun, the second Mughal emperor, this is the
first important example of Mughal architecture in India.

It's also one of the most beautiful buildings in the city and should not be missed. The elements in its design – a squat building, lighted by high arched entrances, topped by a bulbous dome and surrounded by formal gardens – were to be refined over the years to the magnificence of the Taj Mahal in Agra. This earlier tomb is thus of great interest for its relation to the later Taj.

It is open daily from sunrise to sunset and entry is Rs 0.50, except on Friday, when it's free. For photographs it's best to visit in the late afternoon, as the main approach to the tomb is from the west.

Tomb of Isa Khan As you enter the tomb area, a crumbling stone gateway on the right leads into the octagonal enclosure which contains the tomb of Isa Khan, a nobleman at the court of Sher Shah. With its octagonal form, small overhanging chajja (eaves) and chhatris (domed kiosks) on the roof, it's a good example of Lodi architecture. A few small patches of blue tilework give a tantalising hint as to how it may have looked when first built. A small mosque stands at the western edge of the enclosure.

Bu Halima's Garden The next feature is the stone gateway that marks the entrance to Bu Halima's Garden, although approaching it from this side it's actually the exit. Bu Halima was a Mughal noble, and the stone structure in the garden on the left is believed to be her tomb.

Arab Serai Once through the gateway, the main entrance (today) to Humayun's Tomb lies straight ahead, but it's worth making a detour through the Arab Serai, the northern gate of which is the impressive soaring structure to the right of the path.

The serai was built by Hamida Banu Begum, Humayun's widow, in the mid-16th century, supposedly to house the 300 Arabs she brought back with her from Mecca. It is unclear whether these men were actually Arab priests or Persian artisans brought in to work on the construction of Humayun's Tomb.

Inside the serai is the **Afsarwala Mosque & Tomb**, but it is not known who the *afsar* (officer) responsible for these buildings was.

Most visitors to Humayun's Tomb spare these buildings barely a passing glance, and virtually none cross the somewhat overgrown serai enclosure to visit the impressive **eastern gate** of the serai, which still has some of its enamelled tilework in place. An inscription over

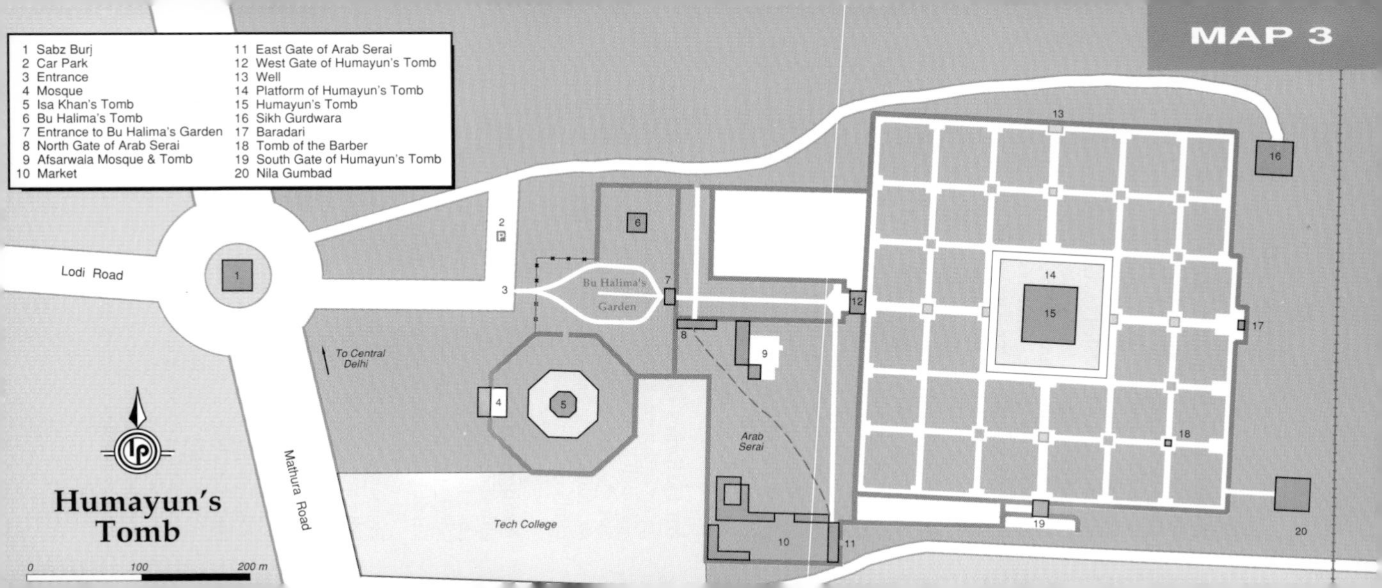

MAP 3

Humayun's Tomb

1 Sabz Burj
2 Car Park
3 Entrance
4 Mosque
5 Isa Khan's Tomb
6 Bu Halima's Tomb
7 Entrance to Bu Halima's Garden
8 North Gate of Arab Serai
9 Afsarwala Mosque & Tomb
10 Market
11 East Gate of Arab Serai
12 West Gate of Humayun's Tomb
13 Well
14 Platform of Humayun's Tomb
15 Humayun's Tomb
16 Sikh Gurdwara
17 Baradari
18 Tomb of the Barber
19 South Gate of Humayun's Tomb
20 Nila Gumbad

Bu Halima's Garden

Arab Serai

Tech College

To Central Delhi

Mathura Road

Lodi Road

0   100   200 m

the gateway indicates it was built by Mihr Banu, a wet-nurse of Jahangir. The gateway gives on to a ruined *mandi* (market).

While you're here, leave the serai enclosure via the eastern gate and walk along the road for about 100 metres and you come to what was the main entrance to Humayun's Tomb, the **southern gate**.

Return along the gravel path which runs alongside the western wall of the main tomb enclosure, and enter the formal garden surrounding the tomb through the western gate.

Humayun's Tomb The tomb itself sits on a red sandstone platform, a practice that was to become a key feature of Mughal tombs. The walls of the platform are marked by arched openings giving onto small cells. In these are many unmarked tombs, which are the graves of members of the Mughal royal family.

The main tomb is built with red sandstone skilfully inlaid with black and white marble. The central octagonal chamber contains the tombstone of Humayun but, as is the case at the Taj, the real tomb is some six metres under the floor on the lower level. (It's possible to enter the lower level, but you'll need a torch and a strong constitution as the smell of bat-shit is overpowering. The entrance is through the first arch to the right of the southern steps.) In each of the four chambers at the corners of the main tomb lie other important Mughal tombs. On the stone platform outside the tomb lie yet

Humayun's Tomb, built of sandstone and marble by his wife, is one of the most beautiful buildings in the city. (HF)

more Mughal bodies in tombs bearing Persian inscriptions; one of these contains the headless remains of Dara Shikoh, Shah Jahan's favoured son and heir.

The huge marble dome on the roof is one of the earliest examples of a 'full dome' in India, although it was in use in Persia from the 13th century. (A 'full' dome is a complete hemisphere; up until then domes in India had only been half hemispheres.) The chhatris on the roof serve to blend the curves of the dome with the angles of the rest of the structure.

The gardens surrounding the tomb are laid out in the typically formal Mughal pattern and still contain the watercourses which divided the garden into 34 small squares around the main platform. It is probably the most complete garden of its type remaining in India.

Other Sights In the south-eastern corner of the garden is the square, twin-domed **Tomb of the Barber**, so called because it is said to be that of Humayun's barber. Outside the enclosure in this corner is the **Nila Gumbad** (Blue Dome), an octagonal tomb with an impressive blue-tiled dome, thought to date from 1625. The domed tomb on the traffic circle on Mathura Rd is known as the **Sabz Burj** (Green Dome) and dates to the 17th century. The blue tiles are courtesy of the Archaeological Survey of India in the 1980s; the green, blue and yellow tiles below the dome are original.

Nizam-ud-din's Shrine

Across Mathura Rd from Humayun's Tomb is the shrine of the Muslim Sufi mystic and saint, Shaikh Hazrat Nizam-ud-din Aulia Chisti, which lies in the tangle of narrow lanes of Nizamuddin village, just off the busy Mathura Rd, near the intersection with Lodi Rd.

Nizam-ud-din was one of a number of Sufi saints who gained a large following in the 14th century. His doctrine was one of renunciation and tolerance of other religions, and this made him popular not only among Muslims but also among Sikhs, Hindus and Buddhists. He is also attributed with saving Delhi on one occasion in 1303 when invading Mughals suddenly upped and left, due, it is said, to Nizam-ud-din's prayers. The saint died in 1325 aged 92, and his shrine (Hazrat Nizam-ud-din Aulia) is a popular pilgrimage site and one of several interesting tombs here.

The village itself, which sprang up around the shrine, obviously predates New Delhi and is unique in the city. It has narrow, crowded lanes which are passable only on foot, and an almost medieval atmosphere.

Hazrat Nizam-ud-din Aulia The saint's shrine sits in a small marble-paved courtyard, surrounded by a mosque and other tombs. The actual grave was built on the saint's death, but the beautiful pavilion with its marble arches and jali screens was added later by Shah Jahan. The grave is draped with green cloth and the faithful shower it with crimson rose petals as part of their supplication.

It's well worth visiting Nizam-ud-din's tomb on Thursday at sunset, as this is when the place is thronged with pilgrims – not only Muslims but Hindus, Sikhs and anyone else seeking the answer to a prayer. After the evening prayer at the **Jama'at Khana** mosque (built in 1325 by Khizr Khan, son of Ala-ud-din Khalji) right next to the tomb, *qawwali* musicians start up, singing Urdu hymns in praise of Nizam-ud-din, and the devotees sit entranced. Out of respect, most people wear a mosque cap or some other head covering, but this is not compulsory.

Pilgrims gather here in great numbers twice a year to celebrate the *urs* (birth anniversary) of Hazrat Nizam-ud-din Aulia and his disciple, Amir Khusru (see below).

Tombs of Jahanara Begum & Muhammad Shah Such was the saint's stature that the area around the shrine became sacred, and many others wanted to be buried near him. Some of those buried here include **Jahanara Begum**, the elder and favourite daughter of Shah Jahan, who stayed with her father during his imprisonment by Aurangzeb in Agra's Red Fort, and **Muhammad Shah**, Delhi's emperor from 1719 to 1748. These are the two tombs surrounded by carved marble jali screens in the same courtyard as Nizam-ud-din's tomb. Jahanara's is the one closer to the mosque, and you'll notice the top of the tombstone is filled with soil rather than stone. The reason for this is found in part of the inscription on her headstone: 'Except with grass and green things let not my tomb be covered; for grass is all-sufficient pall for the graves of the poor'. While grass may have grown there at one time, these days there's just a forlorn, tatty shrub struggling to survive.

Tomb of Amir Khusru At the southern end of the main enclosure, directly behind the tombs of Jahanara and Muhammad Shah, is the tomb of **Amir Khusru**, a renowned poet and Nizam-ud-din's principal disciple. His tomb is also well patronised by the faithful.

Tank To the north of the main enclosure lies the tank (reservoir), the construction of which caused a dispute

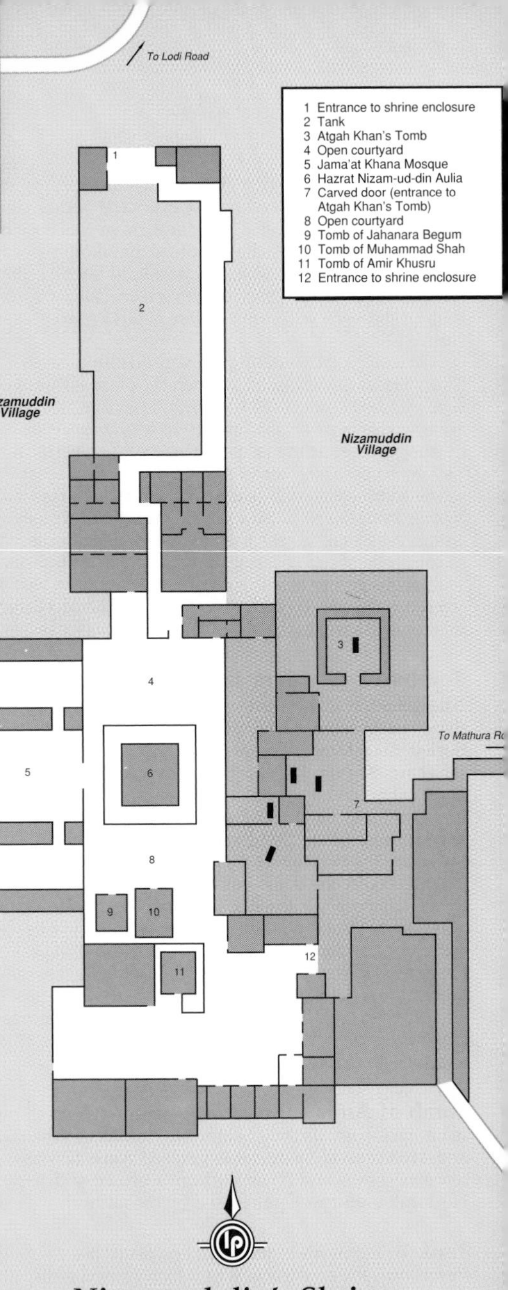

MAP 4

To Lodi Road

1 Entrance to shrine enclosure
2 Tank
3 Atgah Khan's Tomb
4 Open courtyard
5 Jama'at Khana Mosque
6 Hazrat Nizam-ud-din Aulia
7 Carved door (entrance to Atgah Khan's Tomb)
8 Open courtyard
9 Tomb of Jahanara Begum
10 Tomb of Muhammad Shah
11 Tomb of Amir Khusru
12 Entrance to shrine enclosure

Nizamuddin Village

Nizamuddin Village

To Mathura R

Nizam-ud-din's Shrine

0   25   50 m

between the saint and Ghiyas-ud-din, the constructor of Tughlaqabad, further to the south of Delhi (see Tughlaqabad, later in this section, for details).

Atgah Khan's Tomb To the east of the main enclosure is the tomb of Atgah Khan, a great friend of Akbar who was murdered in Agra by Adham Khan, the son of Akbar's wet-nurse. In turn Akbar had Adham Khan killed by having him thrown over the walls of the Red Fort. The six-metre-sq red sandstone tomb sits in a small walled enclosure, and with its original marble and coloured exterior tiles and painted interior must have been quite stunning. These days it's far less impressive.

The entrance to the tomb is from the narrow lanes of the village, just before the entrance to the main enclosure. Try to find the low, ornate sandstone arch with heavy wooden doors. It is through here and to the right, although the family living in the first courtyard may try to charge baksheesh.

Carved sandstone screen on the Chaunsath Khamba. (HF)

Mirza Ghalib's Tomb Another of the tombs in the area belongs to **Mirza Ghalib**, the great writer of *ghazals* (Urdu love poems), who died in 1869. You pass the tomb, which again is surrounded by marble screens, as you pass through the village from Mathura Rd. It is in a small locked courtyard right next to the multi-storey Ghalib Academy, from where the key can be obtained if needed. The academy itself was established by the government to promote the study of Urdu literature.

Chaunsath Khamba Directly behind Ghalib's tomb, and accessed from the other side of the Ghalib Academy, lies the beautiful Chaunsath Khamba, a marble pavilion with, as the name implies, 64 pillars, although it takes a while to figure out how the total is arrived at. In it lies buried (among others) Mirza Aziz Kokaltash, the son of Atgah Khan.

Lodi Garden

About three km to the west of Humayun's Tomb and adjoining the India International Centre is the Lodi Garden. In these well-kept gardens are the tombs of the Sayyid and Lodi rulers. **Muhammad Shah's Tomb** (1450), in the south-western part of the garden, is a prototype for the later Mughal style tomb of Humayun, a design which would eventually develop into the Taj Mahal. Its octagonal form, sloping buttress and projecting chajja (eaves) are typical features of the Lodi style of architecture.

The **Bara Gumbad**, the soaring gateway to the mosque in the centre of the gardens, is a fine example of a square Lodi tomb, although just who it belongs to is unclear as there is no grave within. One interesting feature of the mosque itself, which according to an inscription above the *mihrab* (prayer niche) dates from 1494, is the tapered minarets which form part of the rear (western) wall. These have obviously been inspired by the tapered form of the Qutb Minar.

To the north of the mosque is the **Sheesh Gumbad**, a square tomb with arches on the lower level and corresponding blank arches half-way up the facade that give the tomb a two-storey appearance, the whole surmounted by a dome which was originally covered in dazzling blue tile-work, some of which remains above the main entrance.

Other tombs in the garden include those of Mubarak Shah (1433), Ibrahim Lodi (1526) and Sikander Lodi (1517), the last of which is surrounded by a wall, built to protect the monument from being plundered. Close by is the Tughlaq-era **Athpula** (eight-piered) stone bridge, which crosses the small waterway running through the gardens.

Also in the gardens is a **Kos Mina**, a milestone dating back to Mughal times.

Safdarjang's Tomb

Beside the small Safdarjang Airport, where Indira Gandhi's son Sanjay was killed in a light plane accident in 1980, is Safdarjang's Tomb. It was built in 1753-54 by the Nawab of Avadh for his father, Safdarjang, who was *wazir* (which roughly translates to prime minister) of the Mughal empire during the reign of Ahmed Shah.

Safdarjang's Tomb is the last extant example of a Mughal-style garden-tomb before the final remnants of the great empire collapsed. In many ways it is similar to Humayun's Tomb, but the overall effect is far less pleasing – it is too tall for its width and the dome is overly bulbous. The materials used here were also far inferior – the sandstone is much less red in colour and the poor quality marble of the dome has yellowed. The tomb stands on a high terrace in an extensive garden. The ornate chambers which form part of the perimeter wall were possibly used as the Delhi residence by the nawab's family; today they house the offices of the Archaeological Survey of India (Delhi Circle). Entry is Rs 0.50; free on Friday.

SOUTH DELHI

The rest of Delhi's attractions are in the southern suburbs, south of the Ring Rd. While some of them are accessible by bus, to do any amount of sightseeing you'll need your own transport, or hire an auto rickshaw and negotiate a rate for a full or half day.

Siri

Little remains of Siri, the second city of Delhi. The most interesting monuments are those at Hauz Khas. The remainder of the Siri Fort can be seen near the Asian Games Complex to the east of Hauz Khas; the rest of the site – most of it unexplored by archaeologists – was unfortunately buried under the village when it was built in 1982.

Hauz Khas Midway between Safdarjang and the Qutb Minar, this area was once the tank (reservoir) for Siri, which lies slightly to the east. Feroz Shah Tughlaq built

Safdarjang's Tomb was the last great Mughal building
to be built before the decline of the empire. (HF)

a number of buildings on the south-eastern banks of the
royal (khas) tank (hauz). The monuments today are in a
small, well-tended walled garden at the end of trendy
Hauz Khas Village, a green suburb full of upmarket
boutiques and restaurants.

The main structure here is the somewhat austere,
domed **Tomb of Feroz Shah**, which is partially obscured
by a large tree. Its entrance is from the southern
doorway, over which is an inscription stating that it was
restored during the time of Sikander Lodi.

Adjoining the tomb to the west is a double-storeyed
madrasa, built by Feroz Shah in 1352. The main impression is one of strength and lack of decoration (typical of
the Tughlaq style), but with its balconies overlooking the
tank the madrasa was famous both as a beautiful building and a great place of Islamic learning.

The **tank** itself used to cover about 50 hectares but is
much smaller than that today and no longer has any
water in it for most of the year. It was in this area that
Timur's forces camped after defeating Muhammad
Shah Tughlaq in 1398.

Getting There & Away Bus No 505 will drop you
on Aurobindo Marg, from where it's a pleasant 20-
minutes walk to the village. You can pick this bus up at
Connaught Place (Super Bazar) or opposite the Imperial
Hotel on Janpath.

Bahai House of Worship

Lying to the east of Hauz Khas is this building shaped like a lotus flower. Built between 1980 and 1986, it is set among pools and gardens, and adherents of any faith are free to visit the temple and pray or meditate silently according to their own religion. It looks particularly spectacular at dusk when it is floodlit. The temple is open to visitors from 9 am to 7 pm daily except Monday April to September, and 9.30 am to 5.30 pm from October to March. Fifteen-minute services are held daily at 10 am, noon, and 3 and 5 pm, and you are welcome to sit in on these.

Getting There & Away Bus No 433 from outside the Jantar Mantar on Sansad Marg near Connaught Place will bring you to Nehru Place, from where it's a 15-minute walk to the temple.

Top : The Bahai House of Worship near Hauz Khas (BV)
Bottom : Tomb of Feroz Shah, Hauz Khas (TW)

Ashokan Rock Edict

This rock edict, not far from the Bahai House of Worship, was discovered only in the late 1960s and is important not for the ten-line Brahmi inscription, but because it establishes beyond doubt that this area was a major town in the time of Ashoka (273-232 BC).

Jahanpanah

Jahanpanah (Refuge of the World) was the fourth city of Delhi, built by Muhammad Shah Tughlaq in the 14th century by enclosing the inhabited but unprotected area between the first two cities of Delhi – Siri to the north and Qila Rai Pithora to the south.

The remains of the city today lie in the village of Begumpur, which has been engulfed by the modern housing developments of the suburb of Panchsheel South. The easiest access is from a small road which heads east off Aurobindo Marg between the Outer Ring Rd and the Qutb Minar Complex, right next to the Aurobindo Ashram.

Bijai Mandal The remains of Muhammad Tughlaq's palace, the Bijai Mandal, are impressive, despite being in an advanced state of decay. The whole complex was known as the Thousand-Pillared Palace, the central feature being a massive, squat tower built on a high platform. It was from here that Muhammad Shah is said to have reviewed his troops. As this site sees very few visitors, it's still possible to climb the tower for a great view over southern Delhi.

Adjoining the tower on the platform are the ruins of Muhammad Shah's private apartment and the hall where he gave audiences.

Begumpur Masjid Close to the Bijai Mandal, and visible from the tower, is the rubble-built Begumpur Masjid with its large courtyard and multiplicity of domes. This was one of the seven mosques built by Feroz Shah's prime minister, Khan Jahan. The mosque consists of a large paved courtyard, enclosed on three sides by arched cloisters, while the fourth contains the prayer hall, the large central arch of which is flanked by tapering minarets. Once again decoration is minimal, but the overall effect is powerful.

As at the Bijai Mandal, it's possible to climb the minarets for a sweeping view: the Qutb Minar to the south-west, the distinctive lotus shape of the Bahai House of Worship to the east, and if there's not too much smog you can make out the white marble dome of Humayun's Tomb to the north-east (to the right of the striped shopping complex tower in the middle distance); in the far distance, just to the right of the Bijai Mandal, is the dome of Rashtrapati Bhavan.

Khirki Masjid This interesting mosque with its four open courts dates from 1380 and is another of Khan Jahan's constructions. In each of its four corners stands a massive bastion, which makes the mosque look much more like a fort. The main entrance is the eastern gate, although only the southern gate is unlocked these days. The mosque and nearby village take their names from the latticed windows *(khirkis)* which appear on the upper level of the mosque's exterior wall.

Although still in pretty good condition, this mosque has very few visitors, and consequently the area immediately surrounding it is in danger of becoming a garbage dump. It is just off Press Enclave Marg, which heads east off Aurobindo Marg, about a km north of the Qutb Minar.

Moth-ki-Masjid This 16th-century mosque lies hidden deep in the modern suburb of South Extension Part II, south of the Ring Rd and west of Ashwamegh Gram Rd, but it's well worth seeking out. The mosque stands on a raised platform in a walled enclosure, entered through an impressive red sandstone gateway on its eastern side. It was built in the time of Sikander Lodi (1488-1517) and despite its present-day obscurity is one of the finest period mosques in Delhi. Its five-arched, triple-domed form, and the high level of ornamentation of the *mihrab* and the arches (particularly the central one), are innovative features which make this mosque an important step towards the fine ornamentation of the Mughal mosques.

The mosque takes its name from the lentil *(moth)* seed, picked up by Sikander Lodi and used by his wazir, Miyan Bhuwa, to produce more seed and eventually raise a crop large enough to finance the construction of the mosque.

Tughlaqabad

The massively strong walls of Tughlaqabad, the third city of Delhi, lie eight km east of the Qutb Minar on the Mehrauli-Badarpur road. The walled city and fort with its 13 gateways was built by Ghiyas-ud-din Tughlaq and its construction involved a legendary quarrel with the saint Nizam-ud-din. When the Tughlaq ruler took the workers Nizam-ud-din wanted for work on his tank, the saint cursed the king with the warning that his city would be inhabited only by Gujars (shepherds). Today that is indeed the situation.

The dispute between king and saint did not end with curse and countercurse. When the king prepared to take vengeance on the saint, Nizam-ud-din calmly told his followers (in a saying that is still current in India today): 'Delhi is a long way off'. Indeed it was, for in 1325 the king was murdered coming from Delhi on his way to confront Nizam-ud-din .

The fort walls are constructed of local stone, which was originally faced with plaster. Outside the south wall of the city is an artificial lake (usually dry) with the **Tomb of Ghiyas-ud-din** in its centre. A small causeway connects the tomb and the fort, both of which have walls that slope inward. The tomb is one of the few Tughlaq-era buildings to be built of sandstone rather than the cheaper local stone.

Getting There & Away The easiest way to visit Tughlaqabad is to combine it with a visit to the Qutb Minar Complex, and catch a Badarpur bus from there.

Qutb Minar Complex

The buildings in this complex, 15 km south of New Delhi in Mehrauli, date from the onset of Muslim rule in India and are fine examples of early Afghan architecture.

Qutb Minar The Qutb Minar is a soaring tower of victory nearly 73 metres high, tapering from a 15-metre-diameter base to just 2.5 metres at the top. There are five distinct storeys, each marked by a projecting balcony. The first three storeys are of red sandstone, the fourth and fifth of marble and sandstone. Although Qutb-ud-din (1206-10) began construction of the tower, he only got to the first storey. His son-in-law and successor, Iltutmish, completed it, and in 1368 Feroz Shah Tughlaq replaced the top storey with two more and added a cupola. An earthquake brought the cupola down in 1803 and an English engineer, Major Smith, replaced it with a Mughal-style one in 1829. However, that dome was deemed inappropriate and was removed in 1848. It now stands in the gardens close by.

Today, this impressively ornate tower leans about 60 cm off vertical but otherwise has worn the centuries remarkably well. The tower is closed to visitors and has been for some years after a stampede during a school trip led to a number of deaths.

Top : The Qutb Minar overlooks Imam Zamin's Tomb
at the Qutb Minar Complex. (HF)
Bottom : The carving on the Tomb of Iltutmish is some of
the finest in the Qutb Minar Complex. (HF)

Quwwat-ul-Islam Masjid At the foot of the Qutb Minar stands the first mosque to be built in India, the Might of Islam Mosque. Qutb-ud-din began construction of the mosque in 1192, but it has had a number of additions and extensions over the centuries. The original mosque was built on the foundations of a Hindu temple, and an inscription over the east gate states that it was built with materials obtained from demolishing '27 idolatrous temples'. Many of the elements in the mosque's construction indicate their Hindu or Jain origins – the square pillars around the central courtyard, for example.

Iltutmish, Qutb-ud-din's son-in-law, surrounded the original small mosque with a cloistered court in 1230, thus bringing the Qutb Minar within the mosque enclosure. Ala-ud-din added a court to the east and the magnificent Alai Darwaza gateway in 1300.

This was Delhi's main mosque until 1360, when Feroz Shah built a new mosque in Ferozabad by the banks of the Yamuna.

Iron Pillar This seven-metre-high pillar stands in the courtyard of the mosque but predates it by some centuries. A six-line Sanskrit inscription indicates that it was initially erected outside a Vishnu temple, possibly in Bihar, and was raised in memory of the Gupta king Chandragupta II, who ruled from 375 to 413 AD.

What the inscription does not tell is how it was made, for the iron in the pillar is of quite exceptional purity. Scientists have never discovered how this iron, which is of such purity that it has not rusted after 1600 years, could be cast with the technology of the time. It is said that if you can encircle the pillar with your hands while standing with your back to it, your wish will be fulfilled.

Alai Minar At the same time as Ala-ud-din made his additions to the mosque, he also conceived a far more ambitious construction programme. He would build a second tower of victory, exactly like the Qutb Minar, except it would be twice as high! When he died the tower had reached 27 metres and no-one was willing to continue his overambitious project. The uncompleted tower stands to the north of the Qutb Minar and the mosque.

Alai Darwaza Ala-ud-din's superb Alai Darwaza gateway, just south-east of the Qutb Minar, was the main entrance to the whole complex. Built of red sandstone in 1310, it is richly decorated with geometric patterns and bands of inscriptions in white marble.

Imam Zamin's Tomb This small tomb adjacent to the Alai Darwaza was built in 1537 by Imam Zamin, a Turkestani saint who was involved with the Quwwat-ul-Islam Masjid and who died in 1538. It is a typical Lodi-style tomb – sandstone dome erected on a square base – and features some finely carved sandstone screens.

Tomb of Iltutmish Lying just to the west of the Quwwat-ul-Islam Masjid is the spectacularly decorated tomb of Iltutmish, the successor to Qutb-ud-din. Built by Iltutmish himself in 1235, the tomb shows much less Hindu influence than other buildings in this area, as the reliance on Hindu stonemasons and material from Hindu temples had lessened. The highlight is the amazingly intricate carving which covers virtually the entire interior of the nine-sq-metre tomb.

There has been much speculation as to whether the tomb originally had a dome. It certainly looks unfinished without one, and some experts believe that the original dome collapsed at some stage. If this was the case, it seems almost impossible that the marble tombstone would have escaped major damage – even today it is still in excellent condition.

Ala-ud-din Madrasa The L-shaped ruins in the south-western corner of the compound are believed to be the remains of an Islamic college (madrasa) built by Ala-ud-din. His tomb is thought to be the central room of the southern wing.

Getting There & Away You can get out to the Qutb Minar Complex on a No 505 bus from the Ajmeri Gate side of New Delhi Railway Station or from Janpath opposite the Janpath Hotel.

Mehrauli

Mehrauli is just a small village in southern Delhi, but these days it is also the retreat of the city's ultra-rich, who have 'farms' in the district. These are farms in name only – high walls surround an acre or two, upon which is usually a mansion and an immaculate garden, often complete with swimming pool and fountains.

Although most people head back after visiting the Qutb Minar, there are a few sites in Mehrauli that are worth a quick look.

Adham Khan's Tomb A short distance west of the Qutb Minar enclosure and in Mehrauli village is the imposing Tomb of Adham Khan, the son of the Mughal emperor Akbar's wet nurse, who met an untimely end at the hands of Akbar (see the Nizam-ud-din's Shrine section for more on this incident).

The tomb is built on the remains of the old walls of Lal Kot, the first city of Delhi built by the Tomara Rajputs and consists of an octagonal chamber pierced by three openings on each side and surmounted by a dome. During the 19th century it was used by the British as a police station and a *dak* (postal service) bungalow, but on the orders of Lord Curzon was vacated and maintained as a historical monument.

The local name for the tomb is Bhulbhulaiyan (maze), because it is supposedly easy to get lost in the corridors around the dome.

Gandhak-ki Baoli This step-well is one of a number in the Mehrauli district. It takes its name from the smell of sulphur *(gandh)*, which allegedly emanates from its water. Built during the reign of Iltutmish, it has five levels and a circular well at the southern end.

There is a local tradition of diving into the well, which gives rise to its alternative name, the diving well. The small pool of murky grey water in the bottom hardly makes it an attractive proposition, however.

To find the well, take the small road which runs south from the right of the small line of shops directly opposite Adham Khan's tomb, and follow it for about 250 metres.

Dargah of Qutb Sahib Just off the main road in the heart of Mehrauli village, about half a km beyond Adham Khan's Tomb, is this dargah (shrine) of Qutb Sahib, a Persian Chisti saint who emigrated from Persia in the 12th century and became a disciple of Khwaja Muin-ud-din Chisti of Ajmer.

As was the case with Nizam-ud-din, the saint was highly regarded and his plain grave was decorated by later rulers.

As was also the case with Nizam-ud-din, many people wanted to be buried close to the saint, and so graves close to the shrine include the following late Mughal rulers: Bahadur Shah I, Aurangzeb's son, who ruled from 1707 to 1712; Shah Alam II, who ruled from 1759 to 1806, finally being pensioned off by the British; and Akbar Shah II, who ruled from 1806 to 1837. Between the tombs of Bahadur Shah and Shah Alam is a space which was laid out by Bahadur Shah II, the last of the Mughal rulers, for his own grave. At the age of 82 he was given a dodgy trial by the British following the Mutiny in 1857, then carted off to Rangoon, where he died and was buried in 1862.

Zafar Mahal Close to the western entrance of the dargah of Qutb Sahib are the ruins of the former palace of Bahadur Shah II, who was an ardent admirer of the poet Ghalib and wrote poems under the pen-name Zafar.

This palace, originally built by Akbar II but reconstructed by Bahadur Shah, was used during the monsoon by Bahadur Shah as a hunting lodge. Only the main gateway survives today.

Every year Bahadur Shah would be in Mehrauli for the Phulwalon ki Sair (Procession of the Flower Sellers), when the flower sellers of Mehrauli honoured the Mughal ruler. The festival has been revived in recent years and is held during October.

MUSEUMS

National Museum

On Janpath just south of Rajpath, the National Museum has a good collection of Indian bronzes; terracotta and wood sculptures dating back to the Mauryan period (2nd-3rd century BC); exhibits from the Vijayanagar period in south India; miniature and mural paintings; Mughal clothes, tapestries, ornaments and manuscripts, including Jahangir's memoirs; costumes of the various tribal peoples; and a wide array of musical instruments.

The museum is definitely worth a half-day visit and is open from 10 am to 5 pm daily; closed on Monday. Admission is Rs 0.50. There are film shows most days of the week.

National Gallery of Modern Art

This gallery stands near India Gate at the eastern end of Rajpath and was formerly the Delhi residence of the Maharaja of Jaipur. It houses an excellent collection of works by both Indian and colonial artists, and there's a large reference library.

It is open from 10 am to 5 pm Tuesday to Saturday; admission is free.

Museum of Natural History

The natural history museum is opposite the Nepalese Embassy on Barakhamba Rd. Fronted by a large model dinosaur, it has a collection of fossils, stuffed animals and birds and a 'hands on' discovery room for children. It's open from 9 am to 5 pm; closed Monday.

Nehru Museum & Planetarium

On Teen Murti Rd near Chanakyapuri, the residence of the first Indian prime minister, Teen Murti Bhavan, has been converted into a museum. The building was originally constructed as the home of the British commander in chief.

Photographs and newspaper clippings on display give a fascinating insight into the history of the independence movement, and you can peer through the glass into Nehru's study and bedroom, still laid out with his personal effects. There are even excerpts from his will inscribed on tablets around the wall.

The museum is open from 9.30 am to 5 pm daily; closed on Monday. Admission is free.

Also in the grounds is the Nehru Planetarium, with shows in English at 11.30 am and 3 pm daily except Monday; entry is Rs 5.

The old, square monument on a mound between the main building and the planetarium is the **Kushk Mahal**, thought to have been built during the reign of Feroz Shah (1351-88) as a hunting lodge.

Tibet House

This small museum has a fascinating collection of ceremonial items brought out of Tibet when the Dalai Lama fled following the Chinese occupation. Downstairs is a shop selling a wide range of Tibetan handicrafts. There are often lecture/discussion sessions and there's also a small museum. It's in the Institutional Area, Lodi Rd, and hours are from 10 am to 1 pm and 2 to 5 pm. It's closed Sunday and admission is free.

International Dolls Museum

In Nehru House on Bahadur Shah Zafar Marg, this museum displays 6000 dolls from 85 countries. Over a third of them are from India and one exhibit comprises 500 dolls in the costumes worn all over India. The museum is open from 10 am to 5.30 pm daily; closed Monday.

Crafts Museum

In the Aditi Pavilion at the southern end of the Pragati Maidan Exhibition Grounds, Mathura Rd, this museum contains a collection of traditional Indian crafts in textiles, metal, wood and ceramics, and in many cases you can actually see the artisans at work. The museum is part of a 'village life' complex where you can visit rural India without ever leaving Delhi – there are re-creations of the various styles of huts found throughout the country. There's also a pretty reasonable crafts shop here.

Opening hours are from 10 am to 5 pm daily; admission is free. Entry is from Bhairon Marg, opposite the Purana Qila.

Gandhi Darshan & Gandhi National Museum

Across the road from Raj Ghat, the Gandhi Darshan is a huge but poorly patronised display of paintings and photos about the Mahatma's life and deeds.

On the opposite corner is the Gandhi National Museum, with yet more memorabilia, including photos, the bamboo staff Gandhi carried on the Salt March in Gujarat, the bullet which killed him and even two of his lower teeth extracted in 1936!

Indira Gandhi Memorial Museum

The former residence of Indira Gandhi at 1 Safdarjang Rd has also been converted into a museum. The large number of visitors this place receives says much about the high regard in which Mrs Gandhi was (and is still) held.

On show are some of her personal effects, including the sari (complete with blood stains) she was wearing at the time of her assassination. Her recorded voice wafts eerily through the bungalow, and striking a somewhat macabre note is the crystal plaque in the garden, flanked constantly by two soldiers, which protects a few brown spots of Mrs Gandhi's blood on the spot where she actually fell after being shot by two of her Sikh bodyguards in December 1984.

Gandhi Smriti

This house on Tees January Marg was the former home of the well-known industrialist B D Birla, and is where Mahatma Gandhi used to stay during his many visits to

Delhi. It was during one of these visits that he was assassinated by a Hindu fanatic in 1948.

These days it's yet another museum dedicated to Gandhi. A small pillar in the back garden marks the exact spot where he was shot, and bizarre concrete footprints trace his last walk from the house to the garden. The house is open daily from 10 am to 5.30 pm.

Dara Shikoh Library
(Archaeological Museum)

This small museum in Civil Lines is housed in the old Residency building, which is probably of more interest than the museum itself. The building was originally the library of Dara Shikoh, Shah Jahan's favourite son and chosen successor, whose ascent to the throne was thwarted by his ruthless brother, Aurangzeb, who had him executed and his headless body paraded through the city.

The building is a real curiosity. In 1803, Sir David Ochterlony (the Resident at the time) built a solid mansion, complete with Ionic pillars, over and around the original Mughal building. As you enter the building, the first tell-tale sign that this building is not exactly what it seems is the cusped arch which once formed the main entrance. Traces of Dara Shikoh's original building can also be seen either side of the steps at the rear of the building.

The blend of European exterior and Mughal interior was entirely appropriate for Ochterlony, as he was one of a number of early British administrators who openly adopted Mughal dress and customs, had been given a Mughal *khilat* (title) by the emperor (Nasir-ud-Daula, or Defender of the State), had numerous Indian wives and entertained lavishly in fine Mughal style.

The archaeological displays include pottery shards found recently at Mandoli in east Delhi and Bhorgat in north Delhi. These finds are believed to be from the Gupta period, and so put Delhi's firm founding date back to at least 400 AD. There are also some interesting illustrations on the walls. The museum is open from 10 am to 5 pm Monday to Friday.

Rail Transport Museum

This museum at Chanakyapuri will be of great interest to anyone who becomes fascinated by India's exotic collection of railway engines. The exhibit includes an 1855 steam engine, still in working order, and a large number of oddities such as the skull of an elephant that charged a mail train in 1894 and lost.

There are a number of model displays with buttons to push, and displays on every aspect of rail transport you could possibly think of; there's even a Braille exhibit for the blind. In the grounds a narrow-gauge toy train chugs around a short loop throughout the day (minimum of 10 people required; Rs 4, children Rs 2).

The museum is open from 9.30 am to 5.30 pm (closed on Monday) and there's a small admission fee.

Other Museums

There is a **National Philatelic Museum** hidden in the post office at Dak Bhavan, Sardar Patel Chowk on Sansad Marg (Parliament St). It's closed on Saturday and Sunday.

Near the domestic terminal of the Indira Gandhi International Airport there is an **Air Force Museum**, open from 10 am to 1.30 pm; closed Tuesday.

India Gate is one of the focal points of New Delhi. (HF)

PARKS & GARDENS

Delhi has its fair share of parks and gardens, most of them in the planned areas of New Delhi; the congested layout of Old Delhi makes it difficult to have open spaces.

Connaught Place

The very heart of Connaught Place is a park with lawns, gardens and fountains. It's a very welcome place to relax, or would be if you were not constantly pestered by hawkers – shoe cleaners, ear-cleaners and masseurs seem to descend from nowhere as soon as a foreigner sits down, and each has his own book full of glowing reports from satisfied customers.

India Gate

Rajpath cuts a swathe through New Delhi, and the ornamental lawns and ponds which run along its full length give this part of the city a very open feel. The lawns around India Gate are especially popular, particularly at sunset and early evening in the warm weather. The gate is illuminated nightly from 7 to 9 pm.

Nehru Park

In the diplomatic enclave of Chanakyapuri, Nehru Park is one of the city's major 'lungs'. It has been extensively landscaped with material taken from the nearby Ridge.

Lodi Garden

The central Lodi Garden is a shady and popular retreat – you'll often see members of Delhi's expat community jogging here in the early morning.

The main focus of the gardens are the Lodi and Mughal monuments (described earlier), but with its ponds, paved paths and shady trees, the park is also popular among young couples seeking a few quiet moments together away from the prying eyes of the family.

Talkatora Gardens

These gardens, on Baba Kharak Singh Marg, were once a walled tank (*tal* – tank, *katora* – cup), and it was on this site that the Marathas fought an unsuccessful battle against the Mughals in 1738.

These days it's far more peaceful, and it's also the site of a major indoor stadium, Talkatora Stadium.

Buddha Jayanti Park

This large park occupying a major section of the 650-hectare Southern Ridge, west of Rajpath, commemorates Buddha's attainment of nirvana. The park has been planted out with trees and shrubs associated with the life of Buddha, including of course a Bodhi tree sapling.

Mughal Garden

At the rear of Rashtrapati Bhavan in the President's Estate is the Mughal Garden, laid out along traditional Mughal lines by a British horticulturalist. The gardens contain, among other things, a number of rose varieties found nowhere else in India, and a variety of dahlia named after Zail Singh, the former Indian president. The garden is only open to the public in February.

There are parks around Raj Ghat and many of the sights decried earlier in this chapter include gardens. See also: Roshanara Bagh, Shalimar Bagh, Humayun's Tomb, Red Fort, Qutb Minar Complex, Coronation Durbar Site, Feroz Shah Kotla and Safdarjang's Tomb.

ACTIVITIES

The range of sporting facilities in Delhi is impressive, although many of the clubs are the playgrounds of the city's elite, with restricted membership and astronomical fees. A major exception are the facilities run by the Delhi Development Authority (DDA). At Saket (☎ 65-5742) in south Delhi not far from the Qutb Minar there are facilities for horse-riding, squash, tennis and billiards, and a swimming pool is under construction. Temporary membership is available for Rs 700 for three months. Other DDA complexes are at Siri Fort (☎ 646-7482); Hari Nagar (☎ 544-6683); Paschim Vihar, in the city's north-west (☎ 558-1165); Rohini, north of Paschim Vihar (☎ 726-1986); Maj Dhyan (☎ 724-5338) and Poorvi (☎ 228-1477).

Swimming

The main public swimming pool is in the Talkatora Gardens, but it has a reputation for being less than 100% clean.

The other option is the pools at the major hotels. Unfortunately most are open only to hotel guests and the others discourage outside use by charging exorbitant rates. Those which allow non-guests to use the pool include: Holiday Inn Crowne Plaza (Rs 220 per day), Hotel Claridges (Rs 175), Imperial Hotel (Rs 550!) and Le Meridien (Rs 110 *per hour!*).

Tennis

The Delhi Lawn Tennis Association (☎ 685-7134) has its headquarters in Africa Ave in the Safdarjang Enclave, just north of Hauz Khas. The main centre court stadium has a capacity of 3000 spectators.

Golf

The beautiful 18-hole course of the exclusive Delhi Golf Club (☎ 436-2768) is on Dr Zakir Husain Marg near the Hotel Oberoi. It is open to the public every day, but the greens fees are astronomical – US$35 on weekdays, US$40 on weekends for 18 holes. Club hire is a paltry Rs 15 per set, and balls are available for Rs 75.

Boating

Obviously in a city with no major body of water, boating opportunities are limited. Badhkal Lake, 32 km south of Delhi, is the nearest place with any decent amount of water, and even here it's limited (see the Excursions chapter for details).

Boat Club It's possible to hire little dinghies and go for a paddle in the ornamental ponds which line Rajpath! These cost just a few rupees and are available throughout the day from the north side of Rajpath, where Rafi Marg crosses it.

Delhi Fort (Purana Qila) The old moat at the Purana Qila is also put into use for boating. Although it's little more than a large, stagnant pool, the pedal boats here are a popular source of amusement among the locals.

The boats are available from 10 am to 6 pm daily, and cost Rs 30 per half hour.

Rock Climbing

At the headquarters of the Indian Mountaineering Federation on Benito Juarez Marg, just south of the Ring Rd near Chanakyapuri, there's the country's first artificial climbing wall.

For those who prefer the real thing, Delhi Tourism organises climbing courses at its adventure park at Lado Sarai, near Mehrauli on the southern outskirts of Delhi. The half-day morning courses are held from January to March and October to December and cost Rs 25. Contact the Adventure Tourism Cell (☎ 469-4859) for more details.

Flying & Gliding

The Safdarjang Airport on Aurobindo Marg is the home of the Delhi Gliding Club and the Delhi Flying Club (☎ 462-9210).

Parasailing

It's also possible to try parasailing at the Safdarjang Airport. Delhi Tourism operates this activity here on Sunday from 8 to 11 am, Wednesday from 1 to 4 pm and Friday from 11 am to 1 pm. The cost is Rs 100 per launch, and the only prerequisite is that you have to weigh-in at between 40 and 80 kg.

Places to Stay

PLACES TO STAY – BOTTOM END

Delhi is certainly no bargain when it comes to cheap hotels. There are basically two areas for cheap accommodation. The first is around Janpath on the southern side of Connaught Place in New Delhi. The second area, which is cheaper, more popular and has a greater range of places than Connaught Place, is Paharganj, near New Delhi Railway Station. This is about midway between Old and New Delhi.

There are also a number of possibilities in Old Delhi itself. Although it's generally more noisy and less convenient to stay in Old Delhi, the area does have tremendous colour and atmosphere.

Camping

If you want to camp there are two possibilities in Delhi. The *Tourist Camp* (☎ 327-2898; Map 15) is in Old Delhi, near Delhi Gate on Jawaharlal Nehru Marg, across from the J P Narayan Hospital, only two km from Connaught Place. Managed by retired Indian Army officers, it's a good place if you are seeing India by motorbike or vehicle; most of the overland operators also stay here and it's quite a pleasant place with a shady garden. You can camp with your own tent or sleep in your vehicle (Rs 30), or there are basic brick huts with shared bathrooms for Rs 100/140; air-coolers are available for Rs 30. For a motorcycle there's a Rs 10 daily charge, and for vehicles it's Rs 40. There's a good restaurant and a left-luggage room where you can leave your accumulated junk while you explore elsewhere.

There is a second camping site, the *Qudsia Gardens Tourist Camp* (☎ 252-3121), right across the road from the interstate bus station at Kashmiri Gate (see Map 9). Camping here costs Rs 30 per person, or there are ordinary rooms for Rs 80/100 and deluxe doubles for Rs 150. It's convenient for an early morning bus departure, but little else.

Connaught Place & Janpath Area

There are several cheap lodges or guest houses near the Government of India tourist office. They're often small and cramped but you meet lots of fellow travellers;

they're also conveniently central and there are often dormitories for shoestring travellers. Since many of these places are so popular, you may find that your first choice is full. If that's the case simply stay at one of the others until a room becomes available – it's unlikely you'll have to wait more than a day. (The following hotels are on Map 7 unless otherwise indicated.)

One of the most well known places to stay is the *Ringo Guest House* (☎ 331-0605) at 17 Scindia House, down a small side street near the tourist office. This place has been a travellers' institution for many years, and it has its fair share of detractors as well as fans. Nevertheless, it is still popular. Beds in crowded, 14-bed dorms are Rs 60; small rooms with attached bath are Rs 160/210, or Rs 180/260 for something marginally bigger. You can also sleep on a charpoy on the roof for Rs 50. The rooms are very small but it's clean enough and the showers and toilets are well maintained. Meals are available in the courtyard, although at a higher price than in the nearby restaurants, and there are always plenty of other travellers to talk to. You can also store luggage for Rs 7 per item per day.

Another place with similar prices is the *Sunny Guest House* (☎ 331-2909) at 152 Scindia House, a few doors further along the same side street. Dorm beds are Rs 60; singles/doubles range from Rs 90/170 to Rs 120/190 with common bath and there are doubles with attached bath at Rs 225. Again, the rooms are small but the place has a sort of shabby charm, and this, along with the location, are what attracts so many people. The left-luggage facility is also Rs 7 per item per day.

On the west side of Janpath along Janpath Lane there's a couple of places which have been minor legends among travellers for well over a decade now. *Mrs Colaco's* (☎ 332-8758) at No 3 is the first one you'll come to. A charpoy in the reasonably roomy dormitory costs Rs 55, and there are good doubles for Rs 135 with common bath. There's a safe deposit for valuables, a laundry service and baggage storage. Around the corner, *Mr S C Jain's Guest House*, at 7 Pratap Singh Building also on Janpath Lane, is yet another legend. Extremely plain rooms with common bath cost Rs 150 to Rs 170, depending on the size. The big advantage of both these places is that they are situated in a quiet residential area.

The *Janpath Guest House* (☎ 332-1935) is a few doors down from the tourist office at 82-84 Janpath. It's popular with travellers, reasonably well kept and clean and the staff are friendly; the rooms, though, are claustrophobically small and most don't have a window worth mentioning. Singles/doubles cost Rs 220/250 with air-cooling, Rs 400/450 with air-con.

Across on the east side of Connaught Place is the *Hotel Bright* (☎ 332-0444), 85 M Block, opposite the Super Bazar. There's definitely nothing bright about this place, but it's not too bad. The dark and somewhat grotty rooms cost Rs 250/300 with attached bath, but the ones facing the road can be noisy.

The *Hotel Palace Heights* (☎ 332-1419) in D Block, Connaught Place, is a moderately priced place close to Nirula's. It's on the 3rd floor of an office building and has a huge veranda overlooking Connaught Place – great for breakfast or afternoon tea. Although the facilities are fairly primitive, it's a relaxed place with a small-town atmosphere. Rooms cost Rs 175/285 with air-cooler but common bath and there are air-con double rooms with bath for Rs 480.

The ITDC's *Hotel Ashok Yatri Niwas* (☎ 332-4511; fax 332-4253; Map 6) is just 10 minutes' walk from Connaught Place on Ashoka Rd at the intersection with Janpath. This huge (547 rooms) government-run hotel is a managerial disaster – it's been setting the standard for lousy service for some years now; if your sanity is precious, don't even think about staying here. Simple matters such as checking in and out can easily take half an hour, the service is terrible – surly at best – the whole place is poorly maintained, bed linen is often threadbare, you may have to beg for a blanket and the lifts are hopelessly unreliable. The only saving grace is the views from the upper floor rooms – it's just a pity you can barely see through the filthy windows! All this can be yours for just Rs 275/400. Maximum stay is seven days, but anyone who lasts that long deserves a medal – and a professional assessment of their sanity!

Paharganj Area

Directly opposite New Delhi Railway Station is the start of Main Bazaar, a narrow road which stretches due west for about a km. Because of its proximity to the station it has become a major accommodation centre for Indians and foreigners alike, and these days also seems to be a magnet for Russians on shopping sprees. It has also become a crowded and bustling market selling virtually anything you'd care to name, from incense to washing machines. Because it's so busy, walking along Main Bazaar at any time requires patience. There are any number of cheap hotels along this road, offering varying degrees of comfort and quality. Many are very popular with budget travellers. (The following hotels are on Map 8.)

As you walk along Main Bazaar from the station, one of the first places you come to is the *Hotel Kanishta* (☎ 52-5365). It's not one of the more popular places as it's very close to the station and the accompanying noise of Qutab Rd, but it is reasonable value. Air-cooled rooms with bath, TV and balcony cost Rs 175, and hot water is available by the bucket.

The next place is the *Travellers Guest House* (☎ 354-4849) at 4360A Main Bazaar. The rooms are a good size and have air-cooling in summer. The charge is Rs 160 for a double with attached bath.

A few doors along is the *Kailash Guest House* (☎ 777-4993) at 4469. It's a modern, clean and quite friendly place, although many of the rooms face inwards and tend to be a bit stuffy; those with windows are fine. It's good value at Rs 75/125 with common bath and Rs 150 for a double with attached bath. Hot water is available free by the bucket. The *Kiran Guest House* (☎ 52-6104) next door is virtually an identical twin to the Kailash, and prices are similar at Rs 85/150 with attached bath. Avoid the 1st floor rooms as the TV at reception seems to have only two volume settings – off and full blast.

A short way along the lane opposite the Kailash and Kiran guest houses is the *Delhi Guest House* (☎ 777-6864), a small place with reasonable rooms from Rs 120. The owner can be found in the little electrical store on the ground floor.

Indian handicrafts (GB)

A little further along Main Bazaar on the right is the *Bright Guest House* (☎ 752-5852) at 1089-90. It's one of the cheapest places in Paharganj, and one of the best for the money. Clean rooms around a small courtyard cost Rs 70/80 with common bath, Rs 100 for a double with bath or air-cooler and Rs 130 with both.

Down a narrow alley to the right, not far beyond the Bright Guest House, is the very popular *Hotel Namaskar* (☎ 752-1234, 752-2233), at 917 Chandiwalan. This is a very friendly place run by two brothers, and they go out of their way to make sure you are comfortable. All rooms have windows and attached bath, and there's a geyser on each floor so there's plenty of bucket hot water. There's filtered, cooled drinking water available, and luggage is stored free of charge for guests. It's not the cheapest place, but is well worth the extra. Rooms cost Rs 150/200, and there are also rooms with three (Rs 300) and four (Rs 400) beds, and air-coolers are provided in summer. There are also a couple of air-con doubles at Rs 400. It's an excellent place, and they can also arrange cheap bus and air tickets, and car hire for trips further afield.

Moving further west along Main Bazaar, the next place is the funky old *Camran Lodge* (☎ 52-6053) at 1116, which touts itself as a 'Trusted lodging house for distinguished people'. It's in an old building which is a bit of maze. The rooms are small and shabby, but cheap at Rs 60/120 with common bath, Rs 150 for a double with bath attached. Hot water by the bucket is free.

The *Hotel Vivek* (☎ 777-7062) at 1534-50 is a very popular place, partly because of the restaurant on the ground floor. The rooms are pretty standard – smallish, with and without windows and bathroom – as are the prices at Rs 80/100 with common bath, and with bath for Rs 110/130. There are also air-con rooms for Rs 275/325 with bath.

The *Ankush Guest House* (☎ 751-9000) at 1558 is another place popular with travellers. There are double rooms with common bath at Rs 100, or doubles/triples with attached bath for Rs 120/150.

The popular *Hotel Vishal* (☎ 753-2079), a little further along, is similar and has two good restaurants on the ground floor. Rooms cost Rs 120/160.

The *Hare Krishna Guest House* (☎ 753-3017), next to the Vishal, is another place worth checking out. It has good, clean double rooms for Rs 120, or Rs 150 with attached bath, and there are good views from the rooftop restaurant, which it shares with its sister establishment next door, the *Anoop Hotel* (☎ 73-5219) at 1566. The latter is quite modern and clean, and is also good value for

money. The rooms, which have attached bath and hot
water, are a decent size and are marble-lined, which
makes them cool, although a bit tomb-like. They're well
worth the Rs 120/180. Air-coolers are available for Rs 30.
Checkout at both places is based on the 24-hour system.

On Main Bazaar near Rajguru Rd, the *Sapna Hotel*
(☎ 52-4066) is very basic and a bit tatty around the edges,
but habitable and cheap at Rs 60/80 with common bath,
and Rs 100 for a double with attached bath.

Next door is the *Hotel Satyam* (☎ 73-1155), which is
certainly a step up the scale, with clean rooms for Rs
150/200 with attached bath and hot water. The front
rooms can be noisy, but that's true of all the places along
Main Bazaar.

At the very top of the range is the *Metropolis Tourist
Home* (☎ 52-5492) at 1634 Main Bazaar. This place offers
dorm beds with lockers in air-cooled, four-bed rooms for
Rs 100, or there are air-con doubles for Rs 500 with
attached bath.

Also recommended is *Major's Den* (☎ 752-9599) at
2314 Lakshmi Narain St, near the Imperial Cinema.

Arakashan Rd Still in Paharganj there's a whole group
of places on Arakashan Rd, which is just to the north of
New Delhi Railway Station, past the Desh Bandhu
Gupta Rd flyover and off Qutb Rd (see Map 1). These
are definitely at the top end of the budget category and
charge from Rs 165, but they are all modern and pretty
well equipped.

Pick of the bunch here is the friendly *Hotel Ajanta*
(☎ 752-0925) at 36 Arakashan Rd. This clean and modern
place is popular with travellers looking for a modicum
of comfort and prepared to pay a bit above rock bottom.
The deluxe rooms have colour TV and phone with ISD
facility. The charge is Rs 165/245 for rooms with
common bath, Rs 355/445 for deluxe, and Rs 595 for
deluxe air-con. This hotel also has a taxi available for
trips to the airport, etc.

A few doors along from the Ajanta is the *Hotel Crystal*
(☎ 753-1639) at 8501 Arakashan Rd (I defy you to find
the logic in the numbering system!). The rooms are quite
good, and it's a bit cheaper than the Ajanta, charging Rs
245/325 with attached bath and Rs 50 extra with TV.
Almost next door is the *Hotel Syal* (☎ 51-0091) at 43
Arakashan Rd. It is similar to the Crystal, although none
of the rooms have air-cooling or air-con, which is a major
inconvenience in summer.

The *Hotel Soma* (☎ 752-1002), close by at 33 Arakashan
Rd, boasts a 'gay atmosphere'. The clean and modern
rooms are a good size and cost Rs 200/250, or Rs 250/300

with air-cooler and Rs 350/400 with air-con. Also in this area is the *Krishna Hotel* (☎ 751-0252) at 45 Arakashan Rd. This place offers the standard facilities for Rs 225/250 with TV, attached bath and hot water, and Rs 375 for an air-cooled double room. Another good one is the *Hotel Kalgidhar* (☎ 753-7116) at 7967 Arakashan Rd, with rooms for Rs 150.

Further north along Qutb Rd is the *Hotel Tourist* (☎ 751-0334; fax 777-7446; Map 15), a large place with a deluxe wing by the road and a wing with cheaper rooms set back from the road, behind the large printing house, which is owned by the same people. Rooms in the rear wing are spacious and cost Rs 275/400 with attached bath, and Rs 500/595 with air-con.

Old Delhi

The hotels in Old Delhi (see Map 15) are fine if you like the hustle and bustle and don't mind being away from the business centre of Connaught Place. The advantage is that you get a lot more for your money. Checkout is usually 24 hours.

There's a group of hotels around the south-western corner of the Jama Masjid and many more along Matya Mahal, the road which runs due south of the same mosque.

One of the best places is the *Hotel New City Palace* (☎ 327-9548) right behind the mosque. The front rooms have windows but also get the early morning call from the mosque. The hotel boasts it's a 'home for palatial comfort', which is perhaps overstating things a bit, but it is clean, modern and the management friendly. Double rooms with attached bath with hot water cost Rs 200, and with air-con it's Rs 300.

Also good, and perhaps a bit quieter, is the *Hotel Bombay Orient* (☎ 328-6253) on Matya Mahal, not far from the southern gate of the Jama Masjid. It's also clean and well kept, and single/double rooms with common bath are Rs 75/150, doubles with attached bath are Rs 200 and with air-con Rs 300.

For something a bit cheaper there's the *New Hostel* (☎ 328-6423; fax 328-6205), also on Matya Mahal. Basic double rooms start at Rs 100, but women may not feel too comfortable here.

At the western end of Chandni Chowk, around the Fatehpuri Masjid, there are a few basic hotels. One reasonable place is the *Bharat Hotel* (☎ 23-5326), across the road from the eastern gate of the mosque. It's an old rambling place with a few small courtyards and quite a bit of atmosphere. The rooms are a bit gloomy, and the

25-watt bulbs used to illuminate them certainly don't help. Nevertheless, it's cheap, with rooms for Rs 80/120.

Railway & Airport Retiring Rooms

If all else fails there are railway retiring rooms at both main railway stations (Delhi and New Delhi), with prices for both 24-hour and 12-hour periods. At the (Old) Delhi Railway Station the charges are Rs 30 for a dorm bed for 12 hours, and Rs 75/150 for a single/double room with common bath. As you can imagine, they are noisy places and you deserve a medal if you can actually manage to get some sleep. At New Delhi the cost is Rs 150/250, or Rs 210/500 with air-con, all with common bath.

The *Rail Yatri Niwas* (☎ 331-3484) on the Ajmeri Gate side of New Delhi Railway Station has single/double rooms at Rs 150/250 with common bath, and Rs 210/500 with air-con, all with common bath; there are also dorm beds for Rs 70. To stay there you have to arrive in Delhi by train and have the ticket to prove it.

There are also retiring rooms at both the domestic (Terminal I: ☎ 329-5126) and international (Terminal II: ☎ 545-2011) sections of the airport. You can use them if you have a confirmed departure within 24 hours of your arrival by plane, but you'll need to ring in advance as demand far outstrips supply. They cost Rs 220/250 for an air-con single/double at Terminal II, and Rs 100 for an air-con dorm bed and Rs 220 for a bed in an air-con double at Terminal I. The tourist information officer at the desk at the airport may insist that the retiring rooms are 'full' and try to direct you to a hotel that gives the officer a commission.

Other Places

Out at Chanakyapuri (see Map 10) is the *Vishwa Yuvak Kendra*, or International Youth Centre, (☎ 301-3631) on Teen Murti Marg, at the northern end of the diplomatic enclave. The rooms are very good but not all that cheap, at Rs 341/391, but this does include breakfast. There's also a dormitory at Rs 50. The cafeteria has good food at low prices but lousy service. It's not a bad place to stay if you don't mind the 20-minute bus trip or shorter auto-rickshaw ride from Connaught Place and the sterile, institutional atmosphere. To get there take a No 620 bus from outside the Super Bazar opposite M Block in Connaught Place and get off near the Indonesian Embassy, or take a No 662 from the (Old) Delhi Railway Station and get off at the Ashok Hotel.

There is also a *Youth Hostel* (☎ 301-6285) in Chanakyapuri, at 5 Nyaya Marg, near the Chinese Embassy. Dorm beds cost Rs 50 including breakfast. With the inconvenient location, and the fact that this place takes members only, it's a fairly unattractive proposition for most travellers.

PLACES TO STAY – MIDDLE

Connaught Place & Janpath Area

There are several middle-range hotels around Janpath and Connaught Place (see Map 7).

The *Hotel 55* (☎ 332-1244; fax 332-0769) at 55 H Block, Connaught Circus, is well designed and has central air-conditioning. The rooms are small but have attached bath and cost Rs 600/850. This place suffers from indifferent service and is not great value.

The *Alka Hotel* (☎ 334-4328; fax 373-2796) is also centrally located, at 16 P Block on Connaught Circus, but has shabby and somewhat gloomy air-con singles/doubles for Rs 950/1150 with attached bath and TV. As is typical of many places in this area, most of the rooms don't have windows. There is also a small terrace for 'open air date and get-to-gets'.

Just a few doors along is the easy-to-miss *Prem Sagar Guest House* (☎ 334-5263) on the 1st floor at 11 P Block. This small place has air-con rooms with TV and attached bath for Rs 600/800, which is expensive for what's offered, but not bad by Connaught Place standards. There's a small rooftop terrace where breakfast is served.

The *York Hotel* (☎ 332-3769; fax 335-2419) in K Block is clean but fairly characterless. The rooms are a reasonable size and cost Rs 800/1200. In L Block the more modern *Jukaso Inn* (☎ 332-9694) has very small rooms, although at least most of them have windows. The charge here is Rs 750/1000.

The Ys

There are three YMCA or YWCA places, all of which take either sex. They all have a typically institutional air but are also good value.

The *YMCA Tourist Hostel* (☎ 374-6031; fax 374-6032; Map 7) is on Jai Singh Rd not far from the Jantar Mantar. It's not bad value; rooms have hot and cold water and there are gardens, a swimming pool, a lounge and a restaurant with Western, Indian and Mughlai cuisine. Despite what the touts may tell you if you arrive in Delhi late at night, the hostel is open 24 hours, and credit cards are accepted. The rooms cost Rs 295/500 with common bath, and Rs 525/880 with air-con and attached bath. There's also a temporary membership charge of Rs 10, valid for one month, and maximum stay is 15 days.

The *YWCA International Guest House* (☎ 31-1561; Map 7) at 10 Sansad Marg has singles/doubles for Rs 375/625 including breakfast, and all rooms have bath and air-con. It's conveniently located near Connaught Place and has a reasonable restaurant.

There's a second, lesser-known YWCA, the *YWCA Blue Triangle Family Hostel* (☎ 373-4807), on Ashoka Rd just off Sansad Marg (see Map 6). It's clean, well run and has a restaurant. Rates, including breakfast, are Rs 325/500 with attached bath or Rs 400/650 with air-con. There's also a small temporary membership fee. This place is only about a 10-minute walk from the heart of Connaught Place and, like the YMCA, is open 24 hours.

Guest Houses

There are a number of small guest houses dotted around the suburbs of New Delhi. They are not as convenient as those right in Connaught Place, but this is compensated for by the quieter location, more personal atmosphere and general hassle-free environment which these places offer.

West of Connaught Place There are two excellent family-run guest houses just to the west of Connaught Place.

The first is *Yatri House* (☎ 752-5563; Map 1) at 3/4 Rani Jhansi Rd, which is opposite the junction of Panchkuin Marg (Radial No 3) and Mandir Marg, about one km west of Connaught Place. It's calm, secure and moderately priced, and there are trees, a lawn, and a small courtyard at the back. The good-sized rooms, all with attached bath, are kept spotlessly clean and are good value at Rs 550/650, or Rs 700 for an air-con double. The owner is very friendly and helpful, and there's a car available for sightseeing. Advance bookings are advisable during the high season.

The second place is further to the west but is still only a Rs 20 auto-rickshaw ride from Connaught Place. The family-run *Master Paying Guest House* (☎ 574-1089; Map 1) is at R-500 New Rajendra Nagar. This small and friendly place is in a quiet area and the owner has worked hard to create a homelike atmosphere. It has large, airy and beautifully furnished double rooms from Rs 350 to Rs 550, all with common bath, and there's a

25% discount in summer. Good meals are available, there's a pleasant rooftop terrace and car hire for extended trips can also be arranged.

South Extension The suburb of South Extension straddles the Ring Rd, about a Rs 25, 15-minute auto-rickshaw ride south of Connaught Place. The guest houses here see few foreign visitors, but they offer good value and are very convenient for visiting the sights in the south of the city. There are also plenty of restaurants and cafes close by.

The *B-57 Inn* (☎ 469-4239; Map 1) is at B-57 South Extension Part I, 200 metres north of the Ring Rd. Carpeted, air-cooled single/double rooms with colour TV, direct-dial ISD phone and attached bath cost Rs 495/595, or with air-con Rs 595/695, plus 10% tax. South Indian meals and snacks are available.

Closer to the Ring Rd is the *South Delhi Guest House* (☎ 463-3369) at H-67 South Extension Part I. The rooms are comfortable and cost Rs 400/500 with air-cooling or Rs 495/605 with air-con including taxes.

Sunder Nagar Sunder Nagar is closer to the centre of the city, just off the busy Mathura Rd directly south of the Delhi Zoo. There are a handful of places in this area, all of them at the top of the middle price range and with central air-conditioning; all accept credit cards. Although all these places do serve food, there are no other restaurants in the immediate area, so you'd have to head for somewhere like Khan Market to get a meal outside the hotel.

The *Kailash Inn* (☎ 461-7401; Map 6) at 10 Sunder Nagar is the cheapest of these places, with rooms at Rs 750/950 including taxes.

Just a couple of doors along is the *La Sagrita Tourist Home* (☎ 469-4541; fax 463-6956; Map 6) at 14 Sunder Nagar. The ordinary rooms here cost Rs 995 including taxes, which is somewhat overpriced. The deluxe rooms at Rs 1095 are better value, although all rooms could do with a lick of paint to freshen them up a bit.

In the block behind, with views over the zoo and the Purana Qila, is the *Shervani Fort View* (☎ 463-5831; fax 469-4226; Map 6) at 11 Sunder Nagar. The service is indifferent but the rooms are OK at Rs 775/900 for singles/doubles, including tax.

Also here is the *Maharani Inn* (☎ 469-3128), which is similarly priced, but it's right on Mathura Rd so some rooms could be noisy.

PLACES TO STAY – TOP END

Connaught Place & Janpath Area

Delhi has plenty of expensive hotels, most of them located in the wide, tree-lined avenues of New Delhi south of Rajpath. There are, however, a few choices closer to the city centre, between Connaught Place and Rajpath.

One place right in the centre is the long-running *Nirula's Hotel* (Map 7) in Connaught Place. However, because of its central location it's often full. The *Hotel Marina* (Map 7) is also central but is showing its age, and a glance through the visitors' book suggests maintenance is not what it might be.

Very close to Connaught Place on Sansad Marg is the modern and unremarkable *Park Hotel* (Map 7). It's a five-star deluxe hotel with facilities to match, but it's only the location which saves it from five-star obscurity.

Ornate carvings at Safdarjang's Tomb (HF)

Moving south from Connaught Place along what is essentially New Delhi's main drag, Janpath, is the *Imperial Hotel* (Map 7). This is another of Delhi's older hotels, but it is very well maintained, and its low-rise profile and garden setting give it a much more intimate feel than the large super-deluxe places.

One block to the east is one of the city's more recent additions, the *Holiday Inn Crowne Plaza* (Map 1). It's a typical multi-storey deluxe hotel, and while it is not exactly eye-pleasing, the use of the distinctive red Agra sandstone means it's not a total disaster.

Close by on the corner of Kasturba Gandhi Marg and Tolstoy Marg is the *Centre Point Hotel* (Map 7), which has good-sized rooms and represents good value given its central location. It also has a good vegetarian restaurant, the *Kanchi*.

Further south along Janpath is the ageing *Janpath Hotel* (Map 6), another ITDC disaster and definitely one to avoid. Around the corner, and also run by the ITDC, is the much larger and marginally better *Hotel Kanishka*. These two places really only scrape into the top-end category on price alone – the service and facilities do not come up to the mark.

Still on Janpath, just before Rajpath, is another of Delhi's international chain hotels, *Le Meridien* (Map 6). The exterior is atrocious and totally unsympathetic to its surroundings; the interior, however, is very plush and impressive.

South of Rajpath

In this part of the city there are a couple of popular older-style hotels. The *Hotel Claridges* (Map 6) is a small and comfortable five-star hotel, while the *Ambassador Hotel*, a couple of blocks away on Subramanian Bharti Marg, is a four-star hotel with one of Delhi's best-known vegetarian restaurants, the Dasaprakash.

Between these two hotels is the luxury Taj Group's *Taj Mahal Hotel* (Map 6), probably Delhi's best top of the range hotel, with prices to match. It obviously has the corporate traveller in its sights as there are extensive conference facilities.

Another hotel with extensive gardens is the *Hotel Oberoi New Delhi* (Map 6), on the edge of the Delhi Golf Course, south-east of India Gate on Dr Zakir Husain Marg.

On the northern edge of the diplomatic enclave of Chanakyapuri are two more ITDC places, the *Ashok Hotel* and the *Samrat Hotel* (Map 10). Both provide adequate levels of comfort but are overpriced and poorly serviced when compared with what else Delhi has to offer.

Just to the west of Chanakyapuri on the road in from the airport (Sardar Patel Marg) are two of Delhi's top deluxe hotels: the *Maurya Sheraton* and the *Taj Palace Hotel* (Map 1). Both offer the very best in luxury accommodation and service, and have prices to match.

Elsewhere

There's a second Oberoi hotel, the *Oberoi Maidens Hotel* (Map 9), in the old Civil Lines area north of Old Delhi. The building itself is a veranda'd colonial relic, which sets it apart from the other top-end places, and is very pleasant, as is the large garden. Lutyens, the designer of New Delhi, stayed here in the 1930s when the new city was under construction. The main disadvantage with staying here is that there are few places to eat in the immediate vicinity, and it's quite a haul through the traffic snarls of Old Delhi to get to Connaught Place.

Top-End Hotels in Delhi
Four-Star Unless otherwise stated, these four-star places do not have a swimming pool:

The *Ambassador Hotel*, Sujan Singh Park (☎ 463-2600; fax 463-2252; Map 6), is a short distance south of India Gate. There are just 75 rooms costing from Rs 1075/1850. It has a noted vegetarian restaurant, coffee shop, bar and in-house astrologer (!).

The *Centre Point Hotel* (☎ 332-4805; fax 332-9138; Map 7), 13 Kasturba Gandhi Marg, is close to Connaught Place. Centrally air-conditioned, with large rooms with colour TV, direct-dial phone, 24-hour coffee shop and a small garden. Rooms cost from Rs 1100/1400, or bigger 'superior' rooms with fridge at Rs 1300/1800.

The *Connaught Palace Hotel* is due west of Connaught Place on Bhagat Singh Marg (☎ 34-4225; fax 31-0757). It offers restaurants, 24-hour room service and car rental. Rooms cost from Rs 1300/1800 with breakfast.

The *Hotel Diplomat*, 9 Sadar Patel Marg (☎ 301-0204; fax 301-8605; Map 6), south-east of Rashtrapati Bhavan, is a smaller place with just 25 rooms, a restaurant and a bar. All rooms have colour TV, phone and attached bath. The charge is Rs 1090/1550.

The *Hotel Hans Plaza*, Tolstoy Marg (☎ 331-6861; Map 1), is conveniently central, just south of Connaught Place. The rooms are comfortable, well furnished and cost Rs 1900/2400.

The *Janpath Hotel* (☎ 332-0070; fax 332-7083; Map 6) is run by the ITDC with typically indifferent service. This large hotel has a good position on Janpath, but the rooms are musty and in desperate need of a facelift. At Rs 1195/1700 it's poor value.

The *Hotel Kanishka* (☎ 332-4422; fax 332-4242; Map 6) is another ITDC hotel. It's next to the disastrous Hotel Ashok Yatri Niwas, but fortunately this hotel is much better run. It is one of the few places in this class to have a swimming pool. The room rate is Rs 1600/2400. It's popular with affluent Russians in Delhi buying up cheap goods.

The *Oberoi Maidens Hotel*, 7 Sham Nath Marg (☎ 252-5464; fax 292-5134; Map 9), is in the old Civil Lines area north of Old Delhi. It has a swimming pool and tennis courts. Rooms start at US$38/75.

Five-Star If you're looking for a little more luxury, try one of the following hotels:

Hotel Claridges, 12 Aurangzeb Rd (☎ 301-0211; fax 301-0625; Map 6), is south of Rajpath in New Delhi. It's a very comfortable older place, with four restaurants, a swimming pool, a business centre and a travel agency. Rooms start at Rs 3350.

The *Imperial Hotel* (☎ 332-5332; fax 332-4542; Map 7) is conveniently situated on Janpath near the centre of the city. It's a pleasantly old-fashioned, low-rise hotel with a big garden and is surprisingly quiet given its central location. It's one of the cheaper top-end places and represents good value for money at Rs 2800/3000.

The *Park Hotel* on Sansad Marg (☎ 373-2477; fax 373-2025; Map 7) is in a very central location only a block from Connaught Place. This hotel has a swimming pool, a tennis court, a bookshop and a business centre. Rooms are Rs 3200/3500.

Five-Star Deluxe Delhi's top-of-the-range hotels include:

The *Ashok Hotel*, 50B Chanakyapuri (☎ 60-0121; fax 687-3216; Map 10), is the 571-room flagship of the ITDC hotel fleet. It offers everything from restaurants, coffee shops, bars, discos, a travel agent, a post office, a bank, conference rooms and a swimming pool to full air-conditioning, a baby-sitting service and evening music recitals. Singles/doubles start at Rs 2700/2900. Although the prices are five-star deluxe, the service isn't.

The *Centaur Hotel*, on Gurgaon Rd (☎ 545-2223; fax 545-2256; Map 1), is about two km from the international airport and five km from the domestic terminal. It's a big modern hotel with 376 rooms, a swimming pool, a health club, tennis courts, a putting green and a children's park. It also offers weekend package deals pitched at Delhi-ites who want to escape from the city for a weekend; however, with the bleak expanses of flat land all around it's hardly paradise, and the roar of planes overhead at all hours certainly doesn't add to the ambience. It is, however, the closest hotel to the airport. Room rates are reasonable at Rs 1700/1900.

The *Holiday Inn Crowne Plaza* is a modern 500-room hotel which is very centrally located just off Barakhamba Rd, south-east of Connaught Place (☎ 332-0101; fax 332-5335; Map 1). It boasts every conceivable mod con, including an open-air swimming pool on a third-floor terrace, a business centre and a health centre, and it also has a floor of nonsmoking rooms. Standard single/double rooms cost US$170/190, and there are more expensive suites available.

The *Hyatt Regency Hotel*, with 523 rooms, is south of New Delhi on the Ring Rd between Hauz Khas and Chanakyapuri (☎ 688-1234; fax 688-6833; Map 1). Facilities include a fitness centre, in-house movies, restaurants, a bar and a coffee shop. For all this you pay Rs 4750 for a double room.

Le Meridien (☎ 371-0101; fax 371-4545; Map 6) is another very modern place. This 385-room hotel has a fourth-floor swimming pool, a tennis court, four restaurants, a 24-hour cafe with room service and a business centre. The rates are Rs 4200/4500 for standard single/double rooms.

The *Hotel Oberoi New Delhi* is in south Delhi near the Purana Qila (☎ 436-3030; fax 436-0484; Map 6). This 290-room hotel is one of the best-value luxury places. Services include a 24-hour business centre, a travel desk, a swimming pool and secretarial services. Rooms start at Rs 3850.

The *Maurya Sheraton* is on Sardar Patel Marg (☎ 301-0101; fax 301-0908; Map 1), the road to the airport. Apart from a high level of comfort, the hotel boasts two excellent restaurants, a solar-heated swimming pool (the only pool in Delhi to be open year-round) and a disco. It has 500 rooms costing from Rs 5000/5800 up to Rs 8000/8500.

The *Taj Mahal Hotel*, at 1 Man Singh Rd (☎ 301-6162; fax 301-7299; Map 6), is one of Delhi's best – a luxurious place that is fairly central but quiet. It has all the usual facilities including a swimming pool, a photographer, a business centre, restaurants and a coffee shop. It even has telephones in the bathrooms! Singles/doubles start at US$220/250. ■

Places to Eat

Delhi has an excellent array of places to eat – from a *dhaba* house with dishes for less than Rs 10 up to top-of-the-range restaurants where a meal for two can easily top Rs 2500!

Connaught Place Area

Bottom-End There are many Indian-style fast-food places around Connaught Place. Their plus point is that they have good food at reasonable prices and are clean and healthy. A minus point for some of them is they have no place to sit – it's stand, eat and run. They serve Indian food (from samosas to dosas) and Western food (burgers to sandwiches).

There are a number of basic eateries in the same lane as the Ringo and Sunny guest houses. *Don't Pass Me By* is a popular little place which caters to international tastes with breakfast standards such as muesli and fruit curd, as well as sandwiches and Chinese dishes. Most dishes are less than Rs 25. Other places close by include the *Anand, New Light, Kalpana, Swaram* and *Vikram* restaurants.

For good, solid, no-frills Indian food there's a string of dhabas on Outer Circle opposite L Block. There's probably not a lot to choose between them, although the *Kaka Da* is clean and has healthy food. Curries are around Rs 40, or you can have a half-chicken for Rs 80.

On Janpath at N Block is a branch of the British *Wimpy* hamburger chain. Until McDonald's is up and running in Delhi, this is the closest you're going to get to a Big Mac (100% lamb!) in India. The burgers are fair imitations but, again, if you're used to Indian prices, spending Rs 60 on a burger and a shake seems like reckless extravagance.

Nirula's Hot Shoppe (☎ 332-2419) is probably the most popular and long-running of these fast-food places and does a wide variety of light snacks, both Indian and Western. It has good cold drinks, milk shakes and ice cream, and you can have a lunch box packed – ideal to take on train trips. Next door to Nirula's snack bar is an ice-cream parlour on one side and good pastry shop on the other. Above the ice-cream parlour there's the fourth part of Nirula's, a sit-down restaurant called *Pot Pourri*, which used to be something of a travellers' Mecca but these days seems to be living off its reputation. The

Places to Eat

smorgasbord salad bar is still good value at Rs 72; other dishes are not so good and the air-con is feeble. It's a good place for breakfast, served from 7.30 am, and it's open until midnight. Also upstairs at Nirula's is the *Chinese Room*, with Chinese dishes in the Rs 100 to Rs 150 range, and a very congenial, if somewhat smoky, bar. The ice-cream parlour is amazingly busy and is open from 10 am to midnight. On Sunday nights the crowd here blocks the whole road and the place takes on a carnival atmosphere – there are balloon hawkers and even a few hopeful ice-cream vendors!

The *Cafe 100* on B Block is one of the newest places around and has good snacks and ice creams. Pizzas are Rs 40, burgers Rs 30, and there's also a reasonable buffet upstairs for Rs 105.

On Outer Circle just around the corner from Janpath is the glossy new *Croissants Etc*, a fast-food place with pretty good filled croissants from Rs 11 to Rs 20, burgers from Rs 35 and cakes and ice-cream. It's open daily from 8.30 am to 10.30 pm.

Another good place around Connaught Place is *Kovil* in E Block (☎ 371-0585), with very good south Indian vegetarian food for Rs 25 to Rs 40.

The *Sona Rupa Restaurant* on Janpath (☎ 332-4980) does good south Indian vegetarian food; however, the self-service system is bizarre. Also on Janpath is the *Bankura Restaurant* (☎ 332-8506, Ext 65), behind the pavement stalls. It makes a welcome retreat from the heat and is popular with office workers at lunchtime.

Delhi Tourism operates the *Coffee Home* on Baba Kharak Singh Marg, near the state emporia. It's a large,

Mobile ice-cream vendors are everywhere. (HF)

airy and very popular cafe featuring coffee and snacks. There's also a branch of the *Indian Coffee House* in the amazingly scruffy Mohan Singh Building on the same street. The cafe is on the 3rd floor and has an outdoor terrace which is great on a sunny winter morning; most of the year it's like a furnace.

The fresh milk is excellent at *Keventers*, the hole-in-the-wall milk bar at the corner of Connaught Place and Radial Rd 3, around the corner from American Express. If you just want a cheap soft drink and somewhere semi-cool to drink it, descend into the air-conditioned underground *Palika Bazaar* between Janpath and Sansad Marg (Parliament St) on Connaught Place.

Middle Moving up a price category, there are several restaurants worth considering. The *Kwality Restaurant* on Sansad Marg (☎ 31-1752) is spotlessly clean and very efficient but the food is only average. The menu is the almost standard non-vegetarian menu you'll find at restaurants all over India. Main courses are mainly in the Rs 40 to Rs 70 range. This is also a good place for non-Indian food if you want a break; you can have breakfast here for Rs 45.

El Arab Restaurant, right on the corner of Sansad Marg and the outer circle of Connaught Place, has an interesting Middle Eastern menu with most dishes in the Rs 55 to Rs 80 bracket, and a good buffet for Rs 110. Downstairs there is the more expensive *Cellar* (☎ 31-1444). A few doors along is the *Gaylord* (☎ 35-2677), which has big mirrors, chandeliers and excellent Indian food, the speciality being kebabs and tandoori dishes, which range from Rs 90 to Rs 120. There are also continental dishes from Rs 120 and a good range of Chinese dishes for Rs 90 to Rs 115.

Also on Connaught Place you can find good vegetarian food at the *Volga Restaurant* (☎ 332-2960); it's a little expensive but it's air-conditioned, and the food and service are excellent.

Another restaurant on Connaught Place is *The Host* (☎ 331-6389), which serves excellent Indian and Chinese food. It's extremely popular with well-heeled Indians, but it's not particularly cheap, with main dishes in the Rs 100 to Rs 130 range. A similar but cheaper place is the *United Coffee House* on E Block. It's a pleasantly relaxed and popular place, with main dishes from Rs 60 to Rs 100, and beers for Rs 60. The *Embassy Restaurant* on D Block (☎ 332-0480) is another similar place that's popular among office workers.

The tastefully decorated *Zen Restaurant* on B Block (☎ 372-4444) is another new place. Its focus is Chinese and Japanese food, with main dishes very reasonably priced from Rs 50 to Rs 100.

On A Block near American Express is *El Rodeo* (☎ 371-3780), serving good Mexican food; it's worth visiting just for the sight of saddle bar-stools and waiters in cowboy suits! There's a range of Mexican dishes from Rs 80 to Rs 125, Italian dishes such as spaghetti from Rs 65 to Rs 110 and steaks from Rs 100 to Rs 125. This is one of the few restaurants around Connaught Place to have a beef (yes, beef!) licence. Beers are Rs 65, and bottles of red and white wine from Maharashtra cost Rs 550. The restaurant is open daily from 11 am to 11 pm.

For Chinese food there's the excellent *Fa Yian* on A Block, Middle Circle (☎ 332-4603). It's owned and run by Chinese, the prices are very reasonable and the air-con is positively Arctic. Main dishes are in the Rs 50 to Rs 90 range, and Australian fish features on the menu. It's open daily from 11 am to 3.30 pm and from 7 to 11 pm; alcohol is not served.

Another Chinese option is the classy *Palki Restaurant* on K Block, Outer Circle (☎ 335-4455). The menu is interesting and features the Dum Phukt cuisine of the Lucknow nawabs. Main dishes range from Rs 90 to Rs 120, but beer is not served here. The Rs 101 buffet lunch is good value.

For an interesting dining experience there's the *Parikrama* revolving restaurant on Kasturba Gandhi Marg (☎ 372-1618). The fare is pretty good and it's moderately priced. A full rotation takes around 1½ hours – time enough for a leisurely three courses. It's open daily for lunch and dinner, and for drinks from 3 to 7 pm. It's probably better not to go in the evenings, as all you can see is your own reflection in the window!

Near the Bengali Market at the traffic circle where Tansen Marg meets Babar Rd, the neat and clean *Nathu's* (☎ 371-9784) is a good place for sweets or for a meal of the Bengali vegetarian snacks known as chat. You could try cholaphatura (puffed rotis with a lentil dip), tikkas (fried stuffed potatoes), papri chat (sweet/hot wafers) or golguppas (hollow puffs you break open and use as a scoop for a peppery liquid accompaniment). They also have excellent dosas and kulfi. The *Bengali Sweet House* opposite is similar, and there's also a branch in South Extension Part I.

Finally there's one Delhi food place that should not be forgotten. *Wenger's* on Connaught Place (☎ 332-4373) is a cake shop with an awesome range of little cakes, which they'll put in a cardboard box and tie up with a bow so you can self-consciously carry them back to your hotel room for private consumption.

Indian Food

Indian food has an international reputation, and sampling the various dishes and regional cuisines is one of the delights of any visit. As might be expected in the national capital, there is a wide variety of Indian restaurants in all price ranges.

Contrary to popular belief, not all Hindus are officially vegetarians. Strict vegetarianism is confined more to the south, which has not had the meat-eating influence of the Aryan and later Muslim invasions, and also to the Gujarati community. Muslims tend to eat a lot of meat, and the cooking is often the very rich 'Mughal style' (often spelt 'Mughlai'), which bears a close relationship to food of the Middle East and central Asia. The emphasis is more on spices and less on chilli, and the cooking is usually done in a clay (tandoori) oven.

For those who do eat meat, it is not always a pleasure to do so in India, as the quality is variable – usually it's quite okay, especially in the better restaurants; in the cheaper places it can be tough. Beef, from the holy cow, is strictly taboo – restaurants need to have a special licence to serve beef, and there are only a handful of restaurants in Delhi with such a licence, most of them at the five-star hotels.

In the most basic Indian restaurants and eating places, known as dhabas or *bhojanalyas*, the cooking is usually done right out front so you can see exactly what is going on and how it is done. Vegetables will be on the simmer all day and tend to be overcooked and mushy to Western tastes. In these basic places dahl is usually free but you pay for chapatis, parathas, puris or rice. *Sabzi* (vegetable preparations), dahl and a few chapatis make a passable meal for around Rs 15. If you order half-plates of the various dishes brewing out front you get half the quantity at half the price and get a little more variety. With chutneys and a small plate of onions, which come free, you can put together a reasonable vegetarian meal for Rs 30 or a non-vegetarian one for Rs 40.

Curry & Spice

Believe it or not, there is no such thing as 'curry' in India. It's an English invention, an all-purpose term to cover the whole range of Indian food spicing. *Carhi*, incidentally, is a Gujarati dish, but never ask for it in Kumaon, where it's a very rude word!

Although not all Indian food is curry, this is the basis of Indian cuisine. Curry doesn't have to be hot enough to blow your head off, although it can if it's made that way. Curry most definitely is not something found in a packet of curry powder. Indian cooks have about 25 spices on their regular list and it is from these that they produce the curry flavour. Normally the spices are freshly ground in a mortar and pestle known as a *sil-vatta*. Spices are usually blended in certain combinations to produce masalas (mixes). Garam masala (hot mix), for example, is a combination of cloves, cinnamon, cardamom, coriander, cumin and peppercorns.

Popular spices include saffron *(kesar)*, an expensive flavouring produced from the stamens of certain crocus flowers. This is used to give rice that yellow colouring and delicate fragrance. (It's an excellent buy in India, where a one-gram packet costs around Rs 35 – you'll pay about 10 times that at home.) Turmeric *(haldi)* also has a colouring property, acts as a preservative and has a distinctive smell and taste. Chillies *(mirch)* are ground, dried or added whole to supply the heat. They come in red and green varieties but the green ones are the hottest. Ginger *(adrak)* is supposed to be good for the digestion, while many masalas contain coriander because it is said to cool the body. Strong and sweet cardamom *(elaichi)* is used in many desserts and in rich meat dishes. See the Shopping chapter for a full list of spices and their Hindi names.

Breads & Grains

Rice is, of course, the basic Indian staple, but although it is eaten throughout the country, it's all-important only in the south. The best Indian rice, it is generally agreed, is found in the north, where Basmati rice grows in the Dehra Dun Valley. It has long grains, is yellowish and has a slightly sweetish, or *bas*, smell. In the north wheat is the staple and rice is supplemented by a whole range of breads known as rotis or chapatis.

Indian breads are varied but always delicious. Simplest is the chapati/roti, which is simply a mixture of flour and water cooked on a hot plate known as a *tawa*. A paratha is also cooked on the hot plate, but ghee is used and the bread is rolled in a different way. There are also parathas that have been stuffed with peas or potato. Bake the bread in a tandoori oven and you have naan, the most popular bread in Mughlai cuisine. Use your chapati or naan to mop or scoop up your curry. A speciality of the restaurants in Old Delhi is the thin *rumali roti* (handkerchiefs), which are large, soft and excellent.

An *idli* is a kind of south Indian rice dumpling, often served with a spicy curd sauce *(dahi idli)* or with spiced lentils and chutney. They're a popular breakfast dish among south Indians. Papadams are crispy deep-fried lentil-flour wafers often served with thalis or other meals.

Popular in Delhi, but originating from the south, are *dosas*. These are basically paper-thin pancakes made from lentil and rice flour. Curried vegetables wrapped inside a dosa makes it a masala dosa – a terrific snack meal. Deep-fried bread which puffs up is known as a *puri*. An *uttapam* is like a dosa.

Basic Dishes

Curries can be vegetable, meat (usually chicken or lamb) or fish, but they are always fried in ghee (clarified butter) or vegetable oil. These can be accompanied by rice or any of the Indian breads.

There are a number of dishes which aren't really curries but are close enough to them for Western tastes. Vindaloos have a vinegar marinade and tend to be hotter than most curries. Kormas, on the other hand, are rich, substantial dishes prepared by braising. There are both meat and vegetable kormas. *Navratan korma* is a very tasty dish using nuts, while a *malai kofta* is a rich, cream-based dish. *Dopiaza* literally means 'two onions' and is a type of korma which uses onions at two stages in its preparation.

Probably the most basic of Indian dishes is dhal, rather like a lentil soup. Dhal is almost always there, whether as an accompaniment to a curry or as a very basic meal in itself with chapatis or rice. In the very small rural towns, dhal and rice is just about all there is on the menu. The favourite dhal of Bengal and Gujarat is yellow *arhar*, whereas in Punjab it is black *urad*; the common red lentils are called *moong*, and *rajma* is the Heinz 57 varieties of dhal!

Other basic dishes include *mattar panir*, peas and cheese in gravy; *saag gosht*, spinach and meat; *alu dum*, potato curry; *palak panir*, spinach and cheese; and *alu chhole*, diced potatoes and spicy-sour chickpeas. Some other vegetables include *gobi* (cauliflower), *brinjal* (eggplant) and *mattar* (peas).

Mughlai Specialities

Those who have the idea that Indian food is always curry and always fiery hot will be pleasantly surprised by tandoori and biryani dishes. Tandoori food is a northern speciality and refers to the clay oven in which the food is cooked after first being marinated in a complex mix of herbs and yoghurt. Tandoori chicken is a favourite. This food is not as hot as curry dishes and usually tastes terrific.

Biryani (again, chicken is a popular biryani dish) is another northern Mughal dish. The meat is mixed with a deliciously flavoured, orange-coloured rice which is sometimes spiced with nuts or dried fruit. A Kashmiri biryani is basically fruit salad with rice.

Pulao is flavoured rice often with pulses and with or without meat. You will also find it in other Asian countries further west.

Rogan josh is a popular, straightforward lamb curry which originated in Kashmir. *Gushtaba*, pounded and spiced meatballs cooked in a yoghurt sauce, is another Kashmiri speciality. *Chicken makhanwala* is a rich dish cooked in a butter sauce.

Another indication of the influence of central Asian cooking style is the popularity of kebabs. The two basic forms are *sikh* (skewered) and *shami* (minced and wrapped on a skewer), but the best are said to be the *kakori* kebabs, which are made from finely ground mutton – a good one will just melt in your mouth!

Side Dishes

Indian food generally has a number of side dishes to go with the main meal. Probably the most popular is *dahi* – curd or yoghurt. It has the useful ability of instantly cooling a fiery curry: either blend it into the curry or, if it's too late, you can administer it straight to your mouth. Curd is often used in the cooking or as a dessert and appears in the popular drink called *lassi. Raita* is another popular side dish consisting of curd mixed with cooked or raw vegetables, particularly cucumber (similar to Greek tzatziki) or tomato.

Sabzi is curried vegetables, and *began bharta* is pured eggplant curry. Mulligatawny is a soup-like dish which is really just a milder, more liquid curry. It's a dish adopted into the English menu by the Raj. Chutney is pickled fruit or vegetables and is the standard relish for a curry.

Thalis

A *thali* is the all-purpose Indian dish. Although it is basically a product of south India, you will find restaurants serving thalis, or 'plate meals' (vegetarian or non-vegetarian), all over Delhi. The name is taken from the 'thali' dish in which the meal is served. This consists of a metal plate with a number of small metal bowls known as *katoris* on it. Sometimes the small bowls will be replaced by simple indentations in the plate; in more basic places the 'plate' will be a big, fresh banana leaf. A thali consists of a variety of curry dishes, relishes, a couple of papadams, puris or chapatis and a mountain of rice. A fancy thali may have a *pata*, a rolled leaf stuffed with fruit and nuts. There will probably be a bowl of curd and possibly even a small dessert or *pan*.

Snacks

Samosas are curried vegetables fried in a pastry triangle. They are very tasty and are found all over India. *Bhujias*, or pakoras, are bite-size pieces of vegetable dipped in chickpea flour batter and deep fried. Along with samosas they're the most popular snack food in the country.

Channa is spiced chickpeas *(gram)* served with small puris. *Sambhar* is a soup-like lentil and vegetable dish with a sour tamarind flavour. *Chat* is the general term for snacks, while *namkin* is the name for the various spiced nibbles that are sold prepackaged.

Desserts & Sweets

Indians have quite a sweet tooth and an amazing selection of desserts and sweets to satisfy it. The desserts are basically rice or milk based and consist of various interesting things in sweet syrup or else sweet pastries. Most are horrendously sweet.

Kulfi is a delicious pistachio-flavoured sweet similar to ice cream and is widely available. You can, of course, also get Western-style ice cream. The major brands, such as Vadelal, Go Cool, Kwality and Havmor, are safe and very good. *Ras gullas* are another very popular Indian dessert; they're sweet little balls of cream cheese flavoured with rose water.

Gulub jamuns are a typical example of the small 'things' in syrup – they're fried and made from thickened boiled-down milk (known as *khoya)* and flavoured with cardamom and rose water. *Jalebis*, the orange-coloured squiggles with syrup inside, are made of flour coloured or flavoured with saffron. *Ladu* are yellow coloured balls made from chickpea flour. *Barfi* is also made from khoya and is available in flavours such as coconut, pistachio, chocolate or almond.

Many of the Indian sweets are covered in a thin layer of silver, as are some of the desserts. It's just that, silver beaten paper-thin. Don't peel it off; it's quite edible. There are countless sweet shops with their goodies all lined up in glass showcases. Prices vary from Rs 40 to Rs 60 for a kg but you can order 50 or 100 grams at a time or simply ask for a couple of pieces. These shops often sell curd, as well as sweet curd, which makes a very pleasant dessert. Sweets include all sorts of unidentifiable goodies; try them and see.

Fruit

If your sweet tooth simply isn't sweet enough to cope with too many Indian desserts, you'll be able to fall back on India's wide variety of fruit. Melons are widely available, particularly watermelons, which are a fine thirst quencher when you're unsure about the water and fed up with soft drinks. Try to get the first slice before the flies discover it.

There are dozens of varieties of mangoes, but they are a summer fruit and only start to appear in Delhi around the beginning of May. Bananas are available all year round, while green-skinned oranges are popular in spring and summer.

Pan

An Indian meal should properly be finished with pan – the name given to the collection of spices and condiments chewed with betel nut. Found throughout eastern Asia, betel is a mildly intoxicating and addictive nut, but by itself it is quite inedible. After a meal you chew pan as a mild digestive.

Pan sellers have a whole collection of little trays, boxes and containers in which they mix either *sadha* (plain) or *mitha* (sweet) pans. The ingredients may include, apart from the betel nut itself, lime paste (the ash, not the fruit), the powder known as *catachu*, various spices and even a dash of opium in a pricey pan. The whole concoction is folded up in a piece of edible leaf, which you pop in your mouth and chew. When finished you spit the leftovers out and add another red blotch to the pavement. Over a long period of time, indulgence in pan will turn your teeth red-black and even addict you to the betel nut. Trying one occasionally won't do you any harm. ■

Paharganj Area

In keeping with its role as a travellers' centre, Main Bazaar in Paharganj has a handful of cheap restaurants which cater almost exclusively to foreign travellers. They are all up towards the western end of Main Bazaar. The *Diamond Cafe* and *Lords Cafe* in the Hotel Vishal both have extensive menus and cheap food. The garlic steaks in Lords Cafe are pretty good, while the Diamond Cafe has a menu full of tortured English. The rooftop *Leema* restaurant in the Hotel Vivek is a popular place.

Next door to Lords Cafe and still in the Hotel Vishal building is the *Appetite Restaurant*. This place has similar food to the others but is a bit more upmarket and has some more sophisticated dishes. The pizzas here are popular, but what is even more popular is the fact that this place has cable TV, and international sports broadcasts, especially cricket, draw big audiences.

Further along Main Bazaar are some very basic eating stalls with tables on the footpath. These are popular for chai, and for the really impecunious they offer cheap snack food.

Lastly there's the air-con *Metropolis Restaurant*, in the hotel of the same name just past Rajguru Rd. The food here is definitely more expensive than the other Main Bazaar cheapies, but it's worth the extra money.

Old Delhi

Even if you're not staying in Old Delhi, it's worth eating here at least once. There are a couple of restaurants which are Delhi institutions, and there's also an active night food market.

Without doubt the first choice is *Karims*, in a small courtyard off Matya Mahal very close to the Jama Masjid (☎ 326-9880). This place has been serving excellent Mughlai food to Delhi-ites for 80-odd years and has a well-deserved reputation. It's so popular that it has taken over a number of rooms in other buildings around the courtyard, while the kitchen is smack in the middle! The food is the same in all the rooms, although the rear one is reserved for women and families. All the food is very rich, and meat features prominently. One of the best dishes is the chicken or mutton stew, although the name hardly inspires. You can also sample superb seekh kebabs or Delhi's famous paper-thin roomali rotis, and even the dhal is great! Main dishes range from Rs 50 to Rs 70, but you can order half serves (at half price), making it very cheap. The restaurant is open from 6 am to midnight – breakfast at Karims early on Sunday morning is very popular.

A vendor offers fresh coconut. (GE)

At the other end of the price range is the famous old *Moti Mahal Restaurant* on Netaji Subhash Marg in Darya Ganj (☎ 327-0077). This open-air restaurant is noted for its tandoori dishes, including murga musalam, but it also serves a wide range of other dishes. Main courses are around Rs 125 to Rs 200, but you can order half serves of tandoori. Adding to the atmosphere is the live *qawwali* singing (nightly except Tuesday). The restaurant is open daily from noon until 12.30 am, and beers are available. There's another branch in Greater Kailash.

Close by are two well-known tandoori restaurants. The *Tandoor*, at the Hotel President on Asaf Ali Rd, near the Tourist Camp (☎ 327-7836), is an excellent place with the usual two waiters-per-diner service and a sitar playing in the background. The tandoor kitchen can be seen through a glass panel.

Just a few doors along in the same street is the Hotel Broadway with its *Chor Bizarre* (Thieves' Market) restaurant (☎ 327-3823). They've certainly put some effort into decorating this place with an eclectic mix of bits and pieces collected from various markets – a four-poster bed, an old sports car (now used as a salad bar) and an old cello. The food is good, although not outstanding, and main dishes range from Rs 60 to Rs 150.

For really cheap eating there are stalls that set up in the evening on the south side of the Jama Masjid. They really only serve fried fish, fried chicken or mutton kebabs, accompanied by roomali roti. It's fairly chaotic but you can eat well here for Rs 30. Around the corner, Matya Mahal is buzzing with activity until midnight, helped in part by more street stalls selling ice creams, sweets and fruit.

If you have a liking for Indian sweets, you can't go past *Ghantewala*, near the Sisganj Gurdwara on Chandni Chowk. This place has been running for over 200 years and is reputed to have some of the best Indian sweets in Delhi.

South Delhi

There are a few good eating options in the area south of Connaught Place, but you'll need transport to get to most of them.

Defence Colony Market Defence Colony is one of the upmarket residential suburbs in south Delhi. The restaurants at the market here draw middle-class Delhi-wallahs and their families in numbers, especially on weekends.

Colonel's Kababz (☎ 462-4384) is a very popular kebab, tandoori and seafood place with tables upstairs, although most diners eat at the tables set up outside or remain in their cars and get served by scurrying waiters!

Next door is the *Arabian Nites*, a fast-food place with a limited range of Middle Eastern snacks – doner kebabs (Rs 35) and felafel ((Rs 20), as well as rotisserie chicken.

The *Sagar* (☎ 461-7832) here offers what is reckoned to be the best south Indian food in Delhi, and on weekends the queue to get in can be 20 metres long! The food is very cheap, with thalis at just Rs 25.

Moët's (☎ 463-5280) is a popular place offering a few choices, the most popular being the restaurant on the top floor where there is live music nightly (except Tuesday), so booking is advisable. On the 1st floor the food is Chinese, while on the ground and lower floor it's Mughlai cuisine. There's a small bar on the lower level but it's smoky and the noisy masala movies do nothing for the ambience.

Hauz Khas Village In trendy Hauz Khas is the Village Bistro (☎ 685-3857), a three-storey restaurant complex incorporating a number of eating places. While it's hardly a gastronomic paradise, the concept is good and the views over the illuminated Hauz Khas monuments in the evenings are superb. For this reason it's best to stick to the two top-floor, open-air restaurants: the *Golconda* (☎ 685-2226) features spicy Hyderabadi cuisine and live *ghazal* music, with main dishes in the Rs 120 to Rs 150 range, and the adjacent *Top of the Village* restaurant has a tandoori and tawa barbecue and live jazz from 9 pm. Both these places are open only in the evening.

On the ground floor is *Al Capone*, a very Indian Italian and continental restaurant with Rajasthani decor! Dishes on offer include pasta (Rs 75 to Rs 90) and chicken steaks, and there's a small salad bar. The *Great Wall of the Village* is a reasonably cheap Chinese restaurant, with main dishes from Rs 85 to Rs 115.

Indian restaurants in this complex include the *Mohalla, Dakshin* (south Indian vegetarian) and the *Khas Bagh*, which has live sitar music.

There is also a handful of independent restaurants in Hauz Khas. One of the classiest is the *Mezze Khana*, where the emphasis is on Swiss, French and Italian food. The atmosphere is intimate, the food excellent and the prices not too extravagant. Dishes include European specialities such as cheese fondue (Rs 360 for two), ravioli (Rs 150), rosti (Rs 65), gnocchi and crêpes.

Duke's Place is an Italian restaurant with live jazz on Wednesday, Friday and Saturday nights from 9 pm.

Elsewhere If you happen to be driving late at night and are in need of a snack, head for the *Alkauzer* (☎ 301-5183) kebab stall on Kautilya Marg in Chanakyapuri. This popular little place draws night-owls from all over south Delhi, who come here for the kakori kebabs, which are made from finely ground mince. You can sit in your car and be served, or sit at the tables set up on the footpath. The stall opens only in the evening, from 6 pm to midnight.

In the swish Santushti Shopping Centre (see the Things to Buy section), also in Chanakyapuri, the *Basil & Thyme* (☎ 688-7179) is Delhi's place to be 'seen' – the swish of expensive silk saris and glitter of gold jewellery, high prices and excellent service; the food is straightforward and very good, but perhaps somewhat overrated.

The Pandara Rd Market, south of India Gate, also has a couple of possibilities, including the *Have More* (☎ 38-7070), which does home deliveries, and the *Gulati* (☎ 38-5559), which specialises in north Indian food and is moderately priced. Also here is the *Ichiban* (☎ 38-6689), featuring Chinese and Japanese dishes. A meal for two would cost about Rs 150.

Dilli Haat (☎ 611-9055) on Aurobindo Marg near the Ring Rd is an open-air food and crafts market operated by Delhi Tourism. Although it has great potential, it's not wildly exciting and is poorly patronised. There are a number of kiosks offering food from all parts of the country – Sikkim, the North East states, Kerala, Himachal Pradesh, Tamil Nadu and Kashmir. It's open daily from 11 am to 9 pm and entry is Rs 3.

In Friends Colony, a suburb in the south-eastern part of the city, is the excellent *Lotus Pond* (☎ 684-9101), a restaurant which serves authentic Chinese dishes at very moderate prices. The ginger chilli prawns are sensational, and also worth trying is the shredded lamb in hot garlic sauce. The restaurant is close to the Surya Sofitel hotel.

International Hotels

Many Delhi residents reckon that the best food in the capital is at the upmarket hotels.

Maurya Sheraton (☎ 301-0136) The Sheraton's *Bukhara* is widely regarded as the city's best Indian restaurant. It has many Central Asian specialities, including tandoori cooking and dishes from the Peshawar region in north-west Pakistan. This is a place for big meat eaters and you can expect to pay around Rs 350 to Rs 500 for a main course.

Khari Baoli, Delhi's wholesale spice market (HF)

Another restaurant here is the formal *Dum Phukt*, named after a cuisine first invented by the nawabs of Avadh (Lucknow) around 300 years ago. It involves the dishes being covered by a pastry cap, so the food is cooked by steaming as much as anything else. It's quite distinctive and absolutely superb; you'd be looking at around Rs 1500 for two, plus drinks.

The *Shatranj* cafe here does a good value buffet lunch for Rs 300 plus tax, and the featured cuisine changes daily.

Hotel Claridges (☎ 301-0211) This older-style hotel has a few unusual theme restaurants: the *Dhaba* offers 'rugged roadside' cuisine and is set up like a typical roadside cafe complete with half a Tata truck! (main dishes Rs 110 to Rs 170); the *Jade Garden* serves Chinese food in a bamboo grove setting; *Pickwicks* offers Western food and the decor is 19th-century England (Rs 110 to Rs 140); and the open-air *Corbetts* gets its inspiration from Jim Corbett of man-eating tiger fame, and so has a hunting camp theme complete with recorded jungle sounds – and plenty of real mosquitoes. As might be expected, meat features prominently on the menu, and main dishes are around Rs 100.

Taj Mahal Hotel (☎ 301-0162) The *House of Ming* is a popular Sichuan and Cantonese Chinese restaurant, with seafood from Rs 300 to Rs 1700 (!), and other dishes such as chicken or pork for a mere Rs 200. The *Haveli* is one of the city's best Indian restaurants. It serves an excellent range of dishes for Rs 150 to Rs 350, specialities include raan-e-haveli (marinated lamb) and reshmi kebab, which are spiced with cumin and saffron (Rs 240). There's also live Indian music and dancing from 8.30 pm.

On the top floor, with excellent views over Delhi's green suburbs, is the *Casa Medici*, which has an excellent Italian buffet at lunchtime for Rs 460, complete with piano accompaniment, and a la carte in the evening with a live band. Main dishes here range from Rs 200 for pasta to Rs 300 to Rs 500 for seafood.

The *Captain's Cabin* is primarily a bar, but it also serves fairly substantial meals such as steaks (Rs 265) and flambé chicken (Rs 265).

For late-nighters, the *Machan* is a 24-hour restaurant with meals and snacks such as pasta and steaks from Rs 125; beers are Rs 125.

Hotel Oberoi (☎ 436-3030) The Oberoi has the *Baan Thai* on the lower ground floor, serving superb Thai food.

La Rochelle is the hotel's speciality French restaurant, with a sumptuous lunchtime buffet for Rs 420 plus tax. The a la carte menu features dishes such as pan-fried duck (Rs 440), smoked chicken (Rs 370), seafood, flambé steak (Rs 380) and venison (Rs 380).

The 24-hour *Palms* cafe has a full-on, bells and whistles breakfast for Rs 250, or south Indian breakfast dishes such as idlis and dosas. After 11 am the menu switches to snacks and meals such as fish & chips (Rs 155) and steak (Rs 145), or more interesting Indian food such as chicken tikka masala (Rs 170).

In addition, there is an Indian and a Chinese restaurant (the *Kandahar* and *Taipan*, respectively) and *The Connaught*, a rooftop bar with live music and dancing in the evening.

Le Meridien (☎ 371-0101) Yes, more choices. Pick of the bunch here is *Pierre*, and no prizes for guessing what cuisine is featured. Flambés are flambéed at your table (Rs 275 to Rs 425); other dishes which stand out include duck (Rs 325), trout (Rs 425) and steak (Rs 625), as well as cheese fondue (Rs 675 for two).

La Belvedere, hanging dramatically over a 20-floor chasm, has live music in the evenings and continental cuisine. If you'd prefer being closer to terra firma there's the 24-hour *La Brasserie* coffee shop on the ground floor.

The Meridien's *Golden Phoenix* is one of the city's best Chinese restaurants, featuring Sichuan and Cantonese cooking. Main dishes are reasonably priced at around Rs 250, although if you're feeling flush there's abalone for Rs 850.

To round it off, the *Pakwan* is an Indian restaurant, with thalis for Rs 300 and other main dishes at Rs 100 to Rs 200.

Holiday Inn Crowne Plaza (☎ 332-0101) Not to be outdone, the Holiday Inn also has a full range of top-notch restaurants. The *Silk Orchid* on the 28th floor has stunning views and features Thai cuisine at Rs 150 to Rs 200 for a main course; there's live music from 9 pm. On the same floor there's the *Grill Room*, where meat eaters can indulge themselves in a big way.

At the *Noble House* Chinese restaurant you can dine relatively modestly on duck (Rs 225), seafood (Rs 380) or steak (Rs 160). The *Baluchi* is an Indian restaurant where the emphasis is on tandoori cooking (main dishes around Rs 200).

You can get a pretty good buffet lunch or dinner for Rs 407 including taxes at the hotel's 24-hour *Rendezvous Cafe* on the ground floor. There's also a wide range of a la carte items.

Park Hotel The Park Hotel, on Sansad Marg near Connaught Place, has a good buffet breakfast at Rs 125, but the service is diabolically bad.

Other Hotels Several cheaper hotels have noted vegetarian restaurants. Thalis at *Dasaprakash* (☎ 469-4966) in the Ambassador Hotel are good value at Rs 110.

The Lodhi Hotel, in south Delhi, is also noted for the vegetarian thalis at its *Woodlands Restaurant* (☎ 436-2422).

The old Imperial Hotel on Janpath is great for an al fresco breakfast (Rs 135) in the casual *Garden Party*.

Entertainment

CINEMAS

For films there are a number of cinemas around Connaught Place, such as the *Regal*, the *Odeon* and the *Plaza*, and the fare is typically Hindi mass-appeal movies.

For something a little more cerebral, the *British Council* (☎ 371-0111) on Kasturba Gandhi Marg often screens good foreign films.

DANCE & THEATRE

The best sources for listings of current performance events are the magazine *First City*, the small tourist-guide booklets such as *Delhi Diary* and the main newspapers such as the *Hindustan Times*.

A classical Indian dancer (HF)

Classical Indian dances are held each evening at 6.45 pm at the *Parsi Anjuman Hall* (☎ 331-7831) on Bahadur Shah Zafar Marg, opposite Ambedkar Stadium.

Theatres & Auditoriums

Most of the performing arts centres are situated around Copernicus Marg at the end of Barakhamba Rd, not far from Connaught Place, in an area known as Mandi House, which is actually the name of Doordarshan's headquarters on Barakhamba Rd.

The *Shri Ram Centre* (☎ 371-4307) has a major auditorium which stages dance and theatre performances. At the rear of the centre, on Tansen Marg, is the *Triveni Kala Sangam* (☎ 371-8833), a centre for the study of dance, art and music. There's also an extensive library, the Triveni Chamber Theatre, the outdoor Triveni Garden Theatre, the Triveni Sculpture Court, the Shridharani Gallery and a small bookshop specialising in dance and art.

Close by is Bhawalpur House on Bhagwan Das Rd, which houses the *National School of Drama* (☎ 38-2821) and the *Kathak Kendra* (☎ 38-5065), both of which often have live performances.

In the same area is Rabindra Bhavan, and here you'll find academies of the performing arts (*Sangeet Natak Akademi*, ☎ 38-7246), literature (*Sahitya Akademi*, ☎ 38-6626) and fine arts and sculpture (*Lalit Kala Akademi*, ☎ 38-7243), which has displays of contemporary art. Also here is the *National School of Drama Repertory Company* (☎ 38-3420).

Next door, at 1 Copernicus Marg, is the *Kamani Auditorium* (☎ 38-8084), which is part of the *Shriram Bharatiya Kala Kendra* (☎ 38-6428) and another important performing arts venue. Next door again is the *LTG Auditorium*.

Sapru House on Barakhamba Rd is an institution devoted to the study of people of the world and has a good library.

DISCOS

Delhi's strict licensing laws certainly don't help its night life scene. Discos are basically limited to the five-star hotels and are quite exclusive. Entry is generally restricted to members and hotel guests, although outside couples and women stand a better chance of being admitted than unaccompanied men. Expect to pay a cover charge of about Rs 300, and once inside the drink prices are sky high.

The main discos in Delhi include *CJ's* at Le Meridien, *Ghungroo* at the Maurya Sheraton and *My Kind of Place* at the Taj Palace. The two most popular are probably the *Oasis* at the Hyatt Regency and *Annabelles* at the Holiday Inn Crowne Plaza.

BARS

The discos are also limited to the five-star hotels. The *Jazz Bar* at the Maurya Sheraton is very good, with live jazz each evening, but drinks are expensive: beers are Rs 170! *The Connaught* at the Oberoi is a classy roof-top bar with live music and dancing from 8 pm to midnight.

Cheaper bars include those at the *Marina* and *Alka* hotels in Connaught Place; however, probably the best bar in this area (although that's not saying much) is *Pegasus* at Nirula's on L Block.

SPECTATOR SPORTS

Horse Racing

The *Delhi Racecourse* is on Kamal Ataturk Marg, just north of the Safdarjang Airport.

Gambling is a popular pastime among the wealthy, and so the events held here are well patronised. Meetings are held on Monday only, and the season runs from October to April.

On other days you may well see big crowds gathering here, but this is only for 'intervenue' betting, that is, betting on races at other venues.

Cricket

The Indian passion for cricket is well known, and it's worth going along to a game to see not only players but spectators in action. The *Ferozshah Stadium*, on Bahadur Shah Zafar Marg just north of Feroz Shah Kotla, is the venue for Test matches.

The *Nehru Stadium* in south Delhi was built for the Asian Games in 1982. It has a crowd capacity of 75,000 and it's here that the popular international one-day matches are held.

Hockey & Soccer

The *National Stadium* at the eastern end of Rajpath is the city's main soccer and hockey venue.

Shopping

The shopping possibilities in Delhi are excellent, the best thing being that you can find almost anything from anywhere in India.

HANDICRAFTS

Two good places to start are in New Delhi, near Connaught Place. The *Central Cottage Industries Emporium* is on the corner of Janpath and Tolstoy Marg. In this building you will find six floors of handicraft items from all over India, generally of good quality and reasonably priced. Whether it's woodcarvings, brassware, paintings, clothes, textiles or furniture, you'll find it here. Although it's not the cheapest place to shop, the prices are fixed at a reasonable level and the quality of the goods is among the best you'll find. It's open Monday to Saturday from 10 am to 6 pm.

Along Baba Kharak Singh Marg, two streets round from Janpath, are the various *state emporiums* run by the state governments. These are similar to the Central Cottage Industries Emporium, except that each displays and sells handicrafts from its own state. The Rajasthan emporium is probably the best; the Delhi emporium has bits and pieces from all over the place.

There are many other shops around Connaught Place and Janpath. Along Janpath outside the Imperial Hotel are a number of permanent stalls and small shops which line the pavement and are known as the *Tibetan Market*. These are run by Tibetan refugees and rapacious Kashmiris selling carpets, jewellery and many (often instant) antiques. On the same side of the road, closer to Connaught Place, is a similar line of handicraft and souvenir shops known as *Janpath Market*.

Also worth checking out is the supposedly air-con *Palika Bazaar*. This utterly confusing underground market with its 400-odd shops is in the centre of Connaught Place. There are plenty of shops here selling cheap leather goods and other handicrafts, but the emphasis is more on cheap consumer goods.

The Chatta Chowk just inside the main gate of the *Red Fort* is lined with souvenir shops overflowing with crafts and souvenirs, much of it tacky and extremely tasteless. Prices are generally way over the top, a reflection of the fact that even the briefest package tour to Delhi brings its punters through here.

A Warning to Shoppers

When shopping for handicrafts take extreme care with the commission merchants – these guys hang around waiting to pick you up and cart you off to their favourite dealers where whatever you pay will have a hefty margin built into it to pay their commission. Stories about 'my family's place', 'my brother's shop' or 'special deal at my friend's place' are just stories and nothing more.

Whatever you might be told, if you are taken to a place, be it a hotel, craft shop, market or even restaurant, by a rickshaw driver or tout, the price you pay will be inflated. This can be by as much as 50%, so try to visit these places on your own. And don't underestimate the persistence of these guys. The high-pressure sales technique of both the runners and the owners is among the best in the world. Should you get up and leave without buying anything, the feigned anger is just that. Next time you turn up (alone), it will be all smiles – and the prices will have dropped dramatically.

Another trap which many foreigners fall into occurs when buying with a credit card. You may well be told that if you buy the goods, the merchant won't forward the credit slip for payment until you have received the goods, even if it is in three months' time – this is total nonsense. No trader will be sending you as much as a postcard until he or she has received the money, in full, for the goods you are buying. What you'll find, in fact, is that within 48 hours of your signing the credit slip, the merchant's account will have been credited.

Also beware of any shop which takes your credit card out the back and returns with the slip for you to sign. It has

Antiques for sale at Sunder Nagar market. (HF)

happened that, while out of sight, the vendor has imprinted a few more forms, forged the buyer's signature and billed them for items they hadn't purchased. Get them to fill out the slip right in front of you.

Be careful when buying items which include delivery to your home country. You may well be given assurances that the price includes home delivery and all customs and handling charges. Often this is not the case, and you may find yourself having to collect the item yourself from your country's main port or airport and to pay customs charges (which could be as much as 20% of the item's value) and handling charges levied by the airline or shipping company (up to 10% of the value). If you can't collect the item promptly, or get someone to do it on your behalf, storage charges may also be charged.

If you believe any stories about buying anything in India to sell at a profit elsewhere, you'll simply be proving (once again) that old adage about separating fools from their money! Precious stones and carpets are favourites for this game. They'll tell you that you can sell the items in Australia, Europe or the USA for several times the purchase price, and will even give you the (often imaginary!) addresses of dealers who will buy them. You'll also be shown written statements, supposedly from other travellers, documenting the money they have supposedly made – it's all a scam. The stones or carpets you buy may be worth only a fraction of what you pay. Don't let greed cloud your judgement.

While it is certainly a minority of traders who are actually involved in dishonest schemes, virtually all are involved in the commission racket, so you need to shop with care – take your time, be firm and bargain hard. Good luck! ■

Terracotta items at Dilli Haat market in south Delhi (HF)

In south Delhi on Aurobindo Marg near the Ring Rd is *Dilli Haat*, an open-air food and crafts market operated by Delhi Tourism. It's poorly promoted and therefore poorly patronised, but there are a number of interesting stalls selling a variety of crafts. Although it doesn't merit a special trip, it's worth a look if you happen to be in the area. It is open daily from 11 am to 9 pm.

The cardinal rule when purchasing handicrafts in Delhi is to bargain and bargain hard, although this doesn't apply at the government emporiums where prices are fixed.

Carpets

It may not surprise you that India produces and exports more hand-crafted carpets than Iran, but it probably is more of a surprise that some of them are of virtually equal quality. In Kashmir, where India's best carpets are produced, the carpet-making techniques and styles were brought from Persia even before the Mughal era. The art flourished under the Mughals and today Kashmir is packed with small carpet producers. There are many carpet dealers in Delhi, as well as in Kashmir. Persian motifs have been much embellished on Kashmiri carpets, which come in a variety of sizes – three by five feet, four by six feet and so on. They are either made of pure wool, wool with a small percentage of silk to give a sheen (known as silk touch) or pure silk. The latter are more for decoration than hard wear. Expect to pay from Rs 5000 for a good quality four-by-six carpet and don't be surprised if the price is more than twice as high.

Other carpet-making areas include Badhoi and Mirzapur in Uttar Pradesh or Warangal and Eluru in Andhra Pradesh. In Kashmir and Rajasthan, the coarsely woven woollen *numdas* are made. These are more primitive and folksy than the fine carpets. Around the Himalaya and Uttar Pradesh *dhurries*, flatweave cotton warp-and-weft rugs, are woven. In Kashmir *gabbas*, appliqué-like rugs, are made.

The many Tibetan refugees in India have brought their craft of making superbly colourful Tibetan rugs with them. A three-by-five Tibetan rug will be less than Rs 1000. Tibet House is a good place to buy.

Unless you're an expert it is best to have expert advice or buy from a reputable dealer if you're spending large amounts of money on carpets. Check prices back home too; many Western carpet dealers sell at prices you would have difficulty matching even at the source.

Some reputable places to purchase carpets include:

Central Cottage Industries Emporium, Janpath, New Delhi
Cashmeir Gallerie, Hauz Khas Village, south Delhi (☎ 685-4503)
Shikara, Hauz Khas Village, south Delhi (☎ 685-1220)
Tibet House, 16 Jor Bagh, Lodi Rd, south Delhi

Metalwork

Copper and brass items are popular and cheap. Candle-holders, trays, bowls, tankards and ashtrays are made in Bombay and other centres. In Rajasthan and Uttar Pradesh the brass is inlaid with exquisite designs in red, green and blue enamel. *Bidri* is a craft of north-eastern Karnataka and Andhra Pradesh, where silver is inlaid into gunmetal. Hookah pipes, lamp bases and jewellery boxes are made in this manner.

The best place for bidri is the *Central Cottage Industries Emporium*. The *Sunder Nagar Market* (see Antiques below) is also worth checking out.

Jewellery

Many Indian women put most of their wealth into jewellery, so it is no wonder that so much of it is available. For Western tastes the heavy folk-art jewellery of Rajasthan has particular appeal. It's widely available in Delhi at handicraft shops around Connaught Place.

For more upmarket silver and gold jewellery there are a number of expensive shops around Connaught Place and south Delhi. In Old Delhi, the street called Dariba Kalan is the old city's traditional jewellery market. The shopping arcades of the five-star hotels are another place to find top-quality fashion jewellery, with prices to match.

Leatherwork

Of course Indian leatherwork is not made from cow-hide but from buffalo-hide, camel, goat or some other substitute. *Chappals*, those basic sandals found all over India, are the most popular purchase. In craft shops in Delhi you can find well-made leather bags, handbags and other items. Leather jackets are another popular buy, but check the workmanship very carefully.

Palika Bazaar and *Janpath Market* are two good places for leatherwork.

Woodcarving

In the south, images of the gods are carved out of san-dalwood. Rosewood is used to carve animals – elephants

Top : Colourful woodcarving of an Indian Guard (GB)
Bottom : Dolls can be purchased in handicraft shops. (GE)

Top : A woodcarving of a traditional musician (GB)
Bottom : Folk-art jewellery is widely available. (HF)

in particular. Carved wooden furniture and other household items, either in natural finish or lacquered, are also made in various locations. In Kashmir intricately carved wooden screens, tables, jewellery boxes, trays and the like are carved from Indian walnut. They follow a similar pattern to that seen on the decorative trim of houseboats. Old temple carvings can be delightful. Again, the government emporiums are good places to start, but handicraft shops also usually stock wooden items.

ANTIQUES

Articles over 100 years old are not allowed to be exported from India without an export clearance certificate. If you have doubts about any item and think it could be defined as an antique, you can check with the Director of Antiquities, Archaeological Survey of India, Janpath.

Just south of the Purana Qila on Mathura Rd and across from the Hotel Oberoi New Delhi, is the *Sunder Nagar Market*, a collection of shops selling antiques, jewellery and brassware. The prices may be high but you'll find fascinating and high quality artefacts.

MUSIC

Musical Instruments

Indian musical instruments always have an attraction for travellers, and Delhi has a good range of specialist shops.

Bina Enterprises, 3578 Netaji Subhash Rd, Daria Ganj, Old Delhi (☎ 463-3075)
Delhi Musical Stores, 1070 Paiwalan, opposite Jama Masjid, Old Delhi (☎ 327-6909)
Rangarsons Music Depot, 12 K Block, Outer Circle, Connaught Place, New Delhi (☎ 332-3831)

Recorded Music

There are plenty of shops selling a wide variety of recorded Indian music. Most of it is on cassette, but CDs are becoming more widely available.

Dass Studios, 12 F Block, Connaught Place, New Delhi (☎ 331-0751)
The Music Shop, 18 Khan Market, Old Delhi (☎ 461-8464)
Rhythm Corner, E-3 South Extension II, south Delhi (☎ 644-7736)

PAINTINGS & SCULPTURE

Reproductions of the beautiful old miniatures are painted in many places, but beware of paintings claimed to be antique; it's highly unlikely that they are. Also note that quality can vary widely; low prices often mean low quality and if you buy before you've had a chance to look at a lot of miniatures and develop some appreciation, you'll inevitably find you have bought unwisely.

There are also a number of galleries specialising in contemporary works.

Anamica, Hauz Khas Village, south Delhi (☎ 696-7619)
Art Today, A Block, Connaught Place, New Delhi
City Art Gallery, Hauz Khas Village, south Delhi (☎ 643-2659)
Dhoomi Mai Art Gallery & Sculpture Court, 8 A Block, Connaught Place, New Delhi (☎ 332-4492)
Kumar Gallery, Sunder Nagar Market, New Delhi (☎ 461-1113)
Poonam Bakliwal, Sunder Nagar Market, New Delhi (☎ 461-1835)
Village Gallery, Hauz Khas Village, south Delhi (☎ 685-3860)

PERFUMES & ESSENTIAL OILS

You can find an interesting variety of perfumes, oils, soaps and incense at two places (both signposted) on *Main Bazaar* in Paharganj, one near the Hotel Vivek and another near the Camran Lodge.

Other areas worth looking in are *Meena Bazaar* near the Jama Masjid, and *Palika Bazaar*.

SILKS & SARIS

Silk is cheap and the quality is often excellent. If you are buying a silk sari, it helps to know a bit about both the silk and the sari. Saris are 5.5 metres long, unless they have an attached blouse (*choli*), in which case they are six metres. Sari silk is graded and sold by weight – in grams per metre. Soft plain silk up to 60 grams per metre costs Rs 3.20 per gram; chiffon silk of 20 grams per metre is Rs 4.50 per gram, but you'll be lucky to find a printed chiffon sari for less than Rs 600. A thin Kanchipuram silk sari weighs around 400 grams, a heavy sari around 600 grams.

Silk is found in shops throughout Delhi. These two stores are good places to start.

Central Cottage Industries Emporium, Janpath, New Delhi
Handloom House, 9 A-Block Connaught Place, New Delhi (☎ 332-3057)

TEA

It's possible to buy quality tea in bulk from the shops in Khari Baoli in Old Delhi – best quality Darjeeling sells for Rs 500 per kg.

There are a couple of specialist tea-tasting and sales salons where you can taste all the best teas, but you'll pay top dollar if you want to buy.

Aap ki Pasand, 15 Netaji Subhash Marg, Darya Ganj, Old Delhi
Kho-Cha Darjeeling Tea Bureau, 11 Kakanagar Market
  (☎ 463-2755)
Golden Tips Tea Co, 1 Kakanagar Market (☎ 462-2442)

Rajasthani women selling colourful embroidered fabric at a pavement market, Janpath (HF)

TEXTILES & CLOTHES

This is still India's major industry and 40% of the total production is at the village level where it is known as *khadi*. The government khadi emporium (*Khadi Gramodyog Bhavan*) at Connaught Place is a good place to buy handmade items of homespun cloth, such as the popular 'Nehru jackets' and the *kurta pajama*. Bedspreads, tablecloths, cushion covers or material for clothes are other popular khadi purchases.

Opposite the Ashok Hotel in Chanakyapuri is the *Santushti Shopping Centre*, which is just inside the gate of the New Wellington airforce camp! There's a string of

The traditional art of henna painting is a novelty for tourists. (AP)

small upmarket boutiques here with a good range of clothes (and crafts) and high prices to match.

Hauz Khas Village in south Delhi has become a very interesting little shopping enclave, with a number of boutiques selling designer gear.

Anokhi, Santushti Shopping Centre, south Delhi
Handloom House, 9 A-Block, Connaught Place, New Delhi
   (☎ 332-3057)
Shyam Ahuja, Santushti Shopping Centre, south Delhi
Vastra, Hauz Khas Village, south Delhi

MARKETS, BAZAARS & SHOPPING CENTRES

Old Delhi

The colourful bazaars of Old Delhi are great for browsing, even if you're not in the market for anything specific. As is the case in most Asian cities, shops specialising in one particular product or trade are concentrated in one area, which means the competition is intense and prices are kept low.

Residents of New Delhi tend to keep their forays into Old Delhi to a minimum, as it's impossible to park the car close by and the noise and congestion is much greater than what they're used to. Nevertheless, they still come, especially for food and household items, simply because the prices and variety are the best in the city.

Bhagirath Palace This is the market for electrical and goods and pharmaceuticals. It's just north of Chandni Chowk at its eastern end, near the former mansion of Begum Samru.

Car Parts Bazaar If you need a new door, horn or anything else for your Maruti or Ambassador this bazaar is concentrated in the lanes around the south-western corner of the Jama Masjid – check out the tree adorned with lights and gauges in the middle of the road, and the Abid Shocker Expert shop against the western wall of the mosque.

Chor Bazaar This huge weekly market, which translates as Thieves Market, takes place each Sunday outside the eastern wall of the Red Fort, between it and the Ring Rd. There are hundreds of stalls selling all sorts of new and second-hand junk, and the story goes that this is where you come to buy back your hubcap stolen earlier in the week.

Dariba Kalan Dariba Kalan, or 'street of the incomparable pearl', off Chandni Chowk has been Old Delhi's gold, silver and jewellery market since the time of Shah Jahan. It's all very low-key, and the jewellery is sold by weight.

Khari Baoli This incredibly busy street runs west from the Fatehpuri Mosque on Chandni Chowk to Lahori Gate at the western edge of the old city, although the gate itself no longer exists. It is the city's wholesale spice market and is the place to come for spices, herbs, pickles, nuts, dried fruit, tea – and soap!

Shopping in Khari Baoli

The sights and smells of the wholesale spice market make it *the* place to shop for herbs, spices and dried fruit and nuts. This is definitely not a tourist market, though, so you need to know the Hindi names for the spices you wish to buy. The following list may help.

Herbs & Spices

Aniseed	*sonf*	Garlic	*lasan*
Basil	*tulsi*	Ginger	*adrak*
Bay leaf	*tejpatta*	Lemon grass	*sera*
Cardamom	*elaichi*	Lime	*nimbu*
Chillies:		Mace	*javatri*
red	*lal mirch*	Mint	*podina*
green	*sabz mirch*	Mustard seeds	*rai*
Cinnamon	*darchini*	Nutmeg	*jaiphal*
Cloves	*laung*	Onion	*peeaaz*
Coriander		Pepper	*kali mirch*
seeds	*dhania*	Poppy seeds	*khas khas*
leaves	*dhania sabz*	Saffron	*kesar*
Cumin	*jeera*	Sesame seeds	*til*
Curry leaves	*kitha neem*	Tamarind	*imli*
Fennel	*sonf*	Turmeric	*haldi*
Fenugreek	*methi*		

Dried Fruit & Nuts

Almonds	*badam*
Cashew nuts	*kaju*
Pistachios	*pista*
Raisins	*kishmish*
Sultanas	*munaca* ∎

Pavement shoe repair (HF)

Kinari Bazaar This small but very colourful street runs off Dariba Kalan. The shops here specialise in festival and wedding paraphernalia, including rupee-note garlands, costume jewellery, hair braids, rosettes and tinsel.

Meena Bazaar The crowded Meena Bazaar hugs the eastern edge of the Jama Masjid. This largely Muslim market really comes alive on Sundays, at other times it's just comfortably crowded. The atmosphere here is quite different from other markets in Old Delhi, as are many of the items on sale – burkhas, mosque caps, colourful calligraphic Koran verses and pictures of Muslim holy places such as Mecca, but also places closer to home such as the shrine of Hazrat Nizam-ud-din in south Delhi.

Sadar Bazaar The wholesale market for household goods is across the railway line west of Lahori Gate. Although the street is quite wide it's still incredibly congested. This is the place to come for everything from a bunch of plastic flowers to a kg of saucepans!

Gauges, dials and dashboard specialist, Car Parts Bazaar (HF)

New Delhi

Connaught Place This is the commercial heart of Delhi and has the greatest concentration of upmarket shops, as well as all the major banks and most of the airlines.

Paharganj North of Connaught Place close to New Delhi Railway Station is the Main Bazaar in Paharganj. In recent years this has become a popular place to buy household goods. With the increasing numbers of foreigners staying in the area, however, shops catering more specifically to tourists have also sprung up.

Khan Market About half a km south of India Gate is Khan Market, a small shopping centre very popular with expats. There are a number of good bookshops, as well as general provision and household goods stores. There are also a couple of mid-range restaurants, but they're not wildly exciting.

Sunder Nagar Just off Mathura Rd south of the zoo is the small cluster of shops known as the Sunder Nagar market. The speciality here is antiques and second-hand goods. There are about half a dozen shops here crammed full of goods and the pavements are piled high with old wooden chests and other furniture. While you're unlikely to find any real bargains, there's enough of interest here to make browsing worthwhile.

South Delhi

The shopping centres in the newer suburbs of south Delhi are becoming increasingly sophisticated.

Defence Colony The popular Defence Colony market has one of the highest concentrations of restaurants in south Delhi, but also has a range of other shops, including a couple of good greengrocers.

South Extension The rapidly growing South Extension market straddles the Ring Rd. It has become one of the most fashionable in the district and so has an excellent range of shops selling quality goods, especially clothes.

INA The Indian National Army (INA) market is on Aurobindo Marg just north of the Ring Rd. This is south Delhi's main food and produce market. It stocks fresh seafood as well as meat, vegetables and fruit. There are also sections devoted to groceries and textiles.

Hauz Khas Village Designer boutiques, galleries and upmarket restaurants are the feature of this exclusive little enclave in Hauz Khas. While prices are definitely on the high side, there's some really imaginative stuff for sale here.

The Village Bistro restaurant complex (see Places to Eat) is worth a visit in the evenings when you can sit on the rooftop terrace and gaze out over the illuminated 14th-century ruins of Hauz Khas.

Nehru Place The half dozen or so multi-storey office blocks of Nehru Place near the Bahai House of Worship are something of an urban disaster. The paved, pedestrian plaza-type area between the buildings has a decidedly shabby and rundown feel. Nevertheless, the huge Skylark Building here is Delhi's computer centre; virtually every shop on the 1st floor deals in some aspect of the computer industry. Ask discreetly and you'll unearth shops selling pirated versions of just about any software package you care to name.

Santushti Shopping Centre In the somewhat unusual setting of the Willingdon Airforce Camp is this modern little shopping complex, which consists of a number of small units set in a well-maintained garden. It is run by the airforce officers' wives and includes a number of interesting boutiques and an exclusive restaurant, Basil & Thyme (see Places to Eat). It is just inside the gates of the airforce camp, close to the Ashok Hotel in Chanakyapuri.

Excursions

There are a number of places in the vicinity of Delhi which make worthwhile excursions.

Badhkal Lake and **Sohna**, both in Haryana state, are to some extent popular with Delhi-ites simply because they offer cheap liquor (the taxes in Haryana are much lower than in Delhi). For this reason they have a slightly sleazy atmosphere but still make a pleasant escape from the city, although you'll need your own transport to get to them.

Further afield are two of the most popular tourism destinations in the country, both of them within striking distance of Delhi. **Agra**, with the incomparable Taj Mahal, is only 200 km south-west of Delhi, while **Jaipur**, a city full of Rajasthani colour, is 300 km to the southwest. Both cities have excellent rail connections with Delhi and can be visited on day trips, although an overnight (or longer) stay is recommended. There are also good rail links between Jaipur and Agra, so a triangular tour of the three cities is a popular option.

The Palace of Jodh Bai at Fatehpur Sikri (BT)

BADHKAL LAKE

The small Badhkal Lake lies in somewhat stark country-side 32 km south of Delhi. While it's hardly Lake Geneva, it's a pleasant enough spot and is popular with day-trippers.

To get out on to the lake itself you can hire four-seater pedal-boats at Rs 40 per half hour; eight-seater row boats are only available with an oarsman, who'll take you out for a quick 20-minute spin for Rs 60.

Other activities include pony and camel rides along the top of the embankment which forms one side of the lake, and there's a gloomy sauna, massage and swimming complex.

Man from Jaipur (GE)

Places to Stay & Eat

Haryana Tourism runs the unexciting *Badhkal Lake Motel* (☎ 821-6901), where the cheapest rooms are Rs 450 for a double, or Rs 500 with TV.

Also run by Haryana Tourism is the air-con *Mayur Restaurant*, which is patronised mainly, it seems, for the cheap beer, although the food is not bad.

SOHNA

Sohna is a small village in Haryana state, 56 km south of Delhi. There's very little to do here, the main attraction once again being the cheap alcohol. Haryana Tourism has a very pleasant resort on the hill overlooking the town, and this is a popular weekend get-away for Delhi residents.

Places to Stay

The *Hotel Barbet* (☎ (01249) 2133) is set in a large, verdant garden with sweeping views over the surrounding countryside. Accommodation is either in good air-con rooms at Rs 400 or in the somewhat rough and ready cabins in the gardens which cost Rs 200. The latter seem to be used mostly by the hour by respectable Delhi-wallahs as somewhere to entertain their girlfriends.

AGRA

Population: 1.05 million

Agra reached its peak at the time of the Mughals and its superb monuments date from that era. It has a magnificent fort and the building which many people come to India solely to see – the Taj Mahal.

Situated on the banks of the Yamuna River, Agra, with its crowded alleys and predatory rickshaw riders, is much like any other north Indian city, once you're away from its imposing Mughal monuments. It's possible to take a day trip to Agra from Delhi (an excellent train service makes this eminently practicable); however, Agra is worth more than a day's visit, particularly if you intend to visit, as you certainly should, the deserted city of Fatehpur Sikri. In any case, the Taj certainly deserves more than just a single visit if you want to appreciate how its appearance changes under different lights.

Orientation & Information

Agra is on the west bank of the Yamuna River, 204 km south of Delhi. The old part of the town, where you'll find the Kinari Bazaar (the main market place) in a narrow street, is north of the fort. The cantonment area to the south is the modern part of town, known as Sadar Bazaar. On The Mall is the Government of India tourist office (☎ 36-3377), GPO and poste restante. In this area you will also find handicraft shops, restaurants and many moderately priced hotels.

Agra's main railway station is Agra Cantonment; trains from New Delhi arrive here. The main bus station for cities in Rajasthan, Delhi and Fatehpur Sikri is Idgah. Buses going to Mathura leave from the Fort bus station. Agra airport is seven km out of town.

Commission, Touts & Rip-Offs Of all the cities in India, Agra is the city most seriously entangled in the nefarious activity of giving commission – it seems virtually everyone is into it. From the minute you step off the train or bus, there'll be a rickshaw driver wanting to take you to a hotel, to a handicraft shop or on a sightseeing tour. Some visitors find that all this rather mars their visit to Agra, but the persistence and tenacity of these touts is understandable – the commission they get from the handicraft shops can be as much as 20%.

If you're shopping in Agra, be ruthless, and read the warning in the Shopping chapter before stepping foot inside a shop.

Taj Mahal

If there's a building which represents a country – like the Eiffel Tower for France and the Sydney Opera House for Australia – then it has to be the Taj Mahal for India.

This most famous Mughal monument was constructed by emperor Shah Jahan in memory of his wife Mumtaz Mahal, Chosen of the Palace. It has been described as the most extravagant monument ever built for love, for the emperor was heartbroken when Mumtaz, to whom he had been married for 17 years, died in 1631 in childbirth, after producing 14 children.

Construction of the Taj began in the same year and was not completed until 1653. Workers were recruited not only from all over India but also from central Asia, and in total 20,000 people worked on the building. Experts were even brought from as far away as Europe – the Frenchman Austin of Bordeaux and the Italian

Veroneo of Venice had a hand in its decoration. The main architect was Isa Khan, who came from Shiraz in Iran.

In 1659 Shah Jahan was deposed by his son, Aurangzeb, and spent the rest of his life imprisoned in the Agra Fort, looking out along the river to the final resting place of his wife, although hardly missing her it seems – he was a lascivious old bastard and plenty of woman were supplied to satisfy his desires.

The Taj is definitely worth more than a single visit as its character changes with the differing lights during the day. Dawn is a magical time, and the Taj is virtually deserted. Friday tends to be impossibly crowded and

The majestic Taj Mahal in Agra (BT)

Detail of the Taj Mahal (BT)

noisy – not very conducive to calm enjoyment of this most serene of buildings.

The main entrance to the Taj is on the western side, open from 6 to 8 am, 8.30 am to 4 pm and 5 to 7 pm. Entry costs Rs 100 for the early morning and evening opening times, Rs 10.50 during the day. You can also enter through the south and east gates, but they're open only between 8.30 am and 5 pm. There's no entry charge on Friday.

The high red sandstone **entrance gateway** is inscribed with verses from the Koran in Arabic, but these days you only exit through here. The entrance is now through a small door to the right of the gate, where everyone has to undergo a security check. The policy on cameras – how close you can photograph the Taj and whether or not there's a charge – varies from year to year. If you are carrying a video camera (permit currently Rs 25), photography is only allowed from inside the main gate; once you have shot from there the camera must be deposited in one of the lockers at the desk inside the main gate.

The Taj Mahal itself stands on a raised marble platform on the northern edge of the ornamental gardens. Tall, purely decorative white **minarets** grace each corner

Taj Pollution Alert

Scientists fear that after centuries of undiminished glory the Taj may soon be irreparably damaged by the city's severe air pollution. From the Red Fort, a distance of only two km, it is often almost impossible to see the Taj through the cloud of smog and haze which envelops it.

The Mathura power station, less than 50 km upstream from the Taj, dumps a tonne of sulphur dioxide into the atmosphere every day. To add to that, there are more than 150 registered iron-foundries in the vicinity. The UP government insists that all is fine, but the amount of suspended particles in the air is more than five times what the government itself says is the maximum the Taj can sustain without being damaged. A band of cleaners scrubs at the yellowing marble with chemicals, and some slabs have been so badly damaged they've had to be replaced. Not that people haven't damaged the Taj in the past – in 1764 silver doors fitted to the entrance gate were ripped off and carted away, and raiders have also made off with the gold sheets that once lined the subterranean vault.

Environmentalists finally managed to get a hearing in the supreme court, which ordered that the state government tackle the problem immediately. New industries within a 50-km radius of the Taj have been banned, but many existing operations remain. In 1994 an article in the British press suggesting that the world's most beautiful building should be put under international control caused a flood of indignant letters in newspapers here.

Indian environmentalists have now launched a petition to save the Taj, aiming to collect a million signatures demanding tougher action. Ideas for limiting pollution in the vicinity include the banning of vehicles of all types within a three-km radius of the Taj; visitors would arrive only by cycle rickshaw or tonga. By refusing to take auto rickshaws or taxis to visit the Taj, tourists can put this idea into immediate effect. ∎

of the platform – as the Taj Mahal is not a mosque, nobody is called to prayer from them. Twin red sandstone buildings frame the building when viewed from the river. The building on the west side is a mosque, but the identical one on the east is purely for symmetry: it cannot be used as a mosque because it faces the wrong direction.

The central Taj structure has four small domes surrounding the huge, bulbous central dome. The **tombs of Mumtaz Mahal and Shah Jahan** are in a basement room. Above them in the main chamber are false tombs, a common practice in mausoleums of this type. Light is admitted into the central chamber by finely cut marble screens. The echo in this high chamber, under the soaring marble dome, is superb and there is always somebody there to demonstrate it.

Although the Taj is amazingly graceful from almost any angle, it's the close-up detail which is really astounding. Semiprecious stones have been inlaid into the marble in beautiful patterns and with superb skill using a process known as *pietra dura*. The precision and care which went into the Taj Mahal's design and construction is just as impressive whether you view it from across the river or from arm's length.

Agra Fort

Construction of the massive Agra Fort was begun by emperor Akbar in 1565, and additions were made up until the time of his grandson, Shah Jahan. While in Akbar's time the fort was principally a military structure, by Shah Jahan's time it had become partially a palace. A visit to the fort is an Agra 'must' since so many of the events which led to the construction of the Taj took place here.

There are many fascinating buildings within the massive walls, which stretch for 2.5 km and are surrounded by a moat over 10 metres wide. Inside, the fort is really a city within a city. Not all of the buildings are open to visitors, and Shah Jahan's beautiful marble Moti Masjid (known as the Pearl Mosque for its perfect proportions) is, unfortunately, closed.

The fort is on the banks of the Yamuna River and the Amar Singh Gate to the south is the only entry point. It's open from sunrise to sunset and admission is Rs 10.50, except on Friday, when there's no charge.

Diwan-i-Am The Hall of Public Audiences was also built by Shah Jahan and replaced an earlier wooden structure. Beside the Diwan-i-Am is the small **Nagina Masjid**, or Gem Mosque, and the **Ladies' Bazaar**, where merchants came to display and sell goods to the ladies of the Mughal court.

Diwan-i-Khas The Hall of Private Audiences was also built by Shah Jahan in 1636-37. Here the emperor would meet important dignitaries or foreign ambassadors. The famous Peacock Throne was kept here before being moved to Delhi. It was later carted off to Iran and its remains are now in Tehran.

Octagonal Tower The Musamman Burj, or Octagonal Tower, stands close to the Diwan-i-Khas and the small, private Mina Masjid. It was here, with its views along the Yamuna to the Taj, that Shah Jahan died in 1666, after eight years of imprisonment. Unfortunately, the tower has been much damaged over the years.

Jehangir's Palace Akbar is believed to have built this palace, the largest private residence in the fort, for his son. This was one of the first constructions demonstrating the fort's changing emphasis from military to luxurious living quarters. The palace is also interesting for its blend of Hindu and central Asian architectural

Top : Agra Fort with the Taj Mahal in the distance (LB)
Bottom : Domes of Agra Fort (LB)

MAP 5

1 Northern Tower	9 Diwan-i-Am
2 Jama Masjid	10 Octagonal Tower
3 Delhi Gate	11 Mina Mosque
4 Elephant Gate	12 Anguri Bagh
5 Moti Masjid	13 Shish Mahal
6 Ladies' Bazaar	14 Khas Mahal
7 Nagina Masjid	15 Jehangir's Palace
8 Diwan-i-Khas	16 Amar Singh Gate

Yamuna River

Railway Station

Agra Fort

0   150   300 m

To Taj Mahal

styles – a contrast to the unique Mughal style which had developed by the time of Shah Jahan.

Other Buildings Shah Jahan's **Khas Mahal** is a beautiful white marble structure that was used as a private palace. The rooms underneath were intended as a cool retreat from the summer heat. The **Shish Mahal**, or Mirror Palace, is reputed to have been the harem dressing room and its walls are inlaid with tiny mirrors. The **Anguri Bagh**, or Grape Garden, probably never had any grapevines but was simply a small, formal Mughal garden. It stood in front of the Khas Mahal. The **Delhi Gate** and **Elephant Gate** (Hathi Pol) are now closed.

In front of Jehangir's Palace is the **Hauz-i-Jehangri**, a huge 'bath' carved out of a single block of stone – by whom and for what purpose is a subject of conjecture. The **Amar Singh Gate** takes its name from a Maharaja of Jodhpur who was killed beside the gate, along with his followers, after a brawl in the Diwan-i-Am in 1644! Justice tended to be summary in those days; there is a shaft leading down to the river into which those who made themselves unpopular with the great Mughals could be hurled without further ado.

Jama Masjid

Across the railway tracks from the Delhi Gate of Agra Fort is the Jama Masjid, built by Shah Jahan in 1648. An inscription over the main gate indicates that it was built in the name of Jahanara, Shah Jahan's daughter, who stayed with her father during his imprisonment. Large though it is, the mosque is not as impressive as Shah Jahan's Jama Masjid in Delhi.

Itimad-ud-daulah

There are several interesting sights on the opposite bank of the Yamuna and north of the fort. You cross the river on a narrow two-level bridge carrying pedestrians, bicycles, rickshaws and bullock carts.

The first place of interest is the exquisite Itimad-ud-daulah – the tomb of Mirza Ghiyas Beg. This Persian gentleman was Jehangir's *wazir*, or chief minister, and his daughter later married the emperor. She then became known as Nur Jahan, the Light of the World, and her niece was Mumtaz Mahal, Chosen of the Palace. The tomb was constructed by Nur Jahan between 1622 and 1628 and is very similar to the tomb she constructed for her husband, Jehangir, near Lahore in Pakistan.

The tomb is of particular interest since many of its design elements foreshadow the Taj, construction of which started only a few years later. The Itimad-ud-daulah was the first Mughal structure totally constructed of marble and the first to make extensive use of pietra dura, the inlay work of marble which is so characteristic of the Taj. The mausoleum is small and squat compared with the soaring Taj, but the smaller, more human scale somehow makes it attractive, and the beautifully patterned surface of the tomb is superb. Extremely fine marble lattice-work passages admit light to the interior. It's well worth a visit.

The Itimad-ud-daulah is open from sunrise to sunset and admission is Rs 5.50; free on Friday.

Chini Ka Rauza

The China Tomb is one km north of the Itimad-ud-daulah. The squat, square tomb, surmounted by a single huge dome, was constructed by Afzal Khan, who died at Lahore in 1639. He was a high official in the court of Shah Jahan. The exterior was once covered in brightly coloured enamelled tiles and the whole building clearly displayed its Persian influence. Today it is much decayed and neglected, and the remaining tile work only hints at the building's former glory.

Ram Bagh

Laid out in 1528 by Babur, first of the Mughal emperors, this is the earliest Mughal garden. It is said that Babur was temporarily buried here before being permanently interred at Kabul in Afghanistan. The Ram Bagh is two to three km further north of the Chini Ka Rauza on the riverside and is open from sunrise to sunset; admission is free. It's rather overgrown and neglected.

Akbar's Mausoleum

At Sikandra, 10 km north-west of Agra, the tomb of Akbar lies in the centre of a large, peaceful garden. Akbar started its construction himself but it was completed by his son, Jehangir, who significantly modified the original plans, which accounts for the somewhat cluttered architectural lines of the tomb.

The building has three-storey minarets at each corner and is built of red sandstone inlaid with white marble polygonal patterns. Four red sandstone gates lead to the tomb complex: one is Muslim, one Hindu, one Christian, and one is Akbar's patent mixture. Like Humayun's

Tomb in New Delhi, it is an interesting place to study the gradual evolution in design that culminated in the Taj Mahal. Akbar's mausoleum is open from sunrise to sunset and entry is Rs 5.50, except on Friday, when it is free. A permit for a video camera costs Rs 25; still cameras are free.

Sikandra is named after Sultan Sikander Lodi, the Delhi ruler who held power from 1489 to 1517, immediately preceding the rise of Mughal power on the subcontinent. The **Baradi Palace**, in the mausoleum gardens, was built by Sikander Lodi. Across the road from the mausoleum is the **Delhi Gate**. Between Sikandra and Agra are several tombs and two *kos minars*, or milestones.

From Agra Cantonment Railway Station auto rickshaws charge Rs 90 for the return trip with two hours at Sikandra. You can also get there on a cycle rickshaw.

Marble inlaid with semiprecious stones, Taj Mahal (BT)

Arches at the mosque, Taj Mahal (RI)

Organised Tours

If you're just day-tripping from Delhi, tours commence from Agra Cantonment Railway Station and tickets are sometimes sold on the *Taj Express* or *Shatabdi Express* trains. The tours start when the trains arrive (10 am for the *Taj Express*, 8.30 am for the *Shatabdi*). They last all day and include visits to the Taj, the Fort and Fatehpur Sikri. Tickets cost Rs 100.

In Agra itself, you can book the tours (and get picked up) at the tourist office in The Mall or at the tourist information counter at Agra Cantonment Railway Station.

Places to Stay – bottom end

The two main areas for cheap accommodation are the Taj Ganj area (a tangle of narrow streets directly south of the Taj) and the Sadar area, close to the Cantonment Railway Station, the tourist office and the GPO, and only a short rickshaw ride from the Taj.

Taj Ganj Area Many of the hotels in this area boast of Taj views, but often it's just wishful thinking. Only two have a truly uninterrupted view from their rooftops; the better of them is the relatively new *Hotel Kamal* (☎ 36-0926). There are singles with common bath for Rs 50, and doubles/triples with attached bath from Rs 80/100. The rooms are clean but a little dark. From the sitting area on the roof, however, there's a superb view of the Taj. Since this place gives commissions to rickshaw-wallahs they may try to charge you a higher price.

The other place with a real Taj view is the *Shanti Lodge* (☎ 36-1644). It's been getting mixed reports lately but the view from the rooftop restaurant is still as wonderful as it's always been. Rooms are Rs 60/80 for singles/doubles with common bath, Rs 80/100 with bath attached; if you stay for a while you may be able to get a cheaper deal. Some rooms are definitely better than others, so try to look at more than one. Check-out is at 10 am.

Another good hotel is the *Hotel Siddhartha* (☎ 26-4711), not far from the western gate. It's a clean place run by very friendly Sikhs and has a pleasant garden courtyard. Rooms range from Rs 60/80 to Rs 80/175, all with bathroom attached (hot water in buckets in the cheaper rooms). There are limited views from the roof. Nearby, the *Hotel Host* is a little cheaper, and they have their own bike hire for Rs 10 per day.

By the eastern gate, the friendly *Hotel Pink* (☎ 36-0677) is indeed pink, and set around a small courtyard draped in crimson bougainvillaea. All rooms have bath attached and range from Rs 40/70 with a bucket shower to Rs 120/150 for a double/triple with attached bath and hot water. Also in this area is the very good *Veshali Lodge* (☎ 26-9673). Recently renovated, the airy rooms lead off a veranda – Rs 50 for a double, Rs 60/80 for rooms with bathroom attached and Rs 100 for the double with a tub in the bathroom.

There's been a mini building boom in the area south of Taj Ganj and there are several reasonable hotels at the top of this price range, as well as numerous middle range places. The popular *Hotel Safari* (☎ 36-0013) is on Shamsabad Rd. It's clean and good value at Rs 75/120 with air-cooling and hot water. There are also rooms with three and four beds for Rs 150 and Rs 175, respectively. Meals are available, and the Taj is visible from the rooftop.

On a quiet residential street just to the east of this area is the very pleasant *Upadhyay's Mumtaz Guest House* (☎ 36-0865), 3/7 Vibhav Nagar. Rooms with attached bath are Rs 75/150, or Rs 200 for a deluxe double with a tub in the bathroom. There's a small garden and sun terrace on the roof.

Sadar The popular and long-running *Tourist Rest House* (☎ 36-3961) is on Kachahari Rd, not far from The Mall. Set around a small garden, it's managed by two helpful brothers who will even make train reservations for you. This pleasant though rather dog-eared hotel has a variety of rooms with and without bath, ranging from Rs 55/65 for their most basic rooms. They don't need to give commissions, so rickshaw drivers may be unwilling to take you there and instead take you to a couple of other places purporting to be the Tourist Rest House.

On Field Marshal Cariappa Rd, in a spacious residential area closer to the Taj and just a few minutes' walk from the Fort, there are a couple of good places. The friendly *Agra Hotel* (☎ 36-3331) would be the perfect setting for a novel; it's a large crumbling old place that people either love or hate. There's a good range of rooms from Rs 110/150, all with attached baths and some with the most amazing antediluvian plumbing. A double air-con suite costs Rs 450. There are views of the Taj from the garden. Right next door is the *Hotel Akbar* (☎ 36-3312), which is a little cheaper and also has a pleasant garden.

Places to Stay – middle

The *New Bakshi House* (☎ 36-8159) is a very pleasant upmarket guest house at 5 Laxman Nagar, between the railway station and the airport. Comfortable rooms in this well-equipped and clean place range from Rs 400/500 to Rs 650. The food is excellent and they can also arrange to pick you up from the station or airport. They're often booked up so you need to ring in advance.

One of the nicest places in this range is the elderly *Lauries Hotel* (☎ 36-4536) in the Sadar area. The management and staff are very pleasant and claim that this was where the Queen stayed on a visit to India in 1963. You'd hardly believe it, it's certainly not by royal appointment now – the rooms are a tad shabby but the ones at the back are OK. They cost Rs 325/450 and discounts may be given in the off season. It has a peaceful garden and a swimming pool (not always full), and camping is possible at Rs 30 per person, including access to a hot shower.

The main group of middle and top-end places is in the area south of Taj Ganj, about 1.5 km from the Taj itself. The *Mayur Tourist Complex* (☎ 36-0302) is one of these places and has very pleasant cottages arranged around a lawn and swimming pool. The cottages cost Rs 400/550 with air-cooling, Rs 500/750 with air-con and Rs 700/950 for air-con deluxe cottages. It's very well done and the food is good.

The *Hotel Amar* (☎ 36-0695) has a popular swimming pool, jacuzzi and sauna. Room rates are Rs 700/900 with air-con. At the top of this price range is the *Hotel Mumtaz*

(☎ 36-1771), under renovation in an attempt to raise itself from three to five-star status. Standard rooms are Rs 1100/1500.

Places to Stay – top end

Agra's five-star hotels are generally in the open area south of the Taj. The Clarks Shiraz, Agra Ashok and Novotel are all in the same price range.

The *Clarks Shiraz Hotel* (☎ 36-1421; fax 36-1620) is a long-standing Agra landmark. It's fully air-conditioned and has a swimming pool; the Indian Airlines office is here. Singles/doubles cost Rs 1195/2380, and it's one of the better expensive Agra hotels.

The *Agra Ashok Hotel* (☎ 36-1223; fax 36-1428), despite being part of the ITDC chain, is well managed and a pleasant place to stay. Room rates are Rs 1195/2000 for single/double rooms. The new *Novotel Agra* (☎ 36-8282), Fatehbad Rd, is a low-rise Mughal-style hotel built around a lawn and swimming pool. Rooms are US$38/75.

The five-star hotel with Taj views from most of its rooms is the *Taj View Hotel* (☎ 36-1171; fax 36-1179). It costs US$135/145 for a room where you can admire the Taj from the comfort of your bed. Standard rooms (no view) are US$110/125.

Agra's top hotel is the *Mughal Sheraton* (☎ 36-1701; fax 36-1730) on Fatehbad Rd. It's a very elegant place, with thick creepers cascading down the brickwork of the fort-like architecture. Facilities include everything you'd expect in a five-star deluxe hotel – plus camel or elephant rides and an in-house astrologer. The rooms, which cost from US$165/180, are all very well appointed, but only the more expensive ones give you that Taj view. For US$275, in the Mughal Chamber Exclusive, you and your loved one can recline on silk cushions before a picture window and contemplate the immortal view.

Places to Eat

In the Taj Ganj area there are several places catering to travellers. Food tends to be mainly vegetarian here and hygiene is not always quite what it might be. The tiny *Joney's Place* is one of the area's longest-running places, although its 'Yum Yum Food' is nothing great. It is, however, a good meeting place. The *Shankari Vegis Restaurant* is a bit better and equally popular. Main dishes are Rs 20 to Rs 30 and there's a pleasant sitting area on the roof. It also has books, magazines and games you can use – and they let you choose the music.

On the same square as Joney's, the small *Gulshan Lodge Restaurant* is good for a snack. Further along this street is the *Lucky Restaurant*, which claims that its food is so good you'll get your money back if you don't agree.

Honey's Restaurant is a small place that's good value – a set breakfast with tomato, eggs, porridge and coffee costs Rs 20. The popular little *Sikander Restaurant* has good food, reasonable prices and a varied menu, although the servings are small.

The *Only Restaurant* is an outdoor place by the round-about on Taj Rd. It has a good reputation for the quality of its ingredients and claims to have a different chef for each of its cuisines – Indian, Chinese and continental. Nearby is the equally good *Sonar Restaurant*, set in a garden with tables inside and out. There's excellent Mughlai food here.

The *Tourist Rest House* in the Sadar area is a pleasant place to eat. The tables are outside and at night the candles are a nice touch.

There's a bunch of middle-range restaurants at the western end of Taj Rd. The *Kwality Restaurant* is air-conditioned and excellent, certainly one of the best in Agra. Main dishes are from Rs 50, and Rs 7 buys you a chocolate éclair from the bakery.

Nearby is the *Lakshmi Vilas*, a vegetarian restaurant highly recommended for its cheap south Indian food. There are 22 varieties of dosa; a thali is Rs 20.

Zorba the Buddha is an interesting Osho-run vegetarian restaurant. There are stars on the ceiling and clouds on the wall, it's spotlessly clean and the food is excellent. Muesli with fruit, nuts and curd is Rs 20 and a lassi is Rs 14.

Things to Buy

Agra is well known for leather goods, jewellery and marble items inlaid like the pietra dura work on the Taj. The Sadar and Taj Ganj areas are the main tourist shopping centres, although the prices there are likely to be more expensive. Around Pratapur there are many jewellery shops, but precious stones are cheaper in Jaipur.

About one km along the road running from the east gate of the Taj is Shilpgram, a crafts village and open-air emporium. At festival times there are live performances by dancers and musicians; the rest of the time there are displays of crafts from all over the country. Prices are certainly on the high side, but the quality is good and the range hard to beat.

Getting There & Away

Air The Indian Airlines office (☎ 36-0948) is at the Clarks Shiraz Hotel. It is open daily from 10 am to 1 pm and from 2 to 5 pm.

Agra is on the popular daily tourist route Delhi/Agra/Khajuraho/Varanasi and return. It's only a 40-minute flight from Delhi to Agra. Fares from Agra are: Delhi US$23, Khajuraho US$39 and Varanasi US$57.

Bus Most buses leave from the Idgah bus station. Buses between Delhi and Agra operate about every hour and cost Rs 49; deluxe buses cost Rs 56 and super deluxe are Rs 60. The trip takes about five hours. In Delhi buses leave from Sarai Kale Khan, the new bus station in the south of the city by Hazrat Nizamuddin Railway Station.

There are deluxe buses between Agra and Jaipur every half hour for Rs 76; there are also air-con buses for Rs 106. They leave from a small booth right outside the Hotel Sheetal on Ajmer Rd, very close to the Idgah bus station.

Train Agra is 200 km from Delhi on the main Delhi to Bombay broad-gauge railway line, so there are plenty of trains coming through. The fastest train between Delhi and Agra is the daily air-con *Shatabdi Express*, which does the trip in a shade under two hours. It leaves Delhi at 6.15 am, returning from Agra at 8.15 pm, and so is ideal for day-tripping. The fare is Rs 235 in a chair car or Rs 470 1st class, and this includes meals.

There is also the daily *Taj Express* to and from Delhi, but this is slower and gives you less time in Agra. Take great care at New Delhi station; pickpockets, muggers and others are very aware that this is a popular tourist route and they work overtime at parting unwary visitors from their goods.

Getting Around

To/From the Airport Agra's airport is seven km from the centre of town. Taxis charge around Rs 90; in an auto rickshaw it's Rs 50.

Taxi & Auto Rickshaw There are set fares from the Cantonment Railway Station. Auto rickshaws charge Rs 15 to any hotel, Rs 45 to the Agra Fort and back with a couple of hours at the fort, and Rs 250 for a full day's sightseeing. A taxi to any hotel is Rs 60. For the Taj, a cycle rickshaw is the most environmentally friendly form of transport.

Cycle Rickshaw & Bicycle Agra is very spread out so walking is really not on – even if you could. It's virtually impossible to walk because Agra's hordes of cycle-rickshaw drivers pursue would-be pedestrians with unbelievable energy and persuasive ability. Beware of rickshaw-wallahs who take you from A to B via a few marble shops, jewellery shops and so on – just great when you want to catch a train, and it can also work out very expensive!

A simple solution to Agra's transport problem is to hire a rickshaw for the day. You can easily negotiate a full-day rate (Rs 60 to Rs 100), for which your rickshaw-wallah will not only take you everywhere but will wait outside while you sight-see or even have a meal. How much you pay depends on your bargaining ability, but never get in a rickshaw here without first establishing a price. Being told you can pay 'as you like' does not mean that.

Agra is so touristy that many rickshaw-wallahs speak fine English and, like Western cabbies, are great sources of amusing information – like how much they can screw out of fat-cat tourists for a little pedal down to the Taj and back to the hotel's air-conditioning. Around Rs 10 should take you from pretty well anywhere in Agra to anywhere else, but the rickshaw drivers will try for much more.

If, however, you really don't want to be pedalled around, Agra is sufficiently traffic-free to make pedalling yourself an easy proposition. There are plenty of bicycle hire places around. The cost is typically Rs 3 per hour and Rs 15 per day.

AROUND AGRA

Fatehpur Sikri

Between 1570 and 1586, during the reign of Emperor Akbar, the capital of the Mughal Empire was situated here, 40 km west of Agra. Then, as suddenly and dramatically as this new city had been built, it was abandoned. Today it's a perfectly preserved example of a Mughal city at the height of the empire's splendour – an attraction no visitor to Agra should miss.

Legend says that Akbar was without a male heir and made a pilgrimage to this spot to see the Sufi saint Shaikh Salim Chisti. The saint foretold the birth of Akbar's son, the future emperor, Jehangir, and in gratitude Akbar named his son Salim. Furthermore, Akbar transferred his capital to Sikri and built a new and splendid city. Later, however, the city was abandoned, mainly because, it is thought, of difficulties with the water supply.

Orientation & Information The deserted city lies along the top of a ridge, while the modern village with its bus stand and railway station is down the ridge's southern side.

Fatehpur Sikri is open from sunrise to sunset and entry is Rs 0.50; free on Friday. There's no charge for a camera unless it's a video (Rs 25). Note that the Jama Masjid and the tomb of Shaikh Salim Chisti are outside the city enclosure; there's no entry fee to visit them.

As Fatehpur Sikri is one of the most perfectly preserved 'ghost towns' imaginable, you may well decide it is worthwhile hiring a guide. Licensed guides are available around the ticket office; the official charge is set at Rs 48, but if business is slack they ask only about half that. At the Buland Darwaza, the gateway to the mosque and shrine, unlicensed guides will try to lure you into hiring them for around Rs 10 to Rs 20.

Day-trippers in search of a toilet or a place to leave their luggage should head for the Maurya Rest House. They charge Rs 2 for left luggage.

The Buland Darwaza (Gate of Victory), Fatehpur Sikri (HF)

Things to See Fatehpur Sikri's **Jama Masjid** (Dargah Mosque) is said to be a copy of the mosque at Mecca and is a beautiful building containing elements of Persian and Hindu design. The main entrance is through the 54-metre-high **Buland Darwaza** (Gate of Victory), constructed to commemorate Akbar's victory in Gujarat. The eastern gate of the mosque is known as the **Shahi Darwaza** (King's Gate) and was the one used by Akbar. In the northern part of the courtyard is the superb white marble dargah or **tomb of Shaikh Salim Chisti**, built in 1570. Just as Akbar came to the saint four centuries ago looking for a son, so do childless women visit his tomb today. The carved marble lattice screens *(jalis)* are prob-

The beautifully proportioned Panch Mahal, Fatehpur Sikri (HF)

ably the finest examples of such work you'll see any-where in the country.

North-east of the mosque is the ticket office and entrance to the old city. The first building inside the gate is the **Palace of Jodh Bai**, named after Jehangir's mother, who was the daughter of the Maharaja of Amber, and was also a Hindu. The **Hawa Mahal** (Palace of the Winds) is a projecting room with walls made entirely of stone latticework. The ladies of the court probably sat in here to keep a quiet eye on events below.

Built either by or for Raja Birbal, Akbar's favourite courtier, the small **Birbal Bhavan** palace is extremely elegant in its design and execution. Enormous **stables** adjoin the Jodh Bai Palace, with nearly 200 enclosures for horses and camels. Some stone rings for the halters are still in place.

The **Karawan Serai**, or Caravanserai, was a large courtyard surrounded by the hostels used by visiting merchants. The **Hiran Minar** (Deer Minaret), which is actually outside the fort grounds, is said to have been erected over the grave of Akbar's favourite elephant.

Close to the Jodh Bai Palace, the **Palace of the Christian Wife** is a house used by Akbar's Goan Christian wife, Maryam, and at one time was gilded throughout – giving it the name 'Golden House'.

The amusing little five-storey **Panch Mahal** palace was probably once used by the ladies of the court and originally had stone screens on the sides. The name of the **Ankh Micholi** building translates as something like 'hide and seek', and the emperor is supposed to have amused himself by playing that game with ladies of the harem! It is more likely that the building was used for storing records.

The exterior of the **Diwan-i-Khas** (Hall of Private Audiences) is plain, but its interior design is unique. A stone column in the centre of the building supports a flat-topped 'throne'. Akbar spent much time here with scholars of many different religious persuasions, discussing and debating.

Just inside the gates at the north-east end of the deserted city is the **Diwan-i-Am** (Hall of Public Audiences). This consists of a large open courtyard surrounded by cloisters. Beside the Diwan-i-Am is the **Pachisi courtyard**, set out like a gigantic gameboard. It is said that Akbar played the game pachisi here, using slave girls as the pieces.

Places to Stay & Eat Just below the Buland Darwaza is the *Maurya Rest House* (☎ 2348), the most pleasant of the budget hotels in the village. There are basic singles/

doubles for Rs 40/60 with common bath, Rs 60/80 with bath attached and Rs 80/120 for the bigger rooms. It's run by a very friendly and helpful family and there's a good vegetarian restaurant in the shady courtyard.

At the top of the scale is the UPSTDC *Gulistan Tourist Complex* (☎ 2490), about half a km back along the main road. The design is sympathetic to the local surroundings and the facilities reasonable. The rooms are large and cost Rs 200/250, or Rs 350/425 with air-con, but during the tourist season they charge the higher price for all rooms.

Getting There & Away The tour buses stop for only an hour or so at Fatehpur Sikri. If you want to spend longer (which is recommended), it is worth taking a bus from Agra's Idgah bus station (Rs 10, one hour).

JAIPUR

Population: 1.7 million
The capital city of the state of Rajasthan is popularly known as the 'pink city' because of the pink paint applied to the buildings in its old walled city. (In Rajput culture, pink was traditionally a colour associated with hospitality.) In contrast to the cities on the Ganges plain, Jaipur has broad avenues and a remarkable harmony. The city sits on a dry lake bed in a wild and somewhat arid landscape, surrounded by barren hills surmounted by fortresses and crenellated walls. Jaipur long ago outstripped the confines of its city wall, yet it retains a less crowded and more relaxed atmosphere than its large size and population might suggest.

The city owes its name, its foundation and its careful planning to the great warrior-astronomer Maharaja Jai Singh II (1699-1744). His predecessors had enjoyed good relations with the Mughals, and he was careful to cultivate this alliance.

Orientation & Information

The walled 'pink city' is in the north-east of Jaipur, while the new parts have spread to the south and west. The city's main tourist attractions are in the old part of town. The principal shopping centre in the old city is Johari Bazaar, the jewellers' market. Unlike other shopping centres in India and elsewhere in Asia, this one is broad and open. All seven gates into the old city remain, but unfortunately much of the wall itself has been torn down for building material.

The main tourist office (☎ 31-5714) is on platform No 1 at the railway station. It's open daily from 6 am to 8 pm.

Hawa Mahal

Built in 1799, the Hawa Mahal, or Palace of the Winds, is one of Jaipur's major landmarks, although it is actually little more than a facade. This five-storey building, which looks out over the main street of the old city, is a stunning example of Rajput artistry with its pink, semi-octagonal and delicately honeycombed sandstone windows. It was originally built to enable ladies of the royal household to watch the everyday life and processions of the city. You can climb to the top of the Hawa Mahal for an excellent view over the city.

The entrance is at the rear of the building. To get there, go back to the intersection on your left as you face the Hawa Mahal, turn right and then take the first right again through an archway. It's signposted. Hours are 9 am to 4.30 pm and there's an entry fee of Rs 2 – plus Rs 50 if you want to use a camera.

City Palace

In the heart of the old city, the City Palace occupies a large area divided into a series of courtyards, gardens and buildings.

The seven-storey Chandra Mahal is the centre of the palace and commands fine views over the gardens and the city. The ground and 1st floor of the Chandra Mahal form the **Maharaja Sawai Man Singh II Museum**. The apartments are maintained in luxurious order and the museum has an extensive collection of art, carpets, enamelware and old weapons. The paintings include miniatures of the Rajasthani, Mughal and Persian schools.

Other points of interest in the palace include the **Diwan-i-Am**, or Hall of Public Audiences, with its intricate decorations and manuscripts in Persian and Sanskrit, and the **Diwan-i-Khas**, or Hall of Private Audiences, with a marble-paved gallery.

Outside the buildings you can see a large silver vessel in which a former maharaja used to take drinking water with him to England. Being a devout Hindu, he could not drink the English water! The palace and museum are open daily, except on public holidays, between 9.30 am and 4.45 pm. Entry is Rs 30, plus Rs 50 if you wish to take photos with a still camera, or Rs 100 for a video.

Top : The stunning Hawa Mahal (Palace of the Winds)
in Jaipur is little more than a facade. (TW)
Bottom : The apartments in the City Palace are maintained
in luxurious order. (GH)

Jantar Mantar

Adjacent to the entrance to the City Palace is the Jantar Mantar, or observatory, begun by Jai Singh in 1728. Jai Singh's passion for astronomy was even more notable than his prowess as a warrior, and before commencing construction he sent scholars abroad to study foreign observatories. The Jaipur observatory is the largest and best preserved of the five he built and was restored in 1901. The others are in Delhi (the oldest, dating from 1724), Varanasi and Ujjain. The fifth, the Muttra observatory, has now disappeared.

Organised Tours

Jaipur City The Rajasthan Tourism Development Corporation offers half-day and full-day bus tours of Jaipur. They visit the Hawa Mahal, Amber Fort, Jantar Mantar, City Palace and Museum (except Friday) and include the inevitable stop at a craftshop.

The half-day tours are a little rushed but otherwise OK. If possible, take a full-day tour. Times are 8 am to 1 pm, 11.30 am to 4.30 pm and 1.30 to 6.30 pm. The full-day tours are from 9 am to 6 pm, including a lunch break at Nahagarh Fort. Half-day tours cost Rs 50 and full-day tours cost Rs 80. They all depart from the railway station, but you can arrange to be collected from any of the RTDC hotels.

Places to Stay

Getting to the hotel of your choice in Jaipur can be a problem. Auto-rickshaw drivers besiege every traveller who arrives at the railway station (it's less of a problem if you come by bus). If you don't want to go to a hotel of their choice, they'll either refuse to take you at all or they'll demand at least double the normal fare. If you do go to the hotel of their choice, you'll pay through the nose for accommodation because the manager will be paying them a commission of at least 30% of what you are charged for a bed (and the charge won't go down for subsequent nights).

Most hotels will give discounts of 25% to 40% in the off season (April to September).

Places to Stay – bottom end

One of the most popular of Jaipur's budget hotels is the *Jaipur Inn* (☎ 31-6157) in the Bani Park area, about a km west of Chandpol. It's clean, well run, helpful and friendly. Large dormitories cost Rs 40 per person and there's a range of rooms from Rs 80 for a single or double or Rs 120 for some slightly larger rooms. Their most expensive rooms are Rs 250/300. You can even camp on the lawn (Rs 25) if you have your own tent.

The ever-expanding *Evergreen Guest House* (☎ 36-3446), off Mirza Ismail (MI) Rd opposite the GPO, is another popular option. Formerly a small guest house, it's now a large hotel, complete with restaurant and buildings of various vintages arranged around a cramped garden courtyard. All rooms are doubles with bath attached and range from Rs 70 to Rs 120 with bucket hot water (Rs 5), or Rs 150 to Rs 250 with constant hot water; there's a dorm for Rs 50. The more expensive rooms have air-cooling and there is also a small swimming pool.

One of the most pleasant places to stay is the *Hotel Diggi Palace* (☎ 37-3091), just off Sawai Ram Singh Marg, less than a km south of Ajmeri Gate. The building is the former palace of the *thakur* (similar to a lord or baron) of Diggi, and has a huge lawn area which gives the place a very spacious and peaceful ambience. The part which has been turned into a hotel is basically the old servant's quarters, but it's quite comfortable and the facilities are good. There's a range of rooms starting at Rs 100/150 and some very nice small suites at Rs 350/400. Good meals are available.

Dating from 1882, the *Hotel Kaiser-I-Hind* (☎ 31-0195), near the station, is certainly an interesting place with large dusty rooms for Rs 100/150 and vast bathrooms attached. The manager claims that this was Jaipur's first hotel, Mark Twain stayed in room No 6, Henry Ford was another guest and Mussolini's brother-in-law was kept here as a prisoner of war. If it's all true they wouldn't recognise the place now.

At the top of this range there are four excellent places, two near MI Rd and two in Bani Park. Close to the centre is the deservedly popular *Hotel Arya Niwas* (☎ 37-2456; fax 36-4376), just off Sansar Chandra Rd. It has spotlessly clean, pleasantly furnished and decorated rooms, ranging in price from Rs 150/250 up to Rs 350/450 for deluxe rooms. All rooms have baths and, in the winter months, hot water. The hotel restaurant serves tasty vegetarian food at very reasonable prices. Also available are money exchange facilities, a travel agency, a parking area, bicycle hire (Rs 20), a pleasant front lawn with tables and chairs and a small bookshop.

Equally good as the Arya Niwas, and with a beautiful home atmosphere, is the smaller *Atithi Guest House* (☎ 37-8679), 1 Park House Scheme, Motilal Atal Rd, between MI Rd and Station Rd. Run by the Shukla family, it's superbly maintained, squeaky clean and very friendly, and it offers excellent meals. There are ordinary rooms for Rs 225/250, Rs 325/350 for deluxe rooms. All rooms have air-cooling and attached bath with hot water. The family are very keen to please and nothing is too much trouble.

In the peaceful residential district of Bani Park is the very pleasant *Madhuban Guest House* (☎ 31-9033). This small, family-run place is well run and has a nice garden and lawn area. The air-cooled rooms all have attached bath and cost Rs 200/250, or Rs 350/400 for a large room. There are also some plush deluxe rooms with air-con for Rs 500/550. It's a very relaxing place to stay.

In the same area is *Shapura House* (☎ 31-2293), D-257 Devi Marg (off Jai Singh Highway). All rooms have air-cooling and attached bath; doubles range from Rs 200 to Rs 395. They operate camel safaris and also have a horse-drawn carriage for sightseeing round Jaipur (Rs 1000 for two!).

Places to Stay – middle

The *Hotel Megh Niwas* (☎ 32-2661; fax 32-1018), C-9 Jai Singh Highway, is in Bani Park. It has the homely atmosphere of a large guest house and is very well run and an excellent place to stay. Rooms cost Rs 400/500 with

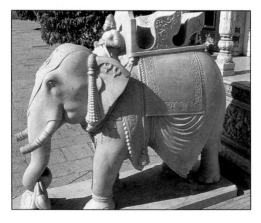

Intricately-carved sandstone Indian elephant
at the City Palace in Jaipur (GH)

air-cooling, Rs 500/600 with air-con and Rs 850 for a suite. There's a peaceful garden and a swimming pool. Meals cost Rs 60 for breakfast and Rs 110 for lunch or dinner.

Also in Bani Park is the *Umaid Bhawan Guest House* (☎ 31-6184), D1-2A. Doubles with attached bath range from Rs 250 to Rs 600; it's also very well run and spotlessly clean, and there's a small garden.

The Jantar Mantar in Jaipur is the best-preserved of Jai Singh's five observatories.
Top : GH, Bottom : RI

Right in the heart of the old city is the *LMB Hotel* (☎ 56-5844) in Johari Bazaar. Although it's probably better known for its restaurant, the hotel does have reasonable rooms, and the location is hard to beat. All rooms have air-con, TV, fridge and attached bath with tub, and cost Rs 625/825.

The *Narain Niwas Palace Hotel* (☎ 56-3448) is a very interesting and peaceful place to stay. In the south of the city, it's yet another former palace, surrounded by the obligatory large garden. The four suites (Rs 1150) are huge and filled with ancient furniture and fittings; some even have four-poster beds. There's an annexe, modern but decorated in style with wall paintings. Rooms here are Rs 650/865. Meals are available at Rs 70/140/140 for breakfast/lunch/dinner.

Places to Stay – top end

The superb *Samode Haveli* (tel/fax 42-407) is in the north-east corner of the old city. This 200-year-old building was once the town house of the *rawal* (a sort of nobleman) of Samode, who was also prime minister of Jaipur. It has a beautiful open terrace area, a stunning painted dining room and a couple of amazing suites – one totally covered with original mirrorwork, the other one painted. The charge is Rs 1000/1200 for ordinary rooms or Rs 1100/1800 for the suites. It's the perfect film set and was, in fact, a location for the movie *Far Pavilions*. The Samode Haveli is a delightful place to stay.

The *Rambagh Palace* (☎ 38-1919; fax 38-1098) is one of India's most prestigious and romantic hotels, offering the elegance of cool white marble, endless terraces over-looking manicured lawns, fountains and browsing peacocks. Formerly the palace of the Maharaja of Jaipur, it's an impressive place to stay by any standard. The cheapest singles/doubles are US$140/160, but they are poor value. The luxury rooms, at US$275, are much more sumptuous and spacious – if you're going to splurge, take one of these. However, it's important to note that, even within the same price category, some rooms are very much nicer than others. Try to see more than one. From May to July the prices of the cheaper rooms drop by around 40%. If you can't afford to stay here, at least come for an evening drink at the terrace bar.

Only a little more modest is the very pleasant *Jai Mahal Palace Hotel* (☎ 37-1616; fax 36-5237) on the corner of Jacob Rd and Ajmer Marg, south of the railway station. This building also used to belong to the Maharaja of Jaipur and has rooms ranging from US$115/135 all the way up to US$425 for luxury suites. From May to September the cheapest rooms are a bargain at US$38/55. There's a swimming pool, a coffee lounge, a bar and a restaurant serving Indian and Western food.

The *Rajmahal Palace* (☎ 52-1757) on Sardar Patel Marg in the south of the city is yet another former important building, this time the former British Residency. It is by no means as luxurious as the previous two, but it still offers top-of-the-range facilities such as a swimming pool and a quality restaurant. It's a much more personal place as it has just 13 rooms and suites, costing US$65/85 (US$38/55 from May to September) for rooms and US$250 for suites. The huge forecourt is used for wedding receptions.

Places to Eat

Two restaurants stand out above the others in Jaipur. The best place for non-veg food is *Niro's*, on MI Rd, popular with Indians and Westerners alike. It's so popular, in fact, that you may have to wait for a table; but since service is fast you don't usually have to wait long. Main dishes range from Rs 70 to Rs 100 and ingredients are of a high quality. They offer Indian, Chinese and continental dishes. Everyone seems to eat here at least once.

For food which 'promotes longevity, intelligence, vigour, health and cheerfulness', head for *LMB* (Laxmi Mishthan Bhandar) in Johari Bazaar, near the centre of the old city. This is the city's best vegetarian restaurant; it also has amazingly pristine '50s 'hip' decor – definitely worth seeing. Main dishes range from Rs 35 to Rs 50. A dessert speciality is LMB kulfi, including dry fruits, saffron and cottage cheese. Out the front, a snack counter serves good snacks and excellent ice cream and offers a wide range of Indian sweets.

Near Niro's are two more good vegetarian places. *Natraj Restaurant* is also famous for its sweets and namkin, and further up MI Rd is the more expensive *Chanakya Restaurant*. A veg steak sizzler (totally vegetarian) is Rs 80, but most of the other main dishes are around Rs 40.

Strict local licensing laws mean that only hotels can serve alcohol. This piece of legislation has been skilfully circumvented by some restaurants, and beer may be served in glasses shrouded in paper napkins – or even served in a teapot and drunk out of cups. 'Special Tea' they call it!

For a splurge, you couldn't find more opulent surroundings than the dining room at the *Rambagh Palace*, although the food gets mixed reports. Main dishes are around Rs 140; jumbo tandoori prawns are Rs 325.

Getting There & Away

Air The Indian Airlines office (☎ 51-4407) in Jaipur is on Tonk Rd. The Air India office (☎ 36-5559) is in Rattan Mansion on MI Rd. Numerous international airlines have offices in Jaipur Towers on MI Rd.

Indian Airlines flies Delhi-Jaipur (US$28) at least daily, and all flights continue to Bombay. For the same price, ModiLuft has daily flights to Delhi, and Jagsan Airlines flies three times weekly.

Bus Buses to all Rajasthan's main population centres and to Delhi and Agra are operated by the Rajasthan State Transport Corporation from the bus station. Some services are deluxe (essentially non-stop). The deluxe buses all leave from platform No 3, which is tucked away in the right-hand rear corner of the bus station yard.

The colourful Teej festival in Jaipur celebrates
the onset of the monsoon. (GE)

A view from the Hawa Mahal in Jaipur (GH)

These buses should be booked in advance, and the booking office, open from 8 am to 10 pm, is also at platform No 3.

State Transport deluxe buses depart every 15 minutes for Delhi (Rs 125, 5½ hours). There are also ordinary buses for Rs 68 and air-con coaches for Rs 215. There are frequent departures for the five-hour trip to Agra (Rs 72 deluxe, Rs 101 air-con).

A number of private companies cover the same routes.

Train Many of the lines into Jaipur have been converted to broad gauge. As other parts of the state's railway are converted, expect disruptions to services.

The computerised railway reservation office, at the station entrance, is open from 8 am to 8 pm Monday to Saturday and from 8 am to 2 pm Sunday. Join the queue for 'Freedom Fighters & Foreign Tourists'. For metre-gauge trains the booking office is on platform No 6.

There's a swift *Shatabdi Express* service leaving New Delhi at 5.50 am, reaching Jaipur at 10.15 am and then departing at 5.50 pm to reach New Delhi at 10.15 pm. It runs daily except Thursday and tickets cost Rs 300/600 for chair car/1st class. There's also a new daily *Intercity* service on the same route, leaving daily from Jaipur at 5.30 am.

Since schedules will be changing as broad gauge conversion proceeds, you need to enquire about trains such as the *Pink City Express*, which used to leave Old Delhi at 6 am for Jaipur.

The daily superfast express between Jaipur and Agra (the *Jaipur-Agra Fort Express*) takes under five hours, leaving Jaipur at 6.10 am and Agra at 5 pm. Reservations should be made one day in advance. Fares for the 208-km journey are Rs 53/189 in 2nd/1st class.

Getting Around

To/From the Airport The airport is 15 km out of town. The airport bus costs Rs 20; a taxi costs about Rs 120.

Local Transport Jaipur has taxis (unmetered), auto rickshaws and a city bus service. A cycle rickshaw from the station to the Jaipur Inn or Arya Niwas Hotel should cost about Rs 6, and from the station to Johari Bazaar Rs 12, or Rs 12 and Rs 18 for an auto rickshaw on these trips. However, if you're going to a hotel with your baggage and the hotel doesn't pay the driver's commission, you'll be extremely lucky to get a ride for these prices. In such cases, expect to pay two to three times the usual price. If they quote you the normal fare to a hotel whose rates you don't know, it probably means they're guaranteed an especially big commission at your expense.

Bicycles can be hired from several of the budget hotels, as well as from the Arya Niwas Hotel, at Rs 20 per day.

Glossary

The glossary that follows is just a sample of words you may come across during your time in Delhi.

acha – OK or 'I understand'.
acharya – revered teacher; originally a spiritual guide or preceptor.
agarbathi – incense.
Agni – fire, a major deity in the *Vedas*, mediator between men and the gods.
ahimsa – discipline of non-violence.
AIR – All India Radio, the national broadcaster.
Amir – Muslim nobleman.
Anglo-Indian – an Indian of mixed Asian and European ancestry.
angrezi – foreigner.
anna – a 16th of a rupee; it's now extinct but still occasionally used in marketplace conversation; ie, eight annas are Rs 0.50.
arak – distilled liquor made from coconut sap, potatoes or rice.
apsaras – heavenly nymphs who distracted *rishis* (sages).
Arjuna – *Mahabharata* hero and military commander who married Krishna's sister (Subhadra), took up arms against and overcame all manner of demons, had the *Bhagavad Gita* related to him by Krishna, led Krishna's funeral ceremony at Dwarka and finally retired to the Himalaya.
ashram – spiritual college cum retreat.
astrology – far more than just a newspaper space filler; marriages are not arranged, flights not taken, elections not called without checking the astrological charts.
attar – perfume
auto rickshaw – small, noisy, uncomfortable three-wheeled motorised contraption used to carry passengers short distances; cheaper than taxis.
avatar – incarnation of a deity, usually Vishnu.
ayah – children's nurse or nanny.
ayurveda – Indian natural and herbal medicine.
azan – Muslim call to prayer.

baba – religious master, father, and a term of respect.
babu – lower-level clerical worker (derogatory).
bagh – garden.
baksheesh – tip, bribe or alms.

bandar – monkey.

bandh – general strike.

banian – T-shirt or undervest.

baniya – moneylender.

banyan – Indian fig tree.

baoli – well, particularly a step-well with landings and galleries.

bara – big, important.

basti – shanty settlement.

bazaar – market area.

bearer – rather like a butler.

begum – Muslim woman of high rank.

betel – nut of the betel tree, chewed as a mild intoxicant.

Bhagavad Gita – Song of the Divine One; Krishna's lessons to Arjuna, the main thrust of which was to emphasise the philosophy of *bhakti* (faith); part of the *Mahabharata*.

bhang – dried leaves and flowering shoots of the marijuana plant.

bhang lassi – a blend of lassi with bhang, a drink with a kick.

Bharat – India.

bhavan – house, building.

bhisti (bheesti) – water carrier.

bidi – small, hand-rolled cigarette; really just a rolled-up leaf.

bindi – forehead mark.

black money – undeclared, untaxed money. There's lots of it in India.

bo tree – *Ficus religiosa*, the tree under which the Buddha attained enlightenment.

Bodhisattva – 'one whose essence is perfected wisdom'; one who has almost reached Nirvana but who renounces it in order to help others attain it.

bojnalaya – basic eating house.

Brahma – source of all existence and also worshipped as the creator in the Hindu triad.

Brahmanism – early form of Hinduism which evolved from Vedism; named after the Brahmin priests and the god Brahma.

Brahmin – a member of the priest caste, the highest Hindu caste.

Buddha – 'Awakened One'; originator of Buddhism who lived in the 5th century BC; regarded by Hindus as the ninth reincarnation of Vishnu.

bund – embankment or dike.

burkha – one-piece garment which totally covers Muslim women.

cantonment – administrative and military area of a British Raj-era town.

caste – one's station in life.

chai – tea.

chaitya – Buddhist temple. Also prayer room or assembly hall.

chajja – a small eave or dripstone used on early Muslim monuments in Delhi.

chakra – focus of one's spiritual power; disc-like weapon of Vishnu.

chalo, chalo, chalo – 'let's go, let's go, let's go'.

Chandra – the moon, or the moon as a god.

chapati – unleavened Indian bread.

chappals – sandals.

charas – resinous exudate of the marijuana plant, hashish.

charbagh – formal Persian garden, divided into quarters by watercourses (literally: four gardens).

charkha – hand-operated spinning wheel; it became the symbol of the Congress Party in the lead up to independence.

charpoy – Indian rope bed.

chat – general term for small snacks, papris, etc.

chauri – fly whisk.

chedi – see pagoda.

chela – pupil or follower, as George Harrison was to Ravi Shankar.

chhatri – a small, domed Mughal kiosk (literally: umbrella).

chillum – pipe part of a hookah; commonly used to describe the small pipes for smoking ganja.

Chisti – an order of Muslim Sufi saints.

choli – sari blouse.

chota – small, spirit drink measure (as in 'chota peg').

chowk – a town square, intersection or marketplace.

chowkidar – night-watchman.

Cong (I) – Congress Party of India.

crore – 10 million.

curd – yoghurt.

cutcherry – office or building for public business.

dacoit – robber, particularly armed robber.

dahi – yoghurt.

dagoba – see pagoda.

dak – postal service.

Dalit – preferred term for India's casteless class; see Untouchable.

dargah – shrine or tomb of a Muslim saint.

darshan – offering, or audience with someone, usually a guru; viewing of a deity.

darwaza – gateway or door.
dervish – Islamic mystic, the Islamic equivalent of a Hindu sadhu.
devadasi – temple dancer.
Devi – the Goddess; Siva's wife. She has a variety of other forms.
dhaba – hole-in-the-wall restaurant or snack bar.
dhal – lentils; what most of India lives on.
dharamsala – pilgrim accommodation.
dharma – Hindu/Buddhist moral code of behaviour.
dharna – non-violent protest.
dhobi – person who washes clothes.
dhobi ghat – the place where clothes are washed.
dhoti – like a *lungi*, but the cloth is then pulled up between the legs; worn by Hindu men.
dhurrie – rug.
digambara – 'sky-clad' Jain sect followers who extend their disdain for worldly goods to include not wearing clothes.
diwan – principal officer in a princely state, royal court or council.
dupatta – scarf worn by Punjabi women.
durbar – royal court; also used to describe a government.
dwarpal – doorkeeper; sculpture beside the doorways to Hindu or Buddhist shrines.

election symbols – identifying symbols for the various political parties, used since so many voters are illiterate.
Emergency – the period during which Indira Gandhi suspended many rights and many observers assumed she was intent on establishing a dictatorship.
eve-teasing – the Indian equivalent of Italian bottom-pinching.
export gurus – gurus whose following is principally from the West.

fakir – accurately a Muslim who has taken a vow of poverty, but also applied to Hindu ascetics such as sadhus.
filmee – music or other aspect of Bollywood movies.
freaks – Westerners wandering India. The '60s live!

Ganesh – god of wisdom and prosperity, elephant-headed son of Siva and Parvati, probably the most popular god in the whole Hindu pantheon.
gali – a narrow lane
Ganga – Ganges River, said to flow from the toe of Vishnu; also goddess representing the sacred Ganges River.
ganj – market.

ganja – dried flowering tips of the marijuana plant.

gari – vehicle; motor gari is a car and rail gari is a train.

ghat – steps or landing on a river, a range of hills or a road up hills; literally: 'a slope'.

ghazal – Urdu songs derived from poetry (usually couplets); traditionally with romantic and/or erotic themes.

ghee – clarified butter.

gherao – lock-in, where the workers lock the management in!

giri – hill.

godmen – commercially minded gurus; see export gurus.

godown – warehouse.

goonda – ruffian. Political parties often employ gangs of goondas.

gopi – cowherd girl. Krishna was very fond of them.

gram – chick peas, pulses.

gurdwara – Sikh temple.

guru – teacher or holy person (literally: *'goe* – darkness' and *'roe* – to dispel').

Haji – a Muslim who has made the pilgrimage *(haj)* to Mecca.

hammam – Turkish bath.

Hanuman – monkey god, prominent in the *Ramayana*; follower of Rama.

haram – prayer room in mosque.

Harijan – name given by Gandhi to India's Untouchables. This term is, however, no longer considered acceptable. See Dalit and Untouchable.

hartal – strike.

hathi – elephant.

haveli – traditional mansions with interior courtyards.

havildar – army officer.

hazrat – Islamic honorific title.

hijra – eunuch.

hookah – water pipe for smoking tobacco.

howdah – framework for carrying people on an elephant's back.

hypothecated – Indian equivalent of leased or mortgaged.

imam – Muslim religious leader.

IMFL – Indian Made Foreign Liquor; beer or spirits produced in India.

Indo-Saracenic – style of colonial architecture that melded Western designs with Muslim, Hindu and Jain influences.

Indra – the most important and prestigious of the Vedic gods of India; god of rain, thunder and lightning and war.

Ishwara – Lord; a name given to Siva.

jaggery – hard, brown sugar-like sweetener made from kitul palm sap.

janata – people, thus the Janata Party is the People's Party, and Janpath is the People's Way.

Jat – tribal people from the Delhi region, usually Hindu but also Sikh or Muslim.

Jatakas – tales from the Buddha's various lives.

jawan – policeman or soldier.

jhuggi – shanty settlement.

ji – honorific that can be added to the end of almost anything; thus Babaji, Gandhiji.

juggernauts – huge, extravagantly decorated temple 'cars' dragged through the streets during Hindu festivals.

jumkahs – earrings.

jyoti linga – the most important Siva shrines in India, of which there are 12.

kachahri – see *cutcherry*.

Kali – the Black; a terrible form of Siva's wife Devi.

Kama – the god of love.

kameez – woman's shirt.

karma – fate.

karmachario – workers.

Kartikiya – god of war, Siva's son.

khadi – homespun cloth; Mahatma Gandhi spent much energy in encouraging people to spin their own khadi cloth rather than buy imported English cloth.

khan – Muslim honorific title.

kibla – niche in a mosque wall to which Muslims look when praying in order to face Mecca.

koil – Hindu temple.

kot – fort.

kothi – residence, house or mansion.

kotwali – police station.

Krishna – Vishnu's eighth incarnation, often coloured blue.

kumbh – pitcher.

kund – lake.

kurta – shirt.

lakh – 100,000.

Lakshmi (Laxmi) – Vishnu's consort, goddess of wealth; is also called Padma (lotus).

lassi – very refreshing sweet yoghurt and iced-water drink.

lathi – large bamboo stick; what Indian police hit you with if you get in the way of a lathi charge.

lenga – long skirt with a waist cord.

lingam – phallic symbol; symbol of Siva.

lok – people.

Lok Dal – political party, one of the components of the Janata party.

Lok Sabha – lower house in the Indian parliament, comparable to the House of Representatives or House of Commons.

lungi – like a sarong.

madrasa – Islamic college.

Mahabharata – Great Vedic epic of the Bharata Dynasty; an epic poem, containing around 10,000 verses, describing the battle between the Pandavas and the Kauravas.

Mahadeva – the Great God; a name of Siva.

Mahadevi – the Great Goddess; a name of Devi, Siva's wife.

mahal – palace or large building.

maharaja, maharana, maharao – king.

maharani – wife of a princely ruler or a ruler in her own right.

mahatma – literally: 'great soul'.

Mahavir – the last tirthankar (Jain teacher).

mahout – elephant rider/master.

maidan – open grassed area in a city.

Makara – mythical sea creature, Varuna's vehicle and Capricorn in the Hindu zodiac; also a crocodile.

mali – gardener.

mandala – circle; symbol used in Hindu and Buddhist art to symbolise the universe.

mandi – market.

mandir – Hindu or Jain temple.

mantra – sacred word or chant used by Buddhists and Hindus to aid concentration; also the part of the *Vedas* consisting of hymns of praise.

mantra-shakti – priest-power.

Mara – Buddhist god of death, has three eyes and holds the wheel of life.

Maratha (Mahratta) – warlike central Indian race who controlled much of India at various times and gave the Mughals a lot of trouble.

marg – major road.

masjid – mosque (literally: place of prostration); Jama Masjid is the Friday Mosque or main mosque.

mata – mother.

math – monastery.

memsahib – married European lady, from 'madam-sahib'; still more widely used than you'd think.

mendi – ornate patterns painted on women's hands and feet for important festivals, particularly in Rajasthan. Beauty parlours and bazaar stalls will do it for you.

Meru – mythical mountain found in the centre of the earth; on it is Swarga, the heaven of Indra.

mihrab – see kibla.

minar – tall tower, often associated with a mosque, thus minaret.

mithuna – pairs of men and women often seen in temple sculpture.

Moghul – alternative spelling for Mughal.

Mohini – Vishnu in his female incarnation.

monsoon – rainy season from around June to October, when it rains virtually every day.

morcha – mob march or protest march.

muezzin – one who calls Muslims to prayer from the minaret.

Mughal – the Muslim dynasty of Indian emperors from Babur to Bahadur Shah Zafar; originally from central Asia.

mullah – Muslim scholar, teacher or religious leader.

mund – village (eg, Ootacamund).

munshi – writer, secretary or teacher of languages.

nadi – river.

Naga – mythical snake having a human face and the tail of a serpent; also a person from Nagaland.

nagar – suburb, town.

namaz – Muslim prayers.

Nandi – bull, vehicle of Siva and usually found at Siva temples.

Narasimha (Narsingh) – man-lion incarnation of Vishnu.

nautch girls – dancing girls; a nautch is a dance.

nawab – Muslim ruling prince or powerful landowner.

nirvana – the ultimate aim of Buddhist existence, a state where one leaves the cycle of existence and does not have to suffer further rebirths.

niwas – house, building.

nizam – hereditary title of the rulers of Hyderabad; originally the name of a high official in the Mughal court, roughly equivalent to a modern Justice Minister or Attorney-General.

noth – the Lord (Jain).

NRI – non-resident Indian, the sub-continent's version of Overseas Chinese and of equal economic importance for modern India.

numda – Rajasthani rug.

Om – sacred invocation representing the absolute essence of the divine principle. For Buddhists, if repeated often enough with complete concentration, it should lead to a state of emptiness.

padyatra – 'foot journey' made by politicians to raise support at the village level.
pagoda – Buddhist religious monument composed of a solid hemisphere topped by a spire, containing relics of the Buddha; also known as a dagoba, stupa or chedi.
paan – betel nut plus the chewing additives.
pandit – teacher or wise man. Sometimes used to mean a bookworm.
Parsi – adherent of the Zoroastrian faith.
peepul – fig tree, especially a bo tree.
peon – lowest grade clerical worker.
pice – a quarter of an anna.
pinjrapol – animal hospital maintained by Jains.
pradesh – state.
pranayama – study of breath control.
prasad – food offering.
puja – literally: 'respect'; offering or prayers.
punkah – cloth fan, swung by pulling a cord.
Puranas – set of 18 encyclopaedic Sanskrit stories, written in verse, relating to the three gods, dating from the period of the Guptas (5th century AD).
purdah – isolation in which some Muslim women are kept.

qawwali – rhymed Urdu couplets performed with musical accompaniment, originally sung by Sufis.
qila – fort.

raga – any of several conventional patterns of melody and rhythm that form the basis for freely interpreted compositions.
railhead – station or town at the end of a railway line; termination point.
raj – rule or sovereignty.
raja – king.
Rajput – Hindu warrior castes, royal rulers of central India.
Rama – seventh incarnation of Vishnu, his life story being the central theme of the *Ramayana*.
Ramayana – the story of Rama and Sita and their conflict with Ravana.
rani – wife of a king.
rasta roko – roadblock for protest purposes.
Ravana – demon king of Lanka; he abducted Sita, and the titanic battle between him and Rama is told in the *Ramayana*.

rawal – nobleman.
Resident – British representative in the court of a princely state.
Rig-Veda – the original and longest of the four main *Vedas*, or holy Sanskrit texts.
Rukmini – wife of Krishna; died on his funeral pyre.

sadar – main.
sadhu – ascetic, holy person, one who is trying to achieve enlightenment. They will usually be addressed as 'swamiji' or 'babaji'.
sahib – 'lord', title applied to any gentleman and most Europeans.
Saivaite (Shaivaite) – follower of Lord Siva.
Saivism – the worship of Siva.
salwar – trousers worn by Punjabi women.
samadhi – an ecstatic state, sometimes defined as 'ecstasy, trance, communion with God' or 'ecstatic state of mystic consciousness'. Another definition is the place where a holy man was cremated, usually venerated as a shrine.
sanyasin – like a sadhu.
sarak – road or street.
Saraswati – wife of Brahma, goddess of speech and learning; usually seated on a white swan, holding a *veena*.
Sati – wife of Siva, became a sati (honourable woman) by destroying herself by fire. These days it applies to any woman who does this. Though banned a century or so ago, occasionally sati is still performed.
satsang – discourse by a swami or guru.
satyagraha – non-violent protest involving a fast, popularised by Gandhi. From Sanskrit, literally: 'insistence on truth'.
Scheduled castes – official term for 'Untouchables', or Dalits.
sepoy – private in the infantry.
serai – place for accommodation of travellers, specifically a caravanserai where camel caravans once stopped.
shirting – the material shirts are made out of.
sikhara – Hindu temple-spire or temple.
singh – lion, name of the Rajput caste; adopted by Sikhs as a surname.
sirdar (sardar) – leader or commander.
Sita – in the *Vedas* the goddess of agriculture, but more commonly associated with the *Ramayana*, where she is Rama's wife and is abducted by Ravana and carted off to Lanka.
sitar – Indian stringed instrument.

Siva – (Shiva) the destroyer; also the creator, in which form he is worshipped in the form of the *lingam* (a kind of phallic symbol).

sof – aniseed seeds; comes with the bill after a meal and you chew a pinch of it as a digestive.

sonam – karma built up in successive reincarnations.

sri (sree, shri, shree) – honorific prefix, but these days the Indian equivalent of Mr or Ms.

stupa – see pagoda.

sudra – low Hindu caste.

sufi – ascetic Muslim mystic.

suiting – the material used to make suits.

Surya – the sun, a major deity in the Vedas.

sutra – string; a set of rules expressed in verse. Many exist, the most famous being the Kamasutra.

swami – title given to initiated monks; means 'lord of the self'.

swaraj – independence.

sweeper – lowest caste servant, who performs the most menial of tasks.

tabla – a pair of kettle drums which are played with the fingers.

tank – artificial water-storage lake.

tatty – woven grass screen which is wetted and hung outside windows in the hot season to provide a remarkably effective system of air-cooling.

thakur – Hindu caste.

thali – traditional south Indian and Gujarati 'all-you-can-eat' vegetarian meal.

thanka – rectangular Tibetan painting on cloth.

thiru – holy.

tiffin – snack, particularly around lunchtime.

tika – the spot devout Hindus put on their foreheads with *tika* powder.

tirthankars – the 24 great Jain teachers.

topi – hat, much used by the British in the Raj era.

Trimurti – Triple Form; the Hindu triad – Brahma, Siva and Vishnu.

Tripitaka – the classical Theravada Buddhist scriptures, which are divided into three categories, hence its name the Three Baskets.

tripolia – triple gateway.

Uma – Light; Siva's consort.

Untouchable – lowest caste or 'casteless' for whom the most menial tasks are reserved. The name derives from the belief that higher castes risk defilement if they touch one. Formerly known as *Harijan*, now *Dalit*.

Upanishads – Esoteric Doctrine; ancient texts forming part of the *Vedas* (although of a later date), they delve into weighty matters such as the nature of the universe and the soul.

Valmiki – author of the *Ramayana*.
varna – the concept of caste.
Varuna – supreme Vedic god.
Vedas – the Hindu sacred books; a collection of hymns composed in pre-classical Sanskrit during the second millennium BC and divided into four books: *Rig-Veda*, *Yajur-Veda*, *Sama-Veda* and *Atharva-Veda*.
veena – Indian stringed drone instrument.
vihara – part of monastery; also resting place, garden, cave with cells.
vimana – principal part of a Hindu temple.
Vishnu – the third of the Hindu trinity of gods along with Brahma and Siva, the preserver and restorer, who so far has nine avatars: the fish Matsya; the tortoise Kurma; the wild boar Naraha; the man-lion Narasimha; the dwarf Vamana; the Brahmin Parashu-Rama; Rama (of *Ramayana* fame); Krishna, and the Buddha.

wallah – man, can be added onto almost anything: thus dhobi-wallah (clothes washer), taxi-wallah, Delhi-wallah.
wazir – prime minister of Mughal court.

yatri – tourist.
yoni – vagina, female fertility symbol.

zenana – area of a high-class Muslim household where the women are secluded.

Index

A porter at the railway station (MC)

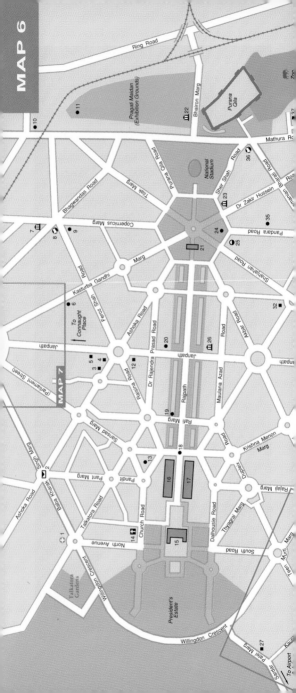

MAP 6

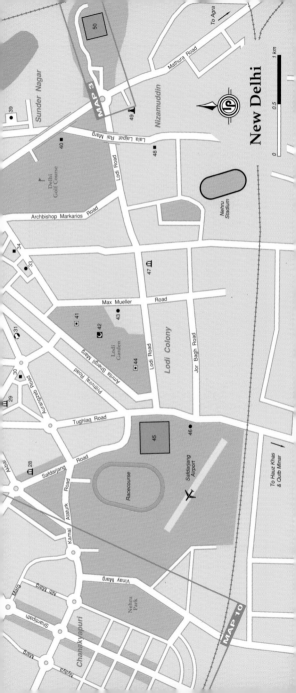

MAP 6 NEW DELHI

PLACES TO STAY

3	Hotel Ashok Yatri Niwas
4	Hotel Kanishka
5	Janpath Hotel
12	Le Meridien
27	Hotel Diplomat
30	Hotel Claridges
32	Taj Mahal Hotel
34	Ambassador Hotel
37	Shervani Fort View
38	Kailash Inn & La Sagrita Tourist Home
40	Hotel Oberoi New Delhi
48	Lodhi Hotel

OTHER

1	Dr Ram Manohar Lohia Hospital
2	GPO
6	Max Mueller Bhavan
7	Museum of Natural History
8	Nepalese Embassy
9	Rabindra Bhavan
10	Hans Bhavan (Foreigners' Registration Office)
11	Appu Ghar
13	Sansad Bhavan (Parliament House)
14	Church of the Redemption
15	Rashtrapati Bhavan (President's residence)
16	Secretariat Building (North Block)
17	Secretariat Building (South Block)
18	Vijay Chowk
19	Boat Club
20	Indira Gandhi National Centre for the Arts
21	India Gate
22	Crafts Museum
23	National Gallery of Modern Art
24	Children's Park
25	Bikaner House (Jaipur Buses)
26	National Museum
28	Indira Gandhi Memorial Museum
29	Gandhi Smriti
31	Israeli Embassy
33	Khan Market
35	Pandara Market
36	Sher Shah's Gate & Khairu'l Manzil Masjid
39	Sunder Nagar Market
41	Sikander Lodi's Tomb
42	Bara Gumbad Tomb & Mosque
43	India International Centre
44	Muhammad Shah's Tomb
45	Safdarjang's Tomb
46	Indian Airlines (24 Hours)
47	Tibet House
49	Nizam-ud-din's Shrine
50	Humayun's Tomb

Detail of a tribal costume (HF)

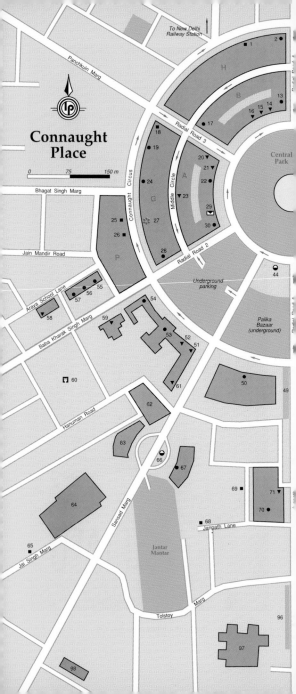

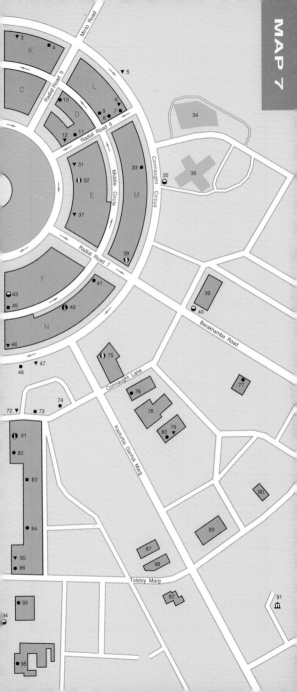

MAP 7

Minto Road

▼ 3
■ 4
K
C

Radial Road 5

▼ 5

L
▶ 10
6 ▼
D
9 ▼ 7 ■
■ 8
12 ■ 11
▼ Radial Road 6

31 ▼
33 ■
35 ■
Middle Circle
32 ✪
E
M
36
34
37 ▼

Connaught Circus

Radial Road 7
38 ■
✪

41 ●
F
39
◐ 43
42 ✪
◐ 40
● 45
N
Barakhamba Road

▼ 46
▼ 47
48 ●

75 ✪
77 ●
Connaught Lane
76 ●
78
74 ■
72 ▼
■ 73
79 ▼
80 ●
81 ✪
82 ●
Kasturba Gandhi Marg
83 ■
90 ●
84 ●
89 ●
85 ▼
67 ●
86 ●
88 ●
Tolstoy Marg
93 ●
92 ●
91 ⊞
94 ◐
95 ●

MAP 7 CONNAUGHT PLACE

PLACES TO STAY

1   Hotel 55
4   York Hotel
7   Nirula's Hotel
9   Jukaso Inn
11 Hotel Palace Heights
18 Hotel Marina
25 Alka Hotel
26 Prem Sagar Guest House
33 Hotel Bright
63 Park Hotel
65 YMCA Tourist Hostel
68 Mr S C Jain's Guest House
69 Mrs Colaco's
73 Ringo Guest House
74 Sunny Guest House
83 Janpath Guest House
92 Centre Point Hotel
97 Imperial Hotel
98 YWCA International Guest House

PLACES TO EAT

3   Palki Restaurant
5   Kaka Da
6   Nirula's Hot Shoppe
12 Embassy Restaurant
14 Zen Restaurant
15 Cafe 100
16 Volga Restaurant
20 Keventers
21 Wenger's
23 Fa Yian
31 Kovil
37 United Coffee House
46 Wimpy
47 Croissants Etc
51 El Arab & Cellar restaurants
52 Gaylord
58 Coffee Home
59 Indian Coffee House
61 Kwality Restaurant
71 Bankura Restaurant
72 Don't Pass Me By
79 Parikrama
85 Sona Rupa Restaurant

OTHER

2   Plaza Cinema
8   ITDC Tours Booking Office
10 Odeon Cinema
13 Bookworm

17	South African Airways & SAS
19	Singapore Airlines
22	American Express
24	Marques & Co
27	Dhoomi Mal Sculpture Garden
28	Malaysia Airlines, Royal Jordanian Airlines, El Al Airlines & Lot Airlines
29	Post Office
30	Art Today
32	ANZ Grindlays Bank
34	Shankar Market
35	Bus 620 to YH & Chanakyapuri, 505 to Qutb Minar & Hauz Khas
36	Super Bazar
38	Bank of Baroda
39	Akash Deep Building
40	Bus No 104, 13 & 160 to Old Delhi
41	Aeroflot
42	Delhi Tourism Corporation office
43	Vayudoot airlines & EATS bus
44	Motorcycle Rickshaws to Old Delhi
45	Indian Airlines
48	Oxford Book Shop
49	Janpath Market
50	Citibank & Air India
53	Regal Cinema
54	Khadi Gramodyog Bhavan
55	Delhi Corporation Emporium
56	Gujarat Government Emporium
57	Maharashtra Government Emporium
60	Hanuman Temple
62	Standard Chartered Bank
64	Delhi Municipal Corporation Office
66	Bus No 433 to Nehru Place, 620 to Youth Hostel
67	British Airways & Swissair
70	Government Map Sales Office
75	Hong Kong Bank
76	Pakistan International Airlines
77	Budget Rent a Car
78	American Center
80	Tarom
81	Government of India tourist office
82	Delhi Photo Company
84	Lufthansa
86	RNAC
87	British Council
88	Credit Lyonnaise
89	Thai Airways International, United Airlines & Sahara India Airlines
90	KLM
91	Ugrasen-ki Baoli
93	Central Cottage Industries Emporium
94	Bus No 505 to Qutb Minar & Hauz Khas
95	UP Tourism, Delta Airlines, Japan Airlines & Shipping Corporation of India
96	Tibetan Market

Dhoomi Mai Sculpture Garden, Connaught Place (HF)

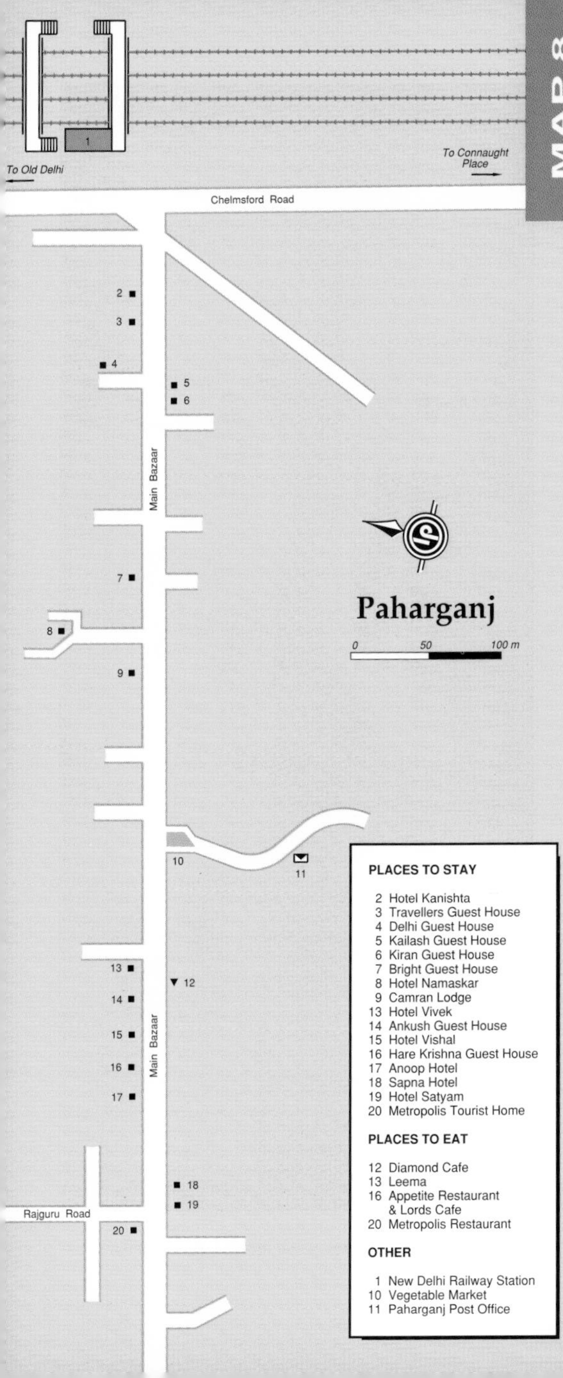

MAP 8

To Old Delhi

To Connaught Place

Chelmsford Road

Main Bazaar

2
3
4
5
6
7
8
9
10
11

Main Bazaar

13
14
15
16
17
18
19

Rajguru Road

20

Paharganj

0   50   100 m

PLACES TO STAY

2 Hotel Kanishta
3 Travellers Guest House
4 Delhi Guest House
5 Kailash Guest House
6 Kiran Guest House
7 Bright Guest House
8 Hotel Namaskar
9 Camran Lodge
13 Hotel Vivek
14 Ankush Guest House
15 Hotel Vishal
16 Hare Krishna Guest House
17 Anoop Hotel
18 Sapna Hotel
19 Hotel Satyam
20 Metropolis Tourist Home

PLACES TO EAT

12 Diamond Cafe
13 Leema
16 Appetite Restaurant
    & Lords Cafe
20 Metropolis Restaurant

OTHER

1 New Delhi Railway Station
10 Vegetable Market
11 Paharganj Post Office

Woodcarving is one of the Indian folk arts. (GB)

MAP 9

1 Flagstaff Tower
2 Old Secretariat Building
3 Metcalfe House
4 Chauburja Masjid
5 Pir Ghaib
6 Hindu Rao Hospital
7 Ashokan Pillar
8 Mutiny Memorial (Ajitgarh)
9 Oberoi Maidens Hotel
10 Mother Theresa's Sisters of Charity Orphanage
11 Nicholson Cemetery
12 Qudsia Masjid
13 Kashmiri Gate ISBT
14 William Fraser's bungalow
15 St James' Church
16 Kashmiri Gate
17 Dara Shikoh Library
18 Delhi GPO, Old Magazine
19 Lothian Cemetery
20 (Old) Delhi Railway Station

Civil Lines

Detail of a tribal costume (HF)

MAP 10

PLACES TO STAY

2 Vishwa Yuvak
   Kendra
7 Youth Hostel
11 Ashok Hotel
12 Samrat Hotel

OTHER

1 Nehru Museum &
   Planetarium
3 Alkauzer Kebab Stall
13 Santushti Shopping
   Centre
42 Railway Transport
   Museum

EMBASSIES

4 Sri Lanka
5 Indonesia
6 Norway
8 Jordan
9 China
10 UK
14 Australia
15 Pakistan
16 USA
17 Switzerland
18 France
19 Finland
20 Myanmar (Burma)
21 Japan
22 Russia
23 Sweden
24 Afghanistan
25 Netherlands
26 Germany
27 Ethiopia
28 Canada
29 Italy
30 South Korea
31 Singapore
32 Thailand
33 New Zealand
34 Belgium
35 Turkey
36 Bhutan
37 Philippines
38 Malaysia
39 Egypt
40 Hungary
41 Czech & Slovak

Chanakyapuri
Diplomatic Enclave

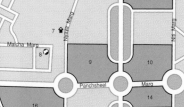
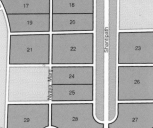

Two girls at New Delhi's Jagannath Temple (SH)

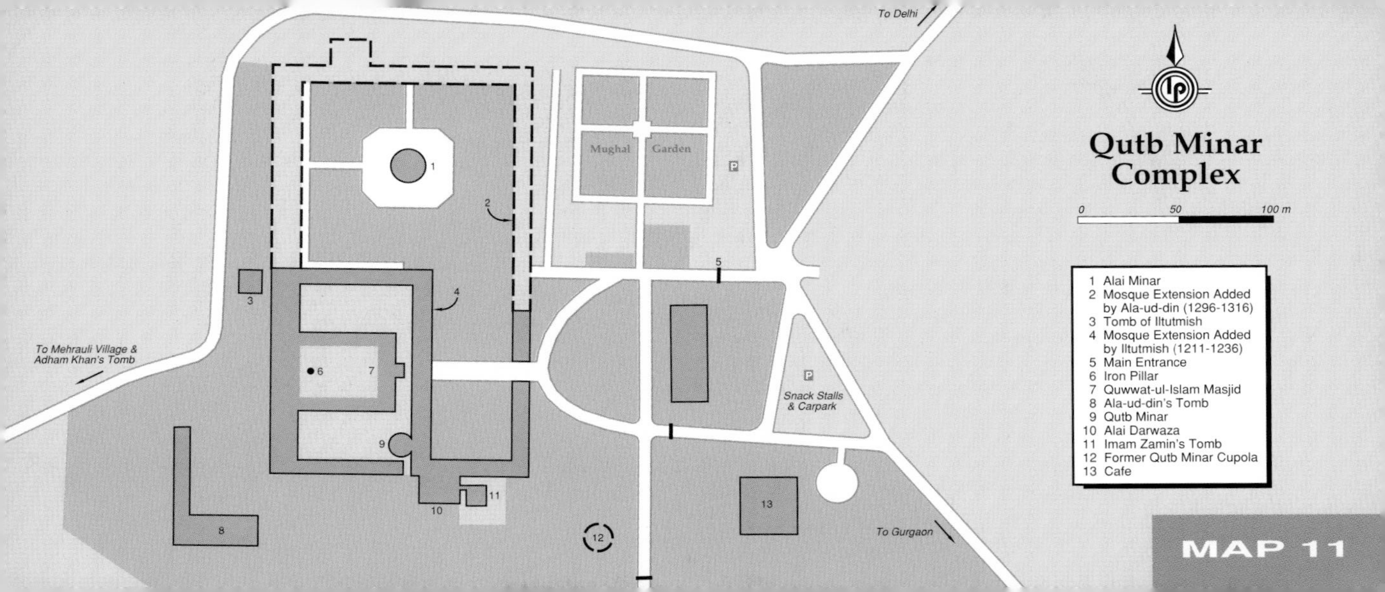

Qutb Minar Complex

0 50 100 m

1 Alai Minar
2 Mosque Extension Added
   by Ala-ud-din (1296-1316)
3 Tomb of Iltutmish
4 Mosque Extension Added
   by Iltutmish (1211-1236)
5 Main Entrance
6 Iron Pillar
7 Quwwat-ul-Islam Masjid
8 Ala-ud-din's Tomb
9 Qutb Minar
10 Alai Darwaza
11 Imam Zamin's Tomb
12 Former Qutb Minar Cupola
13 Cafe

To Delhi

To Gurgaon

To Mehrauli Village &
Adham Khan's Tomb

Mughal Garden

Snack Stalls
& Carpark

MAP 11

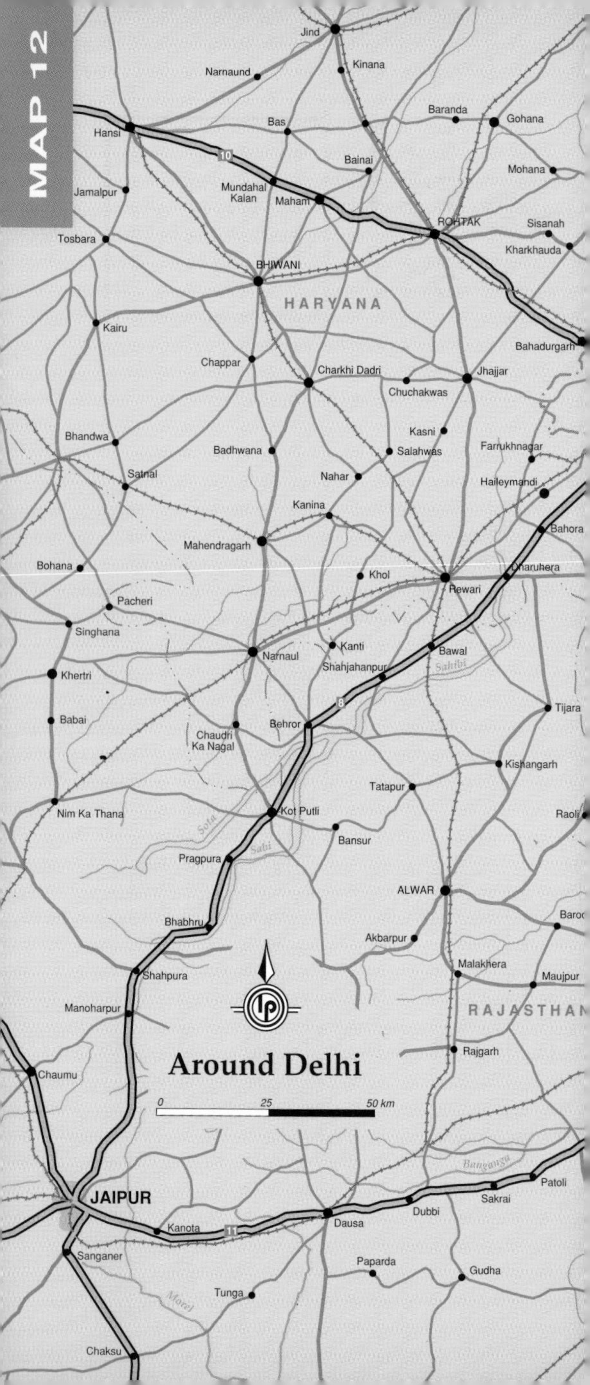

MAP 12

Around Delhi

Jind
Narnaund
Kinana
Baranda
Gohana
Bas
Hansi
Balnai
Mohana
Jamalpur
Mundahal Kalan
Maham
ROHTAK
Sisanah
Tosbara
Kharkhauda
BHIWANI
HARYANA
Kairu
Bahadurgarh
Chappar
Charkhi Dadri
Jhajjar
Chuchakwas
Bhandwa
Kasni
Farrukhnagar
Badhwana
Salahwas
Satnal
Nahar
Haileymandi
Kanina
Bahora
Mahendragarh
Bohana
Khol
Dharuhera
Pacheri
Rewari
Singhana
Narnaul
Kanti
Bawal
Khertri
Shahjahanpur
Sahibi
Babai
Behror
Tijara
Chaudri
Ka Nagal
Tatapur
Kishangarh
Nim Ka Thana
Raoli
Kot Putli
Pragpura
Bansur
Sabi
Bhabhru
ALWAR
Baror
Shahpura
Akbarpur
Malakhera
Maujpur
Manoharpur
RAJASTHAN
Chaumu
Rajgarh
Banganga
0   25   50 km
JAIPUR
Patoli
Kanota
Dausa
Dubbi
Sakrai
Sanganer
Paparda
Gudha
Tunga
Chaksu
Banas

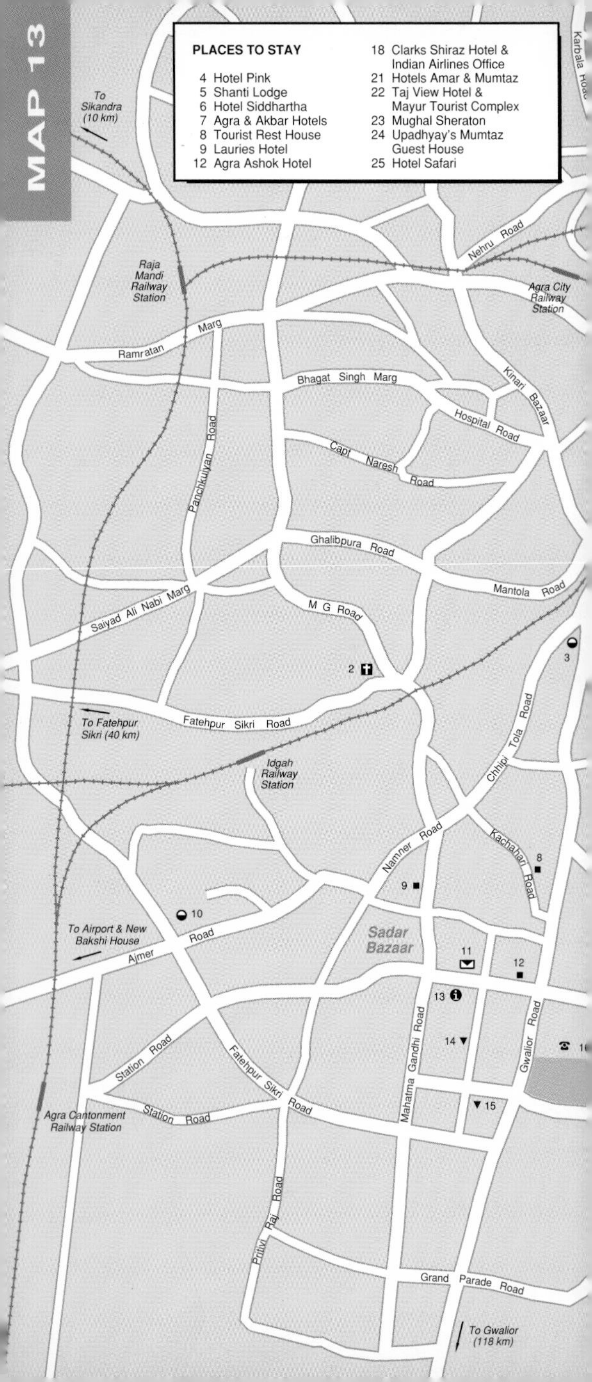

MAP 13

PLACES TO STAY

4 Hotel Pink
5 Shanti Lodge
6 Hotel Siddhartha
7 Agra & Akbar Hotels
8 Tourist Rest House
9 Lauries Hotel
12 Agra Ashok Hotel

18 Clarks Shiraz Hotel &
   Indian Airlines Office
21 Hotels Amar & Mumtaz
22 Taj View Hotel &
   Mayur Tourist Complex
23 Mughal Sheraton
24 Upadhyay's Mumtaz
   Guest House
25 Hotel Safari

Karbala Road

To Sikandra
(10 km)

Nehru Road

Raja Mandi Railway Station

Agra City Railway Station

Ramratan Marg

Bhagat Singh Marg

Kinari Bazaar

Hospital Road

Capt Naresh Road

Panchkuyian Road

Ghalibpura Road

Mantola Road

Saiyad Ali Nabi Marg

M G Road

2

3

To Fatehpur Sikri (40 km)

Fatehpur Sikri Road

Idgah Railway Station

Chhip Tola Road

Namner Road

Kachahari Road

8

9

To Airport & New Bakshi House

10

Road

Ajmer

Sadar Bazaar

11

12

13

14

To Gwalior

16

Mahatma Gandhi Road

Gwalior Road

15

Agra Cantonment Railway Station

Station Road

Station Road

Fatehpur Sikri Road

Prithvi Raj Road

Grand Parade Road

To Gwalior
(118 km)

PLACES TO EAT

14 Zorba the Buddha
15 Lakshmi Vilas
20 Only Restaurant

OTHER

1 Itimad-ud-daulah
2 Central Methodist Church
3 Agra Fort Bus Terminal
10 Idgah Bus Terminal
11 GPO
13 Government of India Tourist Office
16 Telegraph Office
17 Archaeological Survey of India
19 UP Tourist Office

Agra

0   250   500 m

To Aligarh (82 km)

To Shikodabad (63 km)

Ram Bagh

Belanganj Railway Station

Kanpur Road

Pandit Kalicharan Tiwari Road

To Chini Ka Rauza

Yamuna Bridge Railway Station

Belan   Ganj

P. Mandi Road

Chhata Road

Jama Masjid Road

Agra Fort Railway Station

Fort

Yamuna River

MAP 5

Yamuna Kinara Road

Taj Mahal

Shahjahan Park

F M Cariappa Road

Golf Course

Fatehbad Road

The Mall

Taj Road

Gough Road

Taj Road

19

20

21

22

23

24

25

Shamsabad Road

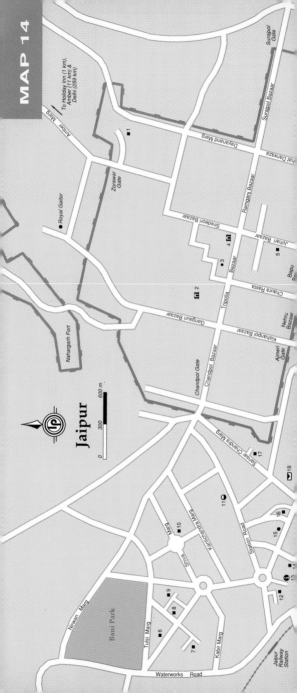